MILLER CENTER SERIES ON THE AMERICAN PRESIDENCY

*for Marge*

*love, Fritz*

Presidential Transitions
and Foreign Affairs

# Presidential Transitions and Foreign Affairs

FREDERICK C. MOSHER
W. DAVID CLINTON
DANIEL G. LANG

Louisiana State University Press
Baton Rouge and London

Designer: Christopher Wilcox
Typeface: Times Roman
Typesetter: G & S Typesetters, Inc.
Printer: Thomson-Shore, Inc.
Binder: John Dekker & Sons, Inc.

10 9 8 7 6 5 4 3 2 1

Library of Congress Cataloging-in-Publication Data

Mosher, Frederick C.
   Presidential transitions and foreign affairs.

   (Miller Center series on the American presidency)
   The recommendations of the Miller Center Commis-
sion on Presidential Transitions and Foreign Policy are
included in the appendix.
   Bibliography: p.
   Includes index.
   1. United States—Foreign relations administration.
2. Executive power—United States. 3. Presidents—
United States—Transition periods.   4. Presidents—
United States—Election.   I. Clinton, W. David.
II. Lang, Daniel George.   III. Miller Center Com-
mission on Presidential Transitions and Foreign Policy.
IV. Title.   V. Series.
JX1706.Z7M67   1987      353.0089      86-20053
ISBN 0-8071-1356-6

# CONTENTS

# FOREWORD

The Miller Center is proud to sponsor this inquiry by Professor Frederick C. Mosher and his colleagues. Not since Laurin Henry's classic study of the history of presidential transitions for the Brookings Institution have leading scholars examined this subject in a systematic way.

It is a subject of foremost concern to the center, whose work concerning it has proceeded along two separate but related lines. We have encouraged independent research and writing by the staff of the Miller Center. At the same time, we have organized a national commission under the cochairmanship of former Secretaries of State William P. Rogers and Cyrus R. Vance. The two interrelated strains of our program represent the Miller Center's response to its mandate both to seek deeper understanding of the American presidency and to contribute to the improvement of the presidency.

For more than four decades, Professor Mosher has been among a handful of leading scholars of public administration recognized internationally as well as nationally. At this stage in his career, he is considered to be the doyen of American authorities in the field. In 1981 Mosher was the second recipient of the Dwight Waldo Award, which is one of the highest honors accorded living scholars of public administration. In 1984 the Miller Center published his *Tale of Two Agencies,* a definitive comparison of the Office of Management and Budget and the General Accounting Office.

Professor W. David Clinton, now of Hamilton College, is an emerging young leader in the field of international relations. His writings on national interest promise to be of an importance matching that of earlier contributions by Hans J. Morgenthau and Charles A. Beard.

Professor Daniel G. Lang's recent volume, *Foreign Policy in the*

*Early Republic: The Law of Nations and the Balance of Power,* published by the Louisiana State University Press, stamps him as a leading interpreter of political theory and international relations. It reexamines the influence of seventeenth- and eighteenth-century European political ideas on the thought of the founders of the American republic. Its contribution to foreign policy studies is comparable to Louis Hartz's in his efforts to illuminate the interconnections between European and American political thought.

The three authors not only have done their own study and writing but also have joined in the discussions of the Presidential Transitions Commission. Thus, they have benefited from a fruitful exchange between theory and practice. Their volume, in its general, historical sections and its specific case studies, reflects this approach. It would be the hope and expectation of the Miller Center staff that this work would be a leading source on transitions for years to come.

Kenneth W. Thompson
Director, Miller Center of Public Affairs

James Sterling Young
Director of the Program on the Presidency

# PREFACE

In the autumn of 1982 a commission was established to examine the problems attending the transfer of power from one American president to another and to make recommendations designed to lessen the difficulties and hazards involved in such transfers. Its particular reference was to foreign affairs. This Commission on Presidential Transitions and Foreign Policy was initiated and sponsored by the White Burkett Miller Center of Public Affairs of the University of Virginia. The Miller Center provided the commission staff and other support, and financial assistance was received from the Ford Foundation. The cochairmen of the commission were two former secretaries of state, William P. Rogers and Cyrus R. Vance. Most of its sixteen other members had been directly involved in one or more of the five interparty presidential transitions since World War II. They were David E. Bell, Harold Brown, Philip W. Buchen, Clark Clifford, Walter Cronkite, David R. Gergen, General Andrew J. Goodpaster, Vernon E. Jordan, Jr., Carol C. Laise, Senator Charles McC. Mathias, Jane Cahill Pfeiffer, Dean Rusk, Theodore C. Sorensen, and Jack H. Watson, Jr. The commission's report, *Transferring Responsibility: The Dangers of Transition,* is expected to be published by the Miller Center in 1987.

The authors of this book, on behalf of the Miller Center, provided such staff help as the commission required. That included, at the beginning, a monograph on the subject of transitions and foreign policy based on such fugitive literature as was available. That monograph formed the basis of Part I of the present volume, now much expanded. At least one of the present authors attended every one of the commission meetings and helped in the drafting of its report.

The current book does not attempt to supersede the report of the commission. Although some recommendations are implicit in the discussion of transition difficulties, our main effort was to be objective and impartial. We have, however, included in the Appendix a complete copy of the commission's recommendations.

An underlying assumption of a study of this kind is that there are common problems or categories of problems that persist through time and can be expected to arise whenever there is a change of leadership. The problems are most acute when a new president succeeds an incumbent of a different political party, and that is the kind of transition with which this study is principally concerned. Although the Republican and Democratic parties bring diverse persons with somewhat different perspectives and values to bear, the basic problems of transitions pertain regardless of which succeeds the other. For a variety of reasons discussed later, leadership changes, always a potential source of conflict and other difficulties, are particularly troublesome in the American national government. We doubt that the difficulties can ever be eliminated, given the structure of our government. But they can be alleviated if the partisans on both sides better understand the nature of the problems and how they have been handled in earlier transitions. This is especially true of incoming administrations, the officials of which typically include few who have ever experienced or had any concern about presidential transitions. It is instructive that the Commission on Presidential Transitions and Foreign Policy recommended no changes in the Constitution and few in the statutes. Its proposals were directed almost entirely to expanding the knowledge and modifying the attitudes and behavior of participants. It is our hope that the present work will help in these aims as well as informing others who are interested in American government and foreign affairs.

The content of this book is oriented to problems that may be expected in future presidential transitions, most of which have been experienced in transitions since World War II. It is not a manual of how to do the multitude of things that must be done to effectuate the transfer of power from one president to another.[1]

1. This is not to suggest that such a manual should not be published. It should. Otherwise every four or eight years a new group will have to rediscover how to construct the wheel. After the 1980–1981 transition, two principal leaders of the process, William Tucker for the Republicans and Harrison Wellford for the Democrats, and a few of their colleagues joined forces to draft such a manual. We hope

Interest in presidential transitions as a focus for objective study was first generated by the transfer of power from President Truman to President Eisenhower in 1952–1953; it was renewed during the contest of 1960 and the subsequent transfer from President Eisenhower to President Kennedy. Leadership came from the Brookings Institution, which initiated several studies and sponsored a bipartisan committee that sought to ease the transition of 1960–1961. The principal enduring product of these endeavors was *Presidential Transitions* by Laurin L. Henry. Published in 1960, it remains the leading authority and the only general work on the subject a quarter of a century later. There have been a good many articles on recent transitions, including several by Henry himself. And there have been studies of particular problems, such as appointments or White House organization, and memoirs containing material about particular transitions. But we have found rather few publications that focus on transitions and foreign affairs, as does this book. Consequently we have relied heavily upon the words and the memories of people who participated in or observed transitions as far back as World War II.

The book is divided into two parts. Part I discusses the nature of presidential transitions and their relation to foreign affairs. It draws upon the five interparty transitions since World War II for its examples and its generalizations. An introductory chapter undertakes to place American transitions in a comparative context and to relate them to the somewhat special problems of foreign affairs. Chapter 2 discusses the constraints and possibilities imposed on our government by the calendar and its punctuation points. Chapter 3 summarizes American historical experience with transitions, giving special emphasis to the efforts to develop and to systematize transition practices since World War II. Chapter 4 explores the problems of communication between outgoing and incoming administrations with emphasis on the education of the latter for their new jobs. Next are two chapters on the means of making the foreign affairs goals of the new team operational: through program development, organization, the budget (in Chapter 5) and personnel (Chapter 6).

Part II opens with a brief prologue on the immediate problems

---

that they will finish and publish it. We are grateful that Mr. Wellford made it available to us, and we have drawn upon it in preparing our own study.

involved in the transfer of power and responsibility during the transition period. There follow five chapters, one on each of the interparty transitions that have occurred since World War II. Each of these chapters begins with a brief summary of the salient features of the transition and is followed by two case summaries on significant foreign affairs problems confronted by the nation during the transition period: how the incoming and the outgoing teams dealt with one another and with the foreign governments concerned. Most of the cases describe events that were well known at the time they occurred. Limitations of space prevent an exhaustive treatment of these episodes, many of which have been the subjects of one or several full books. Despite their brevity, the case studies in some places necessarily overlap with the examples used in Part I. We have endeavored to minimize such overlap, and we hope that references to different aspects of the same episodes will provide amplification rather than repetition. Throughout we have sought to emphasize those features that significantly influenced, or were influenced by, the transition. The book closes with a few observations in which the cases are considered together as illustrations of the generalizations suggested earlier.

# ACKNOWLEDGMENTS

We have been privileged to attend meetings with a number of distinguished groups, most of which were assembled for the immediate purpose of discussing interparty transitions and foreign affairs. With many of the participants we also had individual interviews. The first of these groups was the Commission on Presidential Transitions and Foreign Policy, which met several times over the course of two and one-half years. Its membership, which is listed in the Preface, included high officials in every interparty transition since World War II.

At the instance of David E. Bell and Jack H. Watson, Jr., both members of the commission, a meeting of professors was convened to discuss the federal budget in relation to transitions. The participants included, in addition to Bell, Watson, and Mosher, William M. Capron of Boston University and Hale Champion, Hugh Heclo, Richard Neustadt, and Don K. Price, all of the John F. Kennedy School of Government, Harvard University.

The Arthur Andersen accounting firm has audited the campaign and transition books of most of the presidential candidates since 1960, and this has involved it in several of the recent transitions. The Honorable Charles A. Bowsher, Comptroller General of the United States and former head of Arthur Andersen's Washington office, suggested and then arranged a luncheon meeting at General Accounting Office headquarters with several current and former Andersen officials to discuss their observations of transitions. Bowsher chaired the meeting. The other participants were Robert Conn, who was then Assistant Secretary of the Navy, and Ron Lynch and David Wooden, both of whom were still with Arthur Andersen.

We invited Harold C. Relyea to bring together a group of his colleagues at the Congressional Research Service to discuss, from their objective perspective, the problems of transition and foreign affairs. They were senior analysts in the fields of foreign affairs, intelligence, national defense, the presidency, and American government generally: Ellen Collier, John Collins, Roger Davidson, Louis Fisher, Sharon Gressle, Richard Grimmett, Frederick Kaiser, Mark Lowenthal, Ronald Moe, Sherry Shapiro, Stephanie Smith, and Stephen Stathis.

Most of the members of the commission and most of the speakers at the Miller Center were political appointees of one or the other party. We therefore invited to a discussion at the National Academy of Public Administration several former officials, with a career rather than a political perspective, from executive agencies and from Congress. They included Norman A. Bailey (National Security Council); Ray S. Cline (CIA and the Department of State); Marian Czarnecki (House Foreign Relations Committee); Ambassador U. Alexis Johnson (State); Carl Marcy (Senate Foreign Relations Committee); Ambassador Edwin M. Martin (State); David A. Phillips (CIA); and Melbourne L. Spector (State).

The Miller Center formed a faculty committee to advise in the preparation of this book. That group, which met a number of times, included Dean Laurin L. Henry of the Virginia Commonwealth University, and University of Virginia Professors John A. Armitage, Inis Claude, Robert H. Evans, Emmett B. Ford, Norman Graebner, Matthew Holden, Jr., Kenneth W. Thompson, and Adam Watson.

During the preparation of this study, the Miller Center has invited a number of leading governmental figures to give talks and conduct discussions relative to the presidency. Some of these have made transitions their primary subject; others have talked less formally with a few of us on that topic following their main presentations. Among these Miller Center visitors have been Lucius Battle, Jacob Beam, Herbert Brownell, Zbigniew Brzezinski, Phillip Buchen, Hedley Bull, McGeorge Bundy, William Bundy, Ellsworth Bunker, Lloyd Cutler, I. M. Destler, Douglas Dillon, Arthur Flemming, Leonard Garment, Roswell Gilpatric, Andrew Goodpaster, Louis Halle, Ken Hechler, Richard Helms, Laurin Henry, Robert Johnson, Nicholas Katzenbach, Carol Laise, John Macy, Leonard Marks, George McGhee, David Newsom, Frank Pace, Bradley Patterson, James Pfiffner, Dean Rusk, Charles Schultze, Hugh Scott, Bromley

Smith, Gerard Smith, Elmer Staats, John Steelman, Herbert Stein, Robert Strauss, Richard Strout, and Jack Watson.

The theme and the contents of this book have borrowed—perhaps a more correct word would be *stolen*—a great deal from the observations and the wisdom of all of those named above. We are particularly indebted to those who arranged, or helped us arrange, the various meetings, including David Bell, Charles Bowsher, Harold Relyea, Melbourne Spector, and Jack Watson.

We are indebted to the staff of the Miller Center: its administrative officers, Clyde Lutz and Reed Davis; its secretarial staff, whose patience, even when sorely tried, matched its effectiveness and good humor—Patricia Dunn, Anne Hobbs, Shirley Kohut, and Nancy Lawson; and several graduate assistants, including especially Joseph Devaney and Matt Dever.

Finally, we are grateful to those who, at our request, read all or part of the manuscript and gave us the benefit of their criticisms and suggestions. They have included General Andrew Goodpaster, Laurin L. Henry, David Newsom, Kenneth W. Thompson, Cyrus Vance, and James S. Young.

Surely if this work could live up to those who have contributed to its making, it would be a very good book.

# PART I

# The Evolving Nature
# and Problems of
# Presidential Transitions

CHAPTER 1

# The Many Faces of
# Political Transitions

---

There is no Death! What seems so is transition.

—Henry Wadsworth Longfellow
"Resignation"

The underlying quest of this study is for the optimum balance between change and continuity in the government of the American people. One purpose of presidential transitions, especially those involving the transfer of power from one political party to the other, is to facilitate change in the course of government. In such transitions, change is inevitably disruptive to continuity and perhaps even to coherence of public policy. How much such disruption can we tolerate without serious damage to our institutions and basic values, to the effective conduct of public business, and to the general public interest? Or, more constructively, how can we best manage political transitions so as to permit real change with minimal damages? In the realm of foreign affairs, presidential transitions are more complex, though not necessarily more difficult, than on the domestic scene. This is because foreign policy decisions must be reached in a worldwide context of over 170 sovereign nations and a great variety of international organizations that we may be able to influence but not directly control.

Like other studies of presidential transitions, this book seems to emphasize the negative: how to minimize the dangers, the potential damage, and the difficulties of change rather than how to maximize the benefits that derive from change. Its goal, like that of most earlier studies of transition, is to promote understanding of the hazards and roadblocks so as to facilitate effective and responsible change. The balance in our government is tilted toward stability and continuity rather than change. Since the adoption of the Bill of Rights, our Constitution has been officially amended only sixteen times in almost two centuries. It has been applied, extended, interpreted, and modified by every branch of the government, but its essence persists. The secretary of state has shelves full of treaties, statutes, executive orders, and court decisions that he and his department must follow. None of these is changed automatically by transition, and during the months succeeding a transition, only a tiny proportion can be changed. There are thousands of personnel engaged in thousands of routine tasks for which they are specially trained. Neither most of the people nor most of the routines are changed by transition. The Department of State handles an average of about three thousand cables every day—far more than all the news services together. This load and the work it represents do not change with transitions. In fact, the bringing about of significant change, often called improvement or reform, is as great a challenge as minimizing the turbulence associated with transitions.

The transfer of leadership can be difficult and occasionally disastrous in any type of organization—from a revolution in an empire to a death in the family. But in few organizations does one find such traumatic transitions as occur periodically in the American national government. Government is different, and transitions in government are also different: they follow vigorous and even vicious political campaigns, they are the epitome of conflict, and they affect public policy questions of extraordinary importance. An American presidential transition from one political party to another is likely to mean the separation of many hundreds of administrators, including most of those at the very top, around January 20, and the identification and appointment of an equal number of replacements who will come in during subsequent days and weeks. Most of them will be strangers to one another and to the career personnel whom they will supervise. Some will be strangers to government itself. There have been a few corporate takeovers in the private sector in which the bulk of top management personnel were replaced, but even those have hardly ever been carried out with the haste and unpreparedness that so often characterize our presidential transitions.

By way of analogy, one might imagine the sudden replacement of a university president in the middle of an academic year. He would be succeeded on a given day by another person who had no prior experience in the governing of any university other, perhaps, than as a member of a board of regents or as president of a small junior college. The new president would have just completed a speaking campaign in which he castigated the incumbent president, his associates, his programs, and perhaps the institution itself. On the same day as this new president entered on duty, all of the vice-presidents, deans, assistant deans, officers in the administration, some department chairmen, most of their secretarial help, and a number of the senior professors closely associated with the preceding president would be removed; a few might be temporarily retained pending appointment of their successors. Many of the replacements would be persons with no previous experience in universities except as students; some would have publicly expressed their opposition to higher education; and some, including the incoming president himself, would be on record as doubting the loyalty, ability, and integrity of the tenured faculty. They would also be publicly committed to changing the curriculum, abolishing some of the academic departments and professional schools, adding some new ones, and modifying the standards of admission and the requirements for graduation. To carry this analogy one step further, amidst all this bedlam the regular activities of the university would have to be carried out: classes must meet, examinations be given, buildings and housing be maintained, research be conducted, and so forth.

A main difference between a transfer of power to a new president of the United States and the university scenario imagined above is that the United States government is many times larger, more complex, and more important. The period between election and inauguration is normally one in which the stature and influence of the incumbent are rapidly shrinking, as are those of most of his aides and other appointees. They are often—though not always—inhibited from undertaking foreign policy initiatives that will commit or bind the behavior of their successors.[1] The latter normally, and quite properly, refuse to accept responsibility for anything that happens within the government prior to their inauguration on January 20.

---

1. Some outgoing presidents, however, take actions for partisan or policy advantage, a practice begun in President John Adams' famous "midnight appointments" in 1801 and further exemplified in the last-minute regulations, contracts, and other commitments of many recent outgoing administrations.

This can be a source of difficulty and embarrassment when decisions simply have to be made. But on many of the more important matters requiring decisions, the period of about eleven weeks following a presidential election and sometimes extending several weeks beyond the inauguration is a hiatus in American government when we have little dynamic leadership. During that period, the outgoing president must produce some of his most important messages: his report on the State of the Union, which normally becomes a review of past accomplishments and of current problems; a budget; and an economic report. But many of the decisions involved in the latter two are really only exhortations. The expiring administration is fully aware that its successors can change them at will if they have the time and knowledge and expertise to do so.

Fortunately—as in the university, where classes must go on— governmental activities proceed during these periods. Checks are written and dispatched; mail and thousands of airgrams are written and delivered; military recruits are trained; existing defense installations are manned and operated; research goes on; contracts and agreements are negotiated, signed, and executed. Perhaps 99 percent of the work of the government is preprogrammed, scheduled, and continuing. The way it is done is prescribed in official documents and the learned behavior of officers and employees.

These constitute a powerful source of continuity, but continuity entails several potential costs. One is that some ongoing activities *should* change or be stopped and that some new activities *should* be started. These often require basic decisions that are difficult in a period of ambiguous leadership. The consequences of neglect or delay may be severe. Another is that unforeseen contingencies and emergencies may arise during the interregnum. These might include the raising of a trade barrier, a run on the dollar, the seizure or murder of American personnel or property, a revolution in a nation in which the United States has a vital interest, the invasion of one foreign country by another, the negotiation of a treaty, and countless others. The period of transition is one of particular vulnerability for this country, because other nations, both foes and friends, may try to take advantage of our difficulties in making and implementing decisions when neither the incumbent president nor the president-elect is in firm control.

## The Importance of Transitions in Building New Administrations

The decisions of an incoming president after his election but before inauguration are often crucial for his administration, but unfortunately they must be made when he is least equipped to make them. He and his campaign aides are tired, perhaps nearly exhausted, physically and emotionally. They have just demonstrated their skill in conducting a successful political campaign, but few if any of them have experience in governing a nation. They are typically encumbered with a variety of slogans, promises, and exhortations about foreign (as well as domestic) affairs, but have little idea how to make them operational—if that is indeed possible. To quote Lyn Nofziger, friend and political adviser of Ronald Reagan, the most pressing question after Reagan's election to the governorship of California was: "My God, what do we do now?" [2] The same question—with an exclamation point as well as a question mark—must occur to all successful presidential candidates and their staffs. Furthermore, they are likely to have been attacking and vilifying the very government they must now lead, including the elements on which they are suddenly most dependent, the Congress and the bureaucracy—a posture not conducive to trust and to effective communications.

In most organizations, these would seem prescriptions for disaster. In America we should probably credit the faith, tolerance, and patience of the people, the politicians, and the bureaucracy for the fact that, so far at least, the Republic has survived all its presidential transitions. And in recent years a good many actions, discussed in later chapters, have been taken to alleviate transition problems and dangers.

But the problems associated with presidential transitions extend well beyond the period between the election and the inauguration, for both the incoming and outgoing administrations. Before the election party platforms have been adopted; both candidates will have made pronouncements on policies and programs; some commitments will have been made; a campaign staff, many of whom expect (and some of whom will receive) high appointments in the new ad-

2. Quoted in Lou Cannon, *Reagan* (New York, 1982), 119.

ministration, has been employed. The promises, the slogans, and the rhetoric of a political campaign—however firm, honest, and realistic—all impinge on decisions reached after the election and actions taken after the inauguration. Much of the thrust and tone of the new administration is set before the election.

Often the hardest part of a transition occurs after the dust from the inaugural parade has settled. Newly appointed, inexperienced officials take their seats, surrounded by a few new acquaintances and a multitude of strangers. Most of the new officials have not as yet been appointed, though their future positions may be temporarily occupied by experienced people on an acting basis. The difficult business of translating philosophy, ideology, and rhetoric into policy and program proposals largely lies ahead, as does that of translating the latter into law, budget, and action. Effective relationships must be established with the appropriate members of Congress, with outside interests, with representatives of foreign nations and international organizations, and among and within the executive organizations themselves. The decisions, actions, and appointments or nominations that are made before and soon after a new president's inaugural are crucial to his entire term or terms in office. Collectively, they outline his general direction, his mode of operating, and the nature of his principal advisers. Individually, his appointments are closer to blueprints: they constitute, in some degree, commitments and investments for the future, some of which may drain his political capital or, more happily, enlarge it. If mistaken, they will sooner or later damage his credibility and confidence in his administration—in the eyes of the executive branch, the Congress, the American people, and governments abroad.

It should not be inferred from these difficulties that political transitions are undesirable. They are inevitable in democracies and indeed in all forms of government—as long as mankind remains mortal. Furthermore, they serve essential purposes. They are part of the processes whereby new blood and fresh ideas are brought more intimately to bear upon public policies and performance. They offer opportunities to alter directions, improve performance, and correct abuses, opportunities that might otherwise be discouraged by the forces of inertia and defensiveness of incumbents. They are essential to the maintenance of some degree of accountability of a president, his appointees, and his party to the people who elected him and who may reelect him or elect a successor who is a member of his party. The possibility of an election loss by an incumbent president or his party undoubtedly influences the motivations, behavior, and responsiveness of an adminstration throughout its term, just as do the hopes and plans for assumption of presidential power influence the statements and actions of all potential candidates prior to nomination and election. Thus, the certainty of elections and the possibilities of transition are having an impact upon the course of democratic government *all the time,* not only during the periods immediately preceding and following the legal transfers of power.

## The Succession of Political Leadership as a General Problem of Government

Problems attending governmental transitions are by no means new or unique. Transition is a part of a larger process involving the modes of terminating the tenure of leaders and selecting their successors as well as vesting them with office. The problem is as old as government, which means that it is as old, in every civilization, as the civilization itself. It is ubiquitous and eternal: all people are mortal, and persons in positions of leadership must be succeeded by others.

Political philosophers have argued the merits of collective leadership, partly to avoid the shock of transferring power from one ruler to another. Some societies have respected the leadership of their oldest members, usually men (convened in senates). The Greek philosophers, particularly Plato, opted for government by the wise and educated but offered rather little in the way of a practical means whereby the wise would be chosen, emplaced, maintained, removed, and succeeded in office. In many societies single leaders—chosen because of their class, their significant achievements, their political maneuverings, or their charisma—became recognized, accepted as leaders, and often anointed with godlike attributes. But they were mortal, and their succession could become a source of chaos and civil disruption. The answer to these dangers hit upon by many societies was the practice of granting the succession to the blood descendants of kings—the passage from generation to generation of divine attributes and kingly prerogatives, usually to the eldest son, often accompanied by a highly complex set of rules for succession if there were no eldest son. The divine right of kings could thus be maintained, despite the mortality of each individual king. "The king is dead; long live the king."

The custom and, later, the law of hereditary succession offered a number of advantages: a predictable succession, continuity, and an opportunity to prepare the successor for his new office, even from childhood. On the other hand, Jean Jacques Rousseau long ago pointed out certain risks—"of having children and monsters and imbeciles as rulers," to whom he might have added tyrants, murderers, sadists, and seniles.[3] Even in cases in which the rules of royal succession were precise and were widely accepted, there was still uncertainty. One could seldom predict when a king or queen would die—whether of natural or unnatural causes—or be otherwise rendered incapable of performing in the sovereign role. There was the possibility of coups, internal rebellions, or external wars, which might result in the displacement of the king or queen and even of the entire royal family. The time of succession arising from death or incapacity could provide the spark for an attack by a foreign power, or a civil war. Such an event, however begun, might result in the succession of a new person or even of a totally new regime or system of government. Even when no domestic upheaval occurred, successions could cause disruptions in foreign policy, for in the fifteenth through the seventeenth centuries, states were regarded as the personal possessions of their rulers, treaties were in practice held to be analogous to private contracts, and thus no international agreement signed by one prince was binding on his successor.

Hereditary monarchs who rule as well as reign are now largely a phenomenon of the past. Some royal families remain as useful symbols of the glories and the continuity of the nation and perform some convenient, usually noncontroversial, governmental functions such as receiving the resignations of ministers, calling upon another party to form a government, visiting among the citizens and explaining the government's policies, and participating in ceremonial events, both domestic and international. More frequent today are dictators, leaders of relatively small groups or committees (often

3. *The Social Contract*, trans. Willmore Kendall (Chicago, 1954), 114.

military), who have seized positions of power or have been appointed by those groups, with or without the facade of popular but noncompetitive elections.[4] Tenure in such offices is, if anything, less certain than among hereditary rulers because of the continuing threat of coups, revolts, or removals by the appointing group. And the choice of successor is far less certain, because the rule of heredity is not respected, nor, ordinarily, is a successor designated by the retiring or dying sovereign. Some dictators remain in office for very long periods. But for others, in the absence of set rules, tenure is short, and transitions are unpredictable and sometimes violent.

The problems attending transition—of determining the time, selecting a successor, and actually transferring power—have long been troublesome for democracies as well as autocracies, both in theory and in practice. The attendant dangers are legion: the temptation of leaders in power, however chosen, to retain it, whatever be the rules of the game; the temptation of those seeking but not chosen for leadership to seize power illegitimately; the danger that hostile foreign parties will seek to overthrow or move against the vital interests of a government that is in the throes of transition; the near paralysis attending the transmittal of power from one leader to a successor; the procedural problems of selecting new leadership; the continuance of knowledge, experience, and expertise within a government while changing its leadership; and many others.

Parliamentary systems seem, on paper at least, able to handle the problems more effectively and expeditiously and with less disruption than the American presidential system.[5] Among their alleged advantages is the very absence of a schedule fixing primaries and

4. For contrasting views of the effect of transitions in the Soviet Union, see Valerie Bunce, *Do New Leaders Make a Difference? Executive Succession and Public Policy Under Capitalism and Socialism* (Princeton, 1981) and Philip G. Roeder, "Do New Soviet Leaders Really Make a Difference? Rethinking the 'Succession Connection,'" *American Political Science Review*, LXXIX (December, 1985), 958–76.

5. For comparative purposes, studies of transitions under the parliamentary system of Great Britain by Don K. Price and the mixed system of France by Robert Evans were commissioned in connection with this project. They have been published in Frederick C. Mosher (ed.), *Political Transitions and Foreign Affairs in Britain and France: Their Relevance for the United States* (Lanham, Md., 1986).

caucuses, conventions and nominations, elections and inaugurations. This period of electoral choice-making is characterized by an increasing concentration of all participants on the contest and its outcome and by a growing neglect of the business of governing. Concomitant is the far shorter length of the process. In most parliamentary governments the whole election and transition season lasts but a few weeks, compared with two years or more for American presidents.[6] A third factor, one of singular importance, is that the leaders who constitute or who will constitute the government—including the president in those parliamentary countries that have that office—normally are drawn entirely from a pool of people with prior experience, usually long experience, in national affairs, in the parliament and (for the majority of them) in the cabinet. A change of government is like a change from one well-worn pair of shoes to another: the wearer may walk in a somewhat different direction, but his footgear nonetheless fits comfortably. In some parliamentary countries, such as Great Britain, the parties themselves have already chosen their leaders, so that all know in advance who will be prime minister if one or another party wins a majority in Parliament. The prime minister possesses long experience on both majority and minority sides of the House, as do most of the ministers in his or her government. Most of the replacements will not be newcomers but "old-comers" returning to familiar haunts, conditions, and problems. They have the advantage, too, of knowing their colleagues in the government and in the civil service. In Great Britain the party out of power has what amounts to a second platoon ready to become the cabinet when there is a shift in party control of Parliament. Further, all current and previous members of British cabinets are kept informed on many developments and problems, whether secret or not, through information provided to them as members of the Privy Council. Thus, the tremendous burdens in America of familiarization, education, and acculturation of new political personnel are substantially alleviated.

Another major advantage of parliamentary systems, at least in most industrialized countries, is the higher degree of trust and confi-

6. Of course, in a less concentrated way, the political campaigns in parliamentary systems are going on all the time. But this is also true in the United States.

dence in the top career public servants up to and including the permanent undersecretaries and the directors general (or their equivalents). There is no such turnover in the upper levels of the civil and foreign services as in the United States, no such distrust, and no such break in communications. Indeed, in some parliamentary countries (Italy, for example) where politics are turbulent and new governments replace old ones every few weeks or months, the bureaucracies provide a welcome stability, carrying out the activities of government placidly and unconcernedly while the parliamentary tempest whirls.

All these alleged advantages of parliamentary systems in expeditiousness, preparedness, and continuity are not without their costs. The American system brings in more new blood, new perspectives, new ideas; it offers more responsiveness to shifting needs and shifting popular wishes. It likely makes the government, including its administration, more reflective of the pluralistic nature of the society. And despite the trauma, the near paralysis, and the amateurism often associated with some of our presidential transitions, it has been no little achievement that this system of government is now approaching its two-hundredth birthday without a break in the presidential and governmental successions and with only one shattering uprising—the Civil War. Few other governments of any kind can boast such a record of continuity—a record all the more impressive in view of the territorial, demographic, and economic growth of this country, the variety and dynamism of its people, and the hazards it has faced from the outside.

## Foreign and Domestic Affairs: Similarities, Differences, and Connections

"Domestic policy can only defeat us; foreign policy can kill us," President Kennedy once said.[7] We Americans, who survived more than a century and a half in the happy confidence that we were protected from potential enemies by two broad oceans, have only recently discovered—and even more recently fully realized—that war might appear and annihilate us any year, any month, any day, any

---

7. Arthur M. Schlesinger, Jr., *A Thousand Days: John F. Kennedy in the White House* (Boston, 1965), 426.

hour. The faith that supported a foreign policy known as isolationism was always somewhat less than certain, as our occasionally bellicose history suggests. But today there can be no doubt. The United States is one of the two dominant and opposed nuclear and conventional powers in the world, and its foreign affairs cannot fail to be high on the list of issues in all our presidential elections and transitions. Such issues may not be the most frequently and publicly argued, but they are always among the most important and by far the most dangerous. There is no single figure more important in world affairs than the president of the United States; there is no single political transition of greater concern to the world than the transition from one president to another.

The supreme, overarching difference between domestic and foreign affairs in their interconnected relation to presidential transitions is that the stakes are so much higher in international relations. Errors, delays, or missed opportunities in public policies and actions can be costly in any arena. In international affairs they may be extremely difficult to correct or modify. Statements or actions by unsophisticated spokesmen of an incoming administration can send signals to different cultures abroad that are totally unintended, and sudden shifts in policy at the time of transitions can confuse other states in ways that leave lasting resentment.[8] Similar statements or actions of incumbents about to leave are likely to be ignored. The consequences may lead to lasting misunderstandings by allies and foes alike and to responses damaging to security, trade, diplomacy, and other relationships. During this same time—the period leading down to inauguration and soon thereafter—the nation is peculiarly vulnerable to those who may want to harm it. The authority and influence of those leaving is declining to zero; the newcomers are lacking in legal authority until inauguration and ill-equipped to exert it immediately afterward.

At one of President Eisenhower's final meetings with his National Security Council, just before the inauguration of President Kennedy, Maurice Stans, then director of the budget, remarked, "For an enemy, January 20 would be the ideal date for an attack on the United

8. Lincoln P. Bloomfield, "What's Wrong with Transitions," *Foreign Policy,* LV (Summer, 1984), 23–39.

States." Eisenhower in his memoirs observed: "A presidential inauguration could be a moment of practical dead center for the federal governmental mechanism. Further, an emergency, arising at home or abroad during the first twenty-four hours after a new President takes his oath of office, would demand decisions and actions which by reason of the unfamiliarity of new officials with their duties and authority, might result in bewilderment and lack of intelligent reaction, with resultant damage to the United States."[9]

At presidential inaugurations, elaborate security precautions are taken, including the requirement that the lowest-ranking member of the cabinet, now the secretary of education, stay in a safe place and not attend the ceremonies. But to this date at least, there seems to be no evidence that any foreign power has sought to attack this nation at its most vulnerable hour. There are abundant examples of attempts of foreign nations to help or hurt an incumbent or a candidate and to speed or delay international negotiations or actions. But the general response to an incoming president, particularly by potential enemies, is not immediately aggressive. Rather it is a cautious wait-and-see, watch-and-test attitude, not one of trying to blow him and his country out of the water.

There is no question that the stakes of presidential transitions are high not only for Americans but for most of the rest of the world. Canadian Prime Minister Lester Pearson was only partly joking when he proposed that, because American actions affected their lives so deeply, foreign citizens should be allowed to vote in American presidential elections. Our linkages, our competitions, our antagonisms with the more than 170 nations of the world reach to almost every subject of potential negotiation and confrontation—economic, social, linguistic, scientific, military, environmental—almost without end.

Foreign nations may take, withhold, or delay actions that might help or damage the chances of an incumbent or a candidate in an American presidential election in ways they perceive to be advantageous to themselves. Some of our foreign relations are thus timed to the regularities of our governmental schedule: presidential prima-

9. Dwight D. Eisenhower, *Waging Peace, 1956–1961* (Garden City, N.Y., 1965), 617–18.

ries, nominations, conventions, campaigns, elections, and inaugurals; the legislative calendar; the budget; and others. But foreign affairs also differ in degree from domestic matters in that many developments arise outside of any American schedule and beyond American control, governmental or otherwise. It is perfectly true that a great many events can and do occur on the domestic scene that are effectively beyond governmental control, but domestic tools of persuasion, compromise, and adjustment probably exceed those in the international scene, where terrorism, confrontation, and even war loom as constant threats, during transition as well as other periods.

Heads of state in the West have long enjoyed a unique position and power in regard to international affairs. They named, instructed, and dispatched their various emissaries to foreign nations, received those accredited to them from abroad, negotiated and signed alliances and agreements, commanded their armed forces, initiated and conducted their wars, and negotiated the terms for peace. This practice and the protocol that it produced were quite well established— though not without qualification—by the time of the American and French revolutions. The framers of the American Constitution were perhaps at their most conservative when they gave the president powers somewhat comparable to other chiefs of state in relation to foreign affairs and national security, powers that seemed far to exceed his authority in domestic affairs. These powers were restrained somewhat by the requirement that the Senate ratify such actions as treaties and diplomatic appointments. But it was of course anticipated by the founders that the Senate would be the more conservative, the less quixotic of the two legislative houses. Among other things, the senators would have six-year terms and would be elected by the legislatures of the states. House members, popularly elected for two-year terms, would be less strongly fortified against the hazards of reelection than either the president or the Senate and therefore were granted a lesser role.

In foreign affairs the president has from the beginning been commander-in-chief of the armed forces, and he has been given sole power to negotiate treaties with foreign powers (subject to approval by two-thirds of the Senate), to nominate diplomatic appointments (subject to approval by a majority of the Senate), and to receive for-

eign representatives (which has come to mean granting or withhold-
ing diplomatic recognition). Under these circumstances the impact
of presidential transitions on the nation's relations with the "outside
world"—if internal and external policy can any longer be so neatly
separated—has become vitally important and its dangers especially
great.

During the decade of the 1970s, Congress took major steps to re-
strain what some saw as "the imperial presidency": the War Powers
Act of 1973; the Case Act, mandating the disclosure of executive
agreements; the Congressional Budget and Impoundment Control
Act of 1974; the requirement that foreign arms sales be approved by
Congress; and closer oversight of intelligence activities. But how
many of these will survive court action is now an open question,
especially in view of the Supreme Court's recent sweeping repudiation of legislative vetoes.[10] These and other developments have tended
to constrain presidential power, and incoming administrations tend
to exaggerate the power and freedom of action they will enjoy (see
Chapter 5). But it appears still to be true that the president has a
freer and a stronger hand in foreign than in domestic matters.

Over the past fifty years at least three presidents (Roosevelt,
Johnson, and Reagan) have demonstrated their ability to grasp dominant leadership in domestic matters, and others have done so successfully in particular areas from time to time. But the president's
constitutional basis in domestic affairs is more fragile, and the political obstacles—in the executive branch, Congress, the media, interest groups, state and local governments, and the private sector—
are more numerous, scattered, and resistant to quick or impulsive
change.

On the other hand, until recently there were some factors that operated to make interparty transitions less traumatic in foreign affairs
than in domestic matters. "Politics stops at the water's edge": for at
least a generation after World War II, this statement expressed not
merely a hope or a prescription but an actual (if only imperfectly
realized) state of affairs. "Politics," in the sense of strong partisan
disagreement and vigorous public debate, operated in full force in
regard to most domestic policy, but questions of foreign policy often

10. *Immigration and Naturalization Service* v. *Chadha*, 462 U.S. 919 (1983).

commanded general agreement and evoked the sense that party rancor challenging the consensus was not only improper but also dangerous. By the time of the first postwar presidential election in 1948, both parties had come to accept a broad doctrine holding that the Soviet Union constituted the primary threat to American interests and to world peace, that its containment through American alliances with noncommunist countries in Western Europe and the Pacific was essential, but also that this rivalry should not preclude such agreements with the Soviet Union as could be reached on such subjects as arms control, decolonization, and trade. The consensus was much less perfectly realized in regard to Asia than in regard to Western Europe. Still, presidential campaigns, for all their bombast, generally did not fundamentally challenge this agreement. Instead—as with Eisenhower's pledge to go to Korea or Nixon's "plan" to end the war in Vietnam—they featured debate on which candidates could better carry out this consensual foreign policy. There was general agreement on many specific foreign policy matters as well. These included the development and support of international organizations; the Atlantic alliance; the provision of economic and military assistance to developing countries outside the Iron Curtain; and the encouragement of trade and of cultural exchange.

To a degree, such basic agreement helped to mask the difficulties of transitions by muting policy differences between the parties. Indeed, in the view of some observers, there was too much continuity, leading to an unwise staleness in outlook and even to the imputation of disloyalty to anyone who challenged the consensus. In all this, foreign policy stood in stark contrast to the frequently raucous disputes and wide swings in opinion that governed domestic politics.

But the consensus, which consisted principally of the centers of both parties, began to crack as the partisan extremes—the Republican right and the Democratic left—gained strength and voice. A first crack was the attack, similarly domestic, upon persons and organizations alleged to be sympathetic to communism, an attack known as McCarthyism, which flourished in the early fifties. The second break was the Goldwater Republican victory in the San Francisco convention in 1964—a victory for those who favored a harder line with the Soviets. The third was begun by Eugene McCarthy in 1968, and carried forward by George McGovern in his campaign against the Vietnam War and his call to "come home, America." Since that time, there seems to have been no comfortable place in between for members of either party. Discussions of foreign and defense policies are now as contentious as of domestic ones, and there does not appear to be a strong solder to link a new consensus in the near future.

The second cementing factor that reduced the traumatic impact of transitions in the postwar generation was the foreign policy establishment (or elite) that largely governed our conduct of foreign affairs after World War II. This group was bipartisan—probably the majority were Republicans. They were lawyers, investment bankers, some foreign service and military officers, scholars at prestigious universities, executives of the larger foundations, a few journalists, and scattered others. Many of them were members of the Council on Foreign Relations, and some were later associated with the Trilateral Commission. Many of them moved in and out of top positions in the Departments of Defense, State, and the Treasury, and in the White House, the Central Intelligence Agency (CIA), the United States Information Agency (USIA), the Agency for International Development (AID), and a few other agencies, and they served on a great variety of committees, panels, and informal assignments for presidents of both parties. These were persons of intellect, knowledge (especially in foreign affairs), and savoir faire who shared a common view on American objectives in the world. They were mostly residents of the large cities of the Northeast—New York, Washington, Boston, and Philadelphia—and in a few cases Chicago and the Far West. Their partisan affiliation was largely irrelevant, and many served in both Democratic and Republican administrations. Although there have been somewhat comparable blocs in certain areas of domestic policy, there has been no such widespread, mutually empathic and bipartisan grouping in domestic affairs.

Some of the same developments that weakened the foreign policy consensus also disturbed the unity of this elite. The establishment splintered along lines much the same as those that fractured the consensus among the broader public. Having drawn different lessons from the Vietnam experience, groups of notables such as the Trilateralists or the Committee on the Present Danger now contend for the leadership of public opinion, offering strikingly different prescriptions for the country's future course.[11] Deprived of their own consensus, these elites also have declined in their ability to influence mass attitudes and, by creating bipartisan agreement, to bridge transitions. Indeed, competing elites that seek to promote the candidacies of those who share their views may even accentuate the ideological divisiveness of campaigns and increase differences between succeeding administrations. Whether the establishment, or something like it, can or should be restored to any comparable degree of usefulness in reducing the trauma of transitions is today questionable.

One further factor that contributed to greater continuity and reliability in foreign than in domestic affairs has been the existence of several corps of career personnel at middle and upper levels of most of the agencies heavily involved in national security and international relations: the Foreign Service in State and comparable services in AID and USIA, the officer contingents in the constituent departments of Defense, the career service of CIA, and others. All of these include many knowledgeable persons who have served under several administrations of both parties and have helped engineer a number of earlier transitions. They probably provide a greater degree of unity and cohesiveness than do the upper levels of the civil service in most (though not all) of the primarily domestic departments and agencies.

There are, however, a few factors that work against smooth transitions in foreign, as compared with domestic, affairs. One of these is simply the inexperience of the incoming president and of all or most of his immediate aides and advisers. Of our recent presidents, all have had significant experience in state or national government and politics, but only one, Dwight Eisenhower, had significant executive responsibility in the conduct of foreign affairs prior to his election. The importance of understanding the background of major international issues, their political and strategic implications, would seem obvious, as would some knowledge of the nuances of diplomatic practice.

11. Ole R. Holsti and James N. Rosenau, *American Leadership in World Affairs: Vietnam and the Breakdown of Consensus* (Boston, 1984); Jerry W. Sanders, "Para-Institutional Elites and Foreign Policy Consensus," in Richard A. Melanson and Kenneth W. Thompson (eds.), *Foreign Policy and Domestic Consensus* (Lanham, Md., 1985), 129–52.

Three other, related factors make transitions particularly difficult in foreign and defense matters. One is the pervasiveness of secrecy, and a second is its counterpoise, the restraints on the provision and transmission of information. A third is the importance of intelligence, particularly about developments and prospective developments beyond the boundaries of the United States. All three present problems for those who would pass on or receive responsibility in foreign and security affairs—before the election, after the election, and after the inauguration. Secrets about agreements or commitments with foreign powers, covert actions, plans for contingencies, and many other matters are frequently confined to a very few top officials in a very few agencies. Making certain that the proper information is provided to everyone who needs it, but only to those persons, becomes a problem even within an administration. When such information must be passed along to others, especially party opponents, the problem is magnified many times. So are the questions of what information should be revealed to the public, the uses of information and intelligence for political purposes, and the applicability of the Freedom of Information Act. Such problems are not unique to national security and foreign affairs, but they are undoubtedly more pervasive and critical in them than in most domestic activities.

Thus, there are numerous differences between foreign and domestic problems as they relate to presidential transitions. Yet, many observers of the American scene have correctly stressed that most important foreign problems are also domestic and vice versa. Their separation is in considerable part artificial. The sale of wheat to Russia is at the same time a domestic farm problem and a basic issue in our relations with the Soviet Union; our manufacturing depends on trade policy, as do our banks on the international financial system and particularly the solvency of developing countries; recessions and inflation ripple around the globe with little regard to national boundaries. The list of examples is endless. This interlocking of foreign and domestic policy is but a further complication of presidential transitions. We have structured our government, both executive and congressional, largely on a domestic-foreign dichotomy. We have also so structured our politics, our advisory systems, and our transition teams. Commitments and promises made by or for a candidate for domestic purposes may, quite unconsciously, contradict commitments made to friends abroad. Problems perceived from a domestic perspective in one agency of the government may be conveyed to relatively naïve newcomers who receive no inkling of the opposing views on the same subject passed along by others in foreign affairs agencies in the outgoing administration. In the past little or no coordinating machinery has been established during transitions, and so existing misunderstandings and parochialism may in fact be intensified at such times.

At the presidential level, the interconnection of domestic politics and foreign policy issues and decisions is most significant and most sensitive. An American president is *ex officio* leader of the Free World, but by election he is the leader of the United States, accountable to a domestic constituency. He can hardly make significant decisions in the international arena without giving major if not primary consideration to the domestic impact upon his popularity, his influence, his political future, and his party. To a lesser extent this same phenomenon operates in the opposite direction: decisions that are primarily of a domestic nature often have an impact on the nation's, as well as the president's, international standing and influence. The foreign affairs agencies are poorly positioned and staffed to advise the president on this interdependence of domestic and international considerations. Decisions for the executive branch are essentially political and must be made by the president and his immediate staff. But the point is that decisions in either the foreign or the domestic realm cannot be made intelligently without due consideration of their probable impact in the other realm, as presidents have learned and relearned in Korea and Cuba and Vietnam and Lebanon and El Salvador, ad infinitum.

## Difficulties in the Study of
## Presidential Transitions

The impossibility of separating foreign and domestic issues is only one of a number of the difficulties in a study of this kind. Another is that most of the problems of transitions are parts of larger governmental issues that continue before and after presidential successions and are endemic in our (or any) political system. The reason they are described as transition problems is that during that period they are particularly intense and critical; but most of them are not unique to transition. The difficulties of timing transitions are part of larger problems of nomination and election and of presidential and Congressional terms. The selection of political appointees goes on throughout a presidential term, but most positions must be filled during the transition process. Some of the situations that plague transitions arise from developments begun well before a transition and with little anticipation of it—like the Iranian hostage crisis and the Bay of Pigs invasion.

By the same token, proposed solutions or improvements of transition difficulties—like lengthening the term of presidents or providing preelection public funding for transition planning—are likely to have ramifications on the governmental process far beyond transitions alone. One must be cautious not only in considering the interdependence of transition problems with other elements of government but also in evaluating the likely broader effects of changes designed to improve the transition process.

Another kind of difficulty is that there are several different types of presidential transitions, and no single generalized description encompasses them all. The type most commonly referred to and also the one to which this study is primarily directed is the transition from one president to another of the opposite political party following and consequent upon an election. In the four decades following the conclusion of World War II, there were five such transitions. They fall into two subcategories that are significantly different from each other. One occurs when an incumbent president runs and loses (Gerald Ford succeeded by Jimmy Carter in 1977, Carter succeeded by Ronald Reagan in 1981). In such cases, the electoral contest swings partly or largely on the challenger's attack on, and the incumbent's defense of, his record. There is normally little or no preelection planning for transition by the incumbent—at least not for public consumption—since such activity would suggest that he doubted he would win the election. But he may, and does, provide information, particularly on foreign affairs and national security, to his potential successor. The latter goes through extensive preparation and planning for a transition process that begins well before the election.

The second subcategory consists of instances in which the incumbent does not run for reelection. His party's candidate is someone other than himself. In all three instances of this type since World War II the incumbent's would-be successor has been defeated (Adlai Stevenson to succeed Truman in 1952, Richard Nixon to succeed Eisenhower in 1960, and Hubert Humphrey to succeed Lyndon Johnson in 1968). One would expect, though there is insufficient evidence to prove it, that interparty transitions when the incumbent president is not a candidate would be easier and smoother than those of the type described earlier, because the confrontations between the aspiring opposition candidate and the incumbent are less direct and vitriolic. There should be a readier return to civility and cooperation between the people coming in and those who are leaving and were not immediately involved in the campaign. The losing candidate and his immediate supporters quickly vanish from the political scene, though of course they may return at a later date.

A second kind of transition occurs when a president is succeeded by another member of his own party. Such an event probably would occasion some of the same problems as the interparty transitions, though with much less intensity. But here there is little recent experience to guide us. The nation has had no such transition since Herbert Hoover succeeded Calvin Coolidge more than a half century ago. The only other such occurrence in this century was the succession from Theodore Roosevelt to William Howard Taft in 1908–1909.

Transitions of a third kind occur when an incumbent dies or resigns, and is succeeded by a vice-president. This has happened three times since the last year of World War II (Franklin D. Roosevelt succeeded by Harry Truman in 1945, John F. Kennedy by Lyndon Johnson in 1963, Richard Nixon by Gerald Ford in 1974). These events have been unscheduled and therefore unplanned, making it difficult to draw conclusions or lessons from them (they are discussed briefly in Chapter 2).

A final variety of transition, ordinarily less drastic than the others, occurs when an incumbent president succeeds himself following a successful election (Truman in 1948–1949, Eisenhower in 1956–1957, Johnson in 1964–1965, Nixon in 1972–1973, and Reagan in 1984–1985). In one sense these are not transitions at all, since the same president and the majority of his appointees continue as before. On the other hand, depending partly on the president's margin of victory in the election and the degree of change in the coloration of the Congress, he may launch a basically different program and change many of his key administrators. This was certainly the case with Truman, Johnson, and Nixon. Prior to the election Johnson appointed a great variety of task forces to develop new legislative initiatives, and following his inauguration, he introduced his Great Society program to an overwhelmingly sympathetic Congress that would vie in its speed and activism with Roosevelt's New Deal Congresses. Nixon in 1972 won by a massive majority, in contrast with his slim victory four years earlier, but he failed to carry either house of Congress. Nonetheless, he undertook a major reorganization of the executive branch on his own initiative after the Congress had failed to accede to his plans. It was short-lived. He also marked his move from a first to a second term by a sweeping replacement of upper-level political appointees in the departments and other agencies, a personnel turnover almost comparable with those of transitions when party control changes. Both the reorganization and the personnel changes were apparently intended to increase White House control and agency loyalty in the executive branch.

Among the various kinds of transitions there might also be a category called "transitions that never happened"—the preparations for transition of nonincumbent candidates who lost the presidential election. As early as 1948, both the challenger, New York Governor Thomas E. Dewey, and the president designated representatives to coordinate planning for a transition from Truman to Dewey, even though President Truman was (almost alone) confident he would win the election. The two designees met on a number of occasions during the campaign, and members of Dewey's staff in Albany visited Washington in preparation for his expected takeover. In 1952 President Truman detailed two members of his staff to work with Illinois Governor Adlai Stevenson, the Democratic candidate, and one of them, David E. Bell, became a working member of the so-called Elks Club group, which wrote speeches for Stevenson's campaign and thus basically outlined what his program would be if he were elected. In 1956 Wilson Wyatt, coordinator of the Stevenson campaign, prepared an elaborate book on the projected transition from

Eisenhower to Stevenson, which died with the election. Since that time, every aspiring presidential candidate of the party out of power has taken some steps prior to election day to plan and prepare for a hoped for transition. In the cases of Goldwater in 1964, Humphrey in 1968, McGovern in 1972, and Mondale in 1984, these efforts were of course wasted.

A closing observation about individual transitions in general is that there are wide differences in their spirit, their impact, and their effectiveness at different levels and for different functions and among different actors. The executive branch of our government is like the proverbial elephant that was so variously described by the blind men, each of whom felt a different sector of its epidermis. Each had a different image of the whole beast, not because his touch gave him an inaccurate reading of the part he felt but because he could not feel the whole and how the different parts related to each other. Some activities of the government and some of its personnel, probably a large majority in both foreign and domestic affairs, are not affected at all by presidential transitions. For a few, there may be hope for or, more frequently, apprehension of, changes that do not in fact occur. Some developments initiated before or immediately following the accession of a new president may have little impact for months, even years. By and large, the things most vulnerable to change in a transition are policies and programs in politically sensitive areas, especially where the two parties have opposing positions. The people most affected by transition are likely to be those in upper-level positions who are involved in the policy determinations and the administering of those sensitive program areas, whether elected, politically appointed, or career. Even at these levels and for some of these debated functions, there is rather little consistency in the impact of transitions. Presidential transitions occasion little disturbance in large parts of the State Department, domestic and overseas, of the Defense Department, and of the CIA. Negotiations on the Panama Canal, begun under President Johnson, continued for fourteen years, surviving two interparty transitions, until the treaty was ratified in 1978. Although Reagan, along with a good many others, bitterly denounced the treaty before and during his candidacy, he did not as president undertake any steps to abrogate it.

There has been a tendency, entirely proper for some purposes, to focus almost all attention in transitions on the relations of the incumbent and the new president. Presidents, of course, symbolize and in some ways embody the changeover. They set a tone for their administrations, through their own relationships. But smoothness and cooperation at that level do not guarantee them elsewhere in the administration; nor do hostility and vitriol. In 1952–1953 it was widely thought that Truman and Eisenhower were utterly cold if not bitter toward each other—to the point that they did not speak when they rode together from the White House to the Capitol for the inaugural. For somewhat different reasons, the relationships between the new and the old teams in the Office of the Secretary of Defense at that time were difficult and distrustful. But in the service departments, notably the Army, the transition was friendly and cooperative. Cordiality reigned in the Bureau of the Budget.

The reverse can occur when the relationships at the top are cooperative and respectful if not intimate, but at lower levels cold and distant or even distrustful and hostile. One secretary of state, who worked for an intensely partisan administration, remarked that the rancor of the campaign ended with the election and that the interregnum was a period of cordiality. Another spoke about the pleasant and friendly dinner he had hosted after the inauguration for the members of both the outgoing and the incoming cabinets, all of whom viewed each other with friendliness and esteem. But it is doubtful, in either case, whether at that level there was much awareness of what was going on down below—between the newcomers and the incumbents and between the newcomers and the career people, particularly the Foreign Service officers. Generalizing about transitions or even about an individual transition can be a slippery undertaking.

CHAPTER 2

# The Discipline
# of Time

◆◆

In a sense, the category of time is more important to the President of the United States than to any other political leader in the world.

—Harold J. Laski

It's very difficult to deal with you people in the West because someone is always having one of those damn elections.

—Nikita Khrushchev

Scholars, journalists, and perhaps Americans in general like to rate and classify presidents as strong or weak, activist or passive, great, good, fair, or poor. It has long been a favorite pastime to debate whether the presidency itself was growing in strength and influence or declining. Most recently, at least until President Reagan assumed office in 1981, the prevailing judgment was that presidential power had been declining since the 1960s. Many of these assessments have recognized that circumstances external to the presidents themselves and beyond their control conditioned or determined the nature, quality, and impact of their performance. Great national emergencies have produced crucial challenges to presidents, and their responses to such challenges have often elicited appraisals of relative greatness. Greatness in presidents requires a good deal of native ability, an emergency—and luck.

What has been left out in the evaluation of presidencies and their powers has been the fluctuation of assessments of their popularity, strength, and achievements before, during, and following their terms in office. In fact, there is a considerable regularity in the degree of approval *within* presidential terms and in the periods before and after them. The influence of a presidential candidate and of a president depends upon a great many factors that are beyond his control.

But in general, a candidate's popularity rises between nomination and election if he is increasingly perceived as a probable winner (e.g., Eisenhower in 1952, Johnson in 1964, Nixon in 1972, and Reagan in 1984) and declines if his chances of election grow bleaker (Truman in 1948, Goldwater in 1964, and McGovern in 1972). Between election and inauguration, popularity and the potential influence of a president-elect rise. This was true in the cases of Eisenhower in 1952–1953, Kennedy in 1960–1961, Nixon in 1968–1969, Carter in 1976–1977, and Reagan in 1980–1981. The converse is true of a president who has been defeated or whose party's nominee has been defeated by the candidate of the other party (or even, presumably, who is being succeeded by a member of his own party). They are the losers and leavers.

Usually the peak of a new president's popularity and influence occurs at his inaugural or soon thereafter. The public-opinion polls over the past several decades are basically consistent: a first winter and spring of high presidential popularity, which, however, begins to decline soon after inauguration; there is a continuing decline thereafter, perhaps temporarily halted or reversed by events and during the midterm congressional campaigns, and a nadir often reached as the fourth year begins. The early wave of popularity may be enhanced or temporarily renewed by specific events, such as Eisenhower's negotiated peace in Korea; an inspiring inaugural address, like that of Kennedy in 1961; a walk down Pennsylvania Avenue following the inauguration by Carter and his family; the courageous response to and recovery from an assassin's bullets by Reagan. A show of strength and will in foreign affairs strengthens the popularity of a president. Kennedy is said to have been appalled that his popularity rose after the disastrous Bay of Pigs attack. Carter enjoyed a massive jump in his popularity soon after the Iranian crisis began, as did Reagan following his triumph in Grenada. Conversely, appearances of American weakness and frustration in foreign affairs over a long period work against a president's popularity: for example, Johnson and Vietnam, and Carter and the Iranian hostages.

The degree to which popularity can be translated into governmental action varies widely, depending upon a great many factors including the organization, the skill, the strategy, and the priorities of the new president and his aides. In the last half century, there have been only three occasions when the Congress, either as bride or mother-in-law, was virtually forced to accompany a president on his "honeymoon"—the early months after the first inaugurations of Presidents Roosevelt, Johnson, and Reagan. Other such opportunities were diminished because of adverse elections in Congress, narrow electoral majorities, or intraparty differences.

The political and psychological climate for presidents-elect and new presidents is nonetheless usually favorable. Barring emergencies, it is better at the beginning than it will be for the rest of their terms. A recent study showed that the percentage of disapproval of presidents from Truman to Carter, as measured by Gallup polls, increased on the average for the duration of their terms with the single exception of Eisenhower, for whom there was no substantial change.[1] High popular support can be a strong inducement, indeed a compulsion, to legislative and bureaucratic cooperation with a president's program. A president-elect is likely to enjoy a loyal, smart, ambitious, and enthusiastic staff. His own enthusiasm and confidence may be enhanced by a higher than usual degree of unity in his party and a mandate or at least an expression of approval from a little more or less than half the voting public. He normally will have ideas, if not a rounded program, that he feels will be good for the country.

But there are other considerations. Many of the successful candidate's closest advisers, campaign staff, and other political adherents may be inexperienced, inept, and totally unprepared for the responsibility of putting his program into effect (as indeed may be the candidate himself). He is likely to be burdened by commitments and promises made during the campaign and by pledges on policy and program that he will sooner or later find are impossible to carry out. He is almost certain to be rushed. If he falls into the trap of trying to put through his entire program the first year, the effort will likely prove counterproductive, overburdening the Congress, the public, and the bureaucracy with too many things at once. But if he does not move quickly, he may be missing opportunities that will not occur

1. Richard A. Brody, "Public Evaluations and Expectations and the Future of the Presidency," in James Sterling Young (ed.), *Problems and Prospects of Presidential Leadership in the Nineteen-Eighties* (3 vols.; Washington, D.C., 1982), I, 37–56. See also Stephen Hess, "Portrait of a President," *Wilson Quarterly*, I (Winter, 1977), 38–48.

again or neglecting things that should be attended to—damaging himself, his party, the nation, even the world.

So the months before and after inauguration are not easy ones for an incoming president. They provide him perhaps his greatest opportunities for achievements and greatness but also for mistakes of commission and omission that may damage his entire presidency.

Very nearly the opposite effect occurs for the incumbent president who is to be replaced. His standing and influence decline, reaching a nadir in the last few days before his successor is to be inaugurated. As recent participants in transitions have observed:

> A lame duck President might look at his authority to govern in the transition period as if it were a large balloon with a slow leak. If he acts with dignity, foresight, and firmness immediately after his defeat, the leak will initially be small and the President will retain the loyalty and good will of most of his government and of the Congress. But he must recognize that the balloon is ineluctably shrinking with each passing week. Therefore, he should try to schedule major decisions during transitions in the first six weeks after the election. By the end of the year, he will have lost the attention of the permanent government and can accomplish very little.[2]

For an incumbent president who decides not to run for reelection, the decline begins when he announces his decision, which may be many months before the election. (Truman in 1952 and Johnson in 1968 both withdrew in March of those years, though Truman seems to have made his decision well before then.) This is probably also true of presidents in their second term who cannot run again because of the limitations of the Twenty-second Amendment, though the evidence is slimmer here (Eisenhower in 1957–1961 and Reagan beginning in 1985). When it is widely expected that a candidate of the party other than the incumbent's will win, the latter's influence may begin its decline long before the election, and foreign governments may behave accordingly, even, it is said, to the point of undertaking

2. William Tucker, Harrison Wellford *et al.*, "Transition of the President and President-elect [1980]" (Typescript of projected manual in Miller Center Transition Files), 13. Jimmy Carter has argued that he was able to obtain Republican backing in Congress in November and December of 1980, after his defeat, that he might not have received had he been reelected. See *Jimmy Carter on the Presidency* (Washington, D.C., 1984), 14.

to negotiate with representatives of the anticipated winner during the campaign. After the election, the losing party, even if its administration is still in office, is likely to become almost irrelevant in major aspects of foreign affairs—to both friends and enemies—except in those occasional instances in which other countries can consummate agreements more favorable to their interests than they would expect from the new administration. One likely case of this in recent history was the release of the hostages from Iran on the day of Reagan's inauguration. But in the main, a party voted out of office encounters attitudes like those described by Dean Acheson when he attended his last NATO Council meeting in December, 1952, after the election of Eisenhower and the Republicans: "Our [foreign] colleagues treated us with the gentle and affectionate solicitude that one might show to the dying, but asked neither help nor advice nor commitment for a future we would not share with them. For this they were waiting for our successors."[3]

It is obvious that other nations follow and study American elections with great care. They are concerned about the political declarations of both candidates during the campaign and about those of the winner after it. Indeed, there is some evidence that there is a periodicity in international relations that synchronizes with American presidential elections. For example, there has long been a belief that the election of a new American president prompts the Soviet Union to "test" his will and the limits to which he can be pushed. On the other hand, there is some evidence that incoming presidents generally take aggressive positions and actions, especially in relation to the Soviets, partly because of statements and popular commitments made during the campaign and earlier, partly to demonstrate that they are tough on communism and to refute the allegation that they are "soft," and partly from conviction.[4] For example, in the first months of their first full terms:

3. Dean Acheson, *Present at the Creation: My Years in the State Department* (New York, 1969), 708.

4. On this point see especially George W. Breslauer, "Soviet Politics and the U.S. Presidential Cycle," a paper presented at the meetings of the American Association for the Advancement of Slavic Studies, Washington, D.C., October 15, 1982. Breslauer also finds a rough coincidence between American presidencies and the power cycles and major domestic policy shifts in the Soviet Union. According

Eisenhower (1953) approved the doctrines of massive retaliation and "liberation" of countries behind the Iron Curtain
and directed tests of hydrogen bombs.

Kennedy (1961) authorized acceleration of missile programs to
"close the missile gap," directed the invasion of Cuba that
came to be known as the Bay of Pigs fiasco, and asked for
substantial increases in the defense budget.

Johnson (1965) began the bombing of North Vietnam and increased American forces there.

Carter (1977) launched his human-rights campaign and proposed that Moscow make large cuts in its strategic forces.

Reagan (1981) sought dramatic increases in defense funds—
"to close the window of vulnerability"—for the MX, the
B1, two nuclear carriers, and other massive weapon systems, and repeatedly denounced Russia.

It is interesting that those presidents who had second terms,
Eisenhower, Nixon, and Reagan, began those terms on much less
hostile and aggressive themes. Nixon at the outset of his first term
(1969) does not fit the pattern, partly because of his promise to end
the Vietnam War and perhaps also because his reputation as an anticommunist was well established nationally and internationally. One
can only guess whether further experience will conclusively verify
that incoming presidents typically increase America's aggressiveness
and hostility in foreign affairs. But it does seem clear that political
transitions from one party to another are usually accompanied by
shifts in strategy and posture.[5]

Under our Constitution, there is a periodicity in American government and politics that is regulated more by the calendar than by

---

to his review of the last thirty years, the key changes in the Soviet power struggle
and in domestic policy occur with some regularity in four-year periods at about the
time of presidential transitions. This regularity may have begun accidentally with
the death of Stalin shortly after the inauguration of Eisenhower in 1953 and the
overthrow of Khrushchev just before the election of Johnson in 1964. That cycle
seems somewhat tenuous and would require a good deal further experience to establish or disprove. See also Richard J. Stoll, "Presidential Reelections and the Use
of Force," *Journal of Conflict Resolution*, XXVIII (June, 1984), 231–46.

5. See John Lewis Gaddis, *Strategies of Containment: A Critical Appraisal of
Postwar American National Security Policy* (New York, 1982).

living people. The effect of that periodicity on American foreign relations has been little analyzed in the scholarly literature. One of the most consistently difficult and critical times for American democracy occurs in the months preceding and following the transfer of the presidency from one party to the other. Presidential transition is only one facet of the broader problem of periodicity in American government, but it is a critical one that deserves much more attention than it has been given.

## Temporal Imperatives

In law and custom and to the naked eye, the sequence of events whereby a president succeeds another (or himself) following an election seems quite logical, orderly, and simple. In the summer of every year divisible by four, the two political parties hold conventions of delegates who have been chosen in various ways in the states and are variously committed. The conventions adopt platforms and select candidates for the presidency and vice-presidency. Following a campaign in the fall, the people elect the candidates of one party or the other on the first Tuesday after the first Monday in November. At the same time they choose congressmen, one-third or more of the senators, and sundry state and local officials. At noon on January 3 of the following year the new Congress meets and organizes itself. During the next fourteen days the incumbent president transmits to the Congress a message on the state of the union, an economic report, and a budget for the fiscal year that will begin the following October. At noon on January 20, a new (or incumbent) president assumes (or resumes) office for the following four years. Forthwith he appoints or nominates his staff in the White House, his cabinet, and a few heads of other agencies. Several hundred other top administrative officials are named during the following weeks or months.[6]

6. For convenience, a few steps and exigencies, such as the convening and vote of the electoral college and the role of third and other minor parties, have been omitted. Also omitted is reference to the succession to the presidency of a vice-president, which is discussed below. It may be noted, too, that the only events cited here that are prescribed and dated by the Constitution are the beginning of Congress (though its date of convening may be changed by law) and the inauguration of the president, both covered in the Twentieth Amendment.

That is it. There is in law no transition, just a point in time. Except in cases of reelection, a new president assumes authority and responsibility totally and abruptly the moment he finishes reciting the oath of office. Most of our incoming and outgoing presidents have sought to emphasize that there is no period when there exists either a vacuum or a sharing of presidential authority. Indeed, President Eisenhower eschewed the word *transition*, preferring to refer to *turnover* to make clear that the change was not a process but an instant. This legal transfer of authority and responsibility will be referred to in this study simply as *inauguration*. But in the attitudes, behavior, and perceptions of both participants and observers, there is a major change that is not instantaneous but lasts over weeks, months, and even years. There are also wrenching personal transitions: for the incoming president, from candidate to president-elect to president; for many successful campaigners and other appointees, from private life to high public office; for those leaving, from official authority and responsibility to private life; and for many career public servants, adjustment to, and education of, new political appointees and additional adjustment to changes in policy, directions, and leadership.

Probably the time most frequently denoted by the word *transition* is the period of about eleven weeks between the election and the inauguration.[7] For reasons of convenience, if not of strict accuracy, this period will be referred to as the *interregnum*, meaning a "pause or interruption in continuity."[8] In this study the word *transition* will be used to cover a period of time that is usually longer and much less definite, for it varies with presidencies and with issues: from the time that candidates or incumbents first consciously begin to plan for the transfer of authority to the time when a new administration is in full swing, with major appointments made and in place, with policies, programs, and budgets for the first year firmed up and ap-

7. This refers only to the succession of new presidents, not reelections or turnovers following the death or resignation of an incumbent president.

8. The first and the etymologically correct definition of *interregnum* is "the period between the departure of one sovereign and the induction of his successor." Presidents of course are not sovereigns, and our system provides virtually no time when we are without a president or vice-president temporarily filling in, though there may be considerable gaps in the exercise of effective power. See *Random House Dictionary of the English Language* (1967).

propriate relations established with institutions and people outside the executive branch. The beginning point may be before or after the nominating convention and in some instances may occur a year or more before inauguration, as in the case of the lame-duck presidents who are constitutionally prohibited from reelection. The ending point is likely to be six or eight months after inauguration in most instances, and for some purposes earlier or even later.

These three different time dimensions for viewing the transfer of the presidency, however, are all useful, for they tend to emphasize its different aspects. The focus on the inauguration concentrates on legal power and the psychological impact on the people who are losing and gaining it. But its most significant feature is an indirect one: the actions and perceptions of those participants during the periods before and immediately after the transfer. This is particularly the case as a consequence of the consistent refusal of both incoming and outgoing administrations to share responsibility, at least for official and public purposes, and the inevitable impingement of the actions of one upon the other during these periods.

The second time dimension, the interregnum, focuses attention upon the relationships of the groups concerned during this period— the declining momentum and influence of the old administration, the formation and education of the new "team," and the differing pressures and commitments on both in taking and revealing positions on issues. It also directs attention to the mechanics of transition: financing, office space, preparation by the incumbents and study by the newcomers of briefing books and other materials, designation and work of transition teams, recruiting and appointing of new personnel, establishing relations with Congress, the problems of career personnel, and others.

The third dimension, which encompasses the whole period from the beginning of planning to the early consequences of transition decisions, encourages more attention to the influence of the political campaign; the nature and content of substantive problems; the planning, implementation, and early effects of changes in policy, program, personnel, budget, and organization; and relationships with foreign countries as well as with Congress, the bureaucracy, and private interests.

Viewed in this longest, third dimension, transitions are governed by punctuation points in time, most of which are beyond the control of the candidates. For a challenger who is successful in both the nomination and election decisions, there are a number of principal deadlines.

## Timing of Key Actions in Transitions

| ACTION | TIME | AUTHORITY |
|---|---|---|
| Decision to run | Up to a year or more before election | By the candidate himself |
| Party campaign for nomination | Primaries, caucuses, and conventions in late winter and spring of election year | By state laws, modified to some extent by pressure from the parties |
| Party convention | Summer of election year | By the two parties |
| Election | First Tuesday after first Monday of November | By law |
| Convening of new Congress | January 3 | By Constitution (Twentieth Amendment) but can be changed by law |
| Economic report of the president | Between January 3 and May 3; normally middle of January | By law |
| State of the Union message | Normally middle of January | Message by Constitution, time by practice |
| Budget | On or before January 18 | By law |
| Inauguration | January 20 | By Constitution (Twentieth Amendment) |
| Beginning of fiscal year | October 1 | By law |

There seems to be wide agreement among politicians, academicians, and other citizens that the whole process whereby we select and install our presidents is too long. In some ways it never ends. In the Republican convention in 1984, there was more interest and intraparty campaigning for 1988 than for 1984, the determination of the candidate for 1984 being a foregone conclusion. Under the liberal definition of transitions used in this book, beginning when a candidate of either party starts seriously to plan for it and ending when the key appointive jobs are filled and the new president's basic programs are announced or emplaced, transitions last a year and a half or more. This is far longer than in the British and other parliamentary systems, where the campaigns and transitions are completed in a matter of weeks. Even in France, where the focus of transition is a presidential election, the process proper lasts only a few weeks. In fact, one journalist complained about the "interminable two months" of the Giscard-Mitterrand campaign in 1981.[9] In a sense, however, the quest for political leadership in many other countries, like our own, is also a continuous, never-ending process, partly because the party leaders in their day-to-day activities in parliament are seeking reputation and advantage for the next election. In Britain, as at least one scholar has observed, the biweekly parliamentary question hour is more important for the next political campaign than for its impact upon current decisions.[10]

# The Special Case of
# Vice-Presidential Succession

Successions to the presidency by vice-presidents as a consequence of assassination, natural death, or resignation are quite unlike other transitions in their relation to time. They are unscheduled, usually unpredicted, and sudden; there is almost no time for preparation. Yet they have occurred with a disturbing frequency and consistency in American history. Beginning with William Henry Harrison, who died a month after his inauguration in 1841, an elected president has left office by reason of death on the average of every twenty years.[11]

9. *Le Monde*, May 8, 1981, quoted in Robert H. Evans, "Presidential Transitions in the French Fifth Republic: Their Impact on Military and Foreign Affairs," in Mosher (ed.), *Political Transitions and Foreign Affairs in Britain and France*, 61–62.

10. Don K. Price, "Transitions in Political Leadership and Their Impact on Foreign Policy: The British Experience," in *ibid.*, 11.

11. For the superstitious, the record is eerie. With the single exception of Ronald Reagan, who barely escaped death from assassination, every president elected or reelected in a year ending in zero and divisible by four between 1840 and 1980 was killed or otherwise died in office. The presidents, with the dates of their election or reelection, were: Harrison, 1840; Lincoln, 1860; Garfield, 1880;

Transitions to vice-presidents are in some ways simpler than other transitions, because vice-presidents in the twentieth century have always been of the same party as the presidents they succeeded, so there is no partisan reversal. But in other ways they are more difficult, because there has been no (or only a very brief) anticipation of the change. A vice-president, whose principal reason for holding the office is to take the place of the president in the case of his death, incapacity, or resignation, is constrained by common courtesy and civility, and by the president's predictable resentment, from making any visible preparations to fulfill his primary role. Some months before President Nixon's resignation in 1974 a small group on Vice-President Ford's staff designated itself a "secret transition team" to prepare for a transition that seemed increasingly probable. Ford learned of the effort a few days before the turnover of the presidency, and later wrote that had he known of it he would have "demanded that they stop. If Nixon or any one of his supporters found out, it would have been construed as an act of disloyalty on my part, and the results could have been disastrous. It was a dangerous and questionable undertaking." It may be noted that the originator of the project, Philip W. Buchen, Ford's close friend and later his counsel to the president, considered the work less than adequate, partly because of the group's fear of detection and its inability to reach outside for information.[12]

In some ways, the vice-presidency is a good spot in which to prepare oneself for the presidency. It is near the center of things, though never quite at it. Vice-presidents can meet important people at home and abroad, observe the workings of the executive branch at first hand, advise the president if asked, and contribute to their party's political health. At least since President Roosevelt named Vice-President Henry Wallace to head his Board of Economic Warfare

---

McKinley, 1900; Harding, 1920; Roosevelt, 1940; and Kennedy, 1960. Four of them (Lincoln, Garfield, McKinley, and Kennedy) were assassinated. In all of the nation's history, the only other president to die in office was Zachary Taylor, who was elected in 1848 and died in 1850.

12. This information is drawn primarily from an unpublished paper by Buchen, "Problems of Unscheduled Presidential Transitions" (Typescript in Miller Center Transition Files). The quotation is from President Ford's memoirs, *A Time to Heal* (New York, 1979), 24.

early in World War II, vice-presidents have usually been given some post of continuing responsibility. During recent presidencies they have met regularly with and advised presidents and participated in meetings of the cabinet and National Security Council, as well as presiding over the Senate from time to time. Four of the eight presidents since World War II had earlier been vice-presidents.

But much of the job remains ministerial, ceremonial, or simply hollow. It includes goodwill visits abroad, political speeches, and attendance at funerals of foreign dignitaries.[13] Vice-presidents seldom play a prominent part in making governmental decisions or in bearing responsibility for them. Over the last half century, presidents in office have made increasing efforts to prepare their potential successors through participation in their councils on public policy. Ford was far better prepared to succeed Nixon than was Truman to succeed Roosevelt.[14] But in neither case was the preparation adequate.

Normally one of the first acts of a president who has succeeded from the vice-presidency is to assure the government and the country of continuity and to promise his loyal pursuit of his predecessor's policies. He also urges the political appointees of the former president to continue in their posts, and he brings into the White House with him only a very few immediate aides. Thereafter some of his predecessor's assistants and cabinet appointees resign or are replaced one by one, and the tone of the administration gradually and partially changes. But there is no such wholesale revolution of policies and people as there is in an interparty transition following an election. The real transition seems to occur at the outset of the next presidential term, after the former vice-president has been elected president in his own right and on his own program. In this century every president who has succeeded to the office in midterm has run to succeed himself in the following election, and in every case but that of Gerald Ford in 1976 he has won.[15]

13. In her remarks at the Gridiron Dinner in Washington in March, 1984, Secretary of Transportation Elizabeth Dole jokingly expressed her dismay that Vice-President Bush was there, since no one had died.

14. Paul C. Light, *Vice Presidential Power* (Baltimore, 1984).

15. Theodore Roosevelt in 1904, Coolidge in 1924, Truman in 1948, and Johnson in 1964.

Vice-presidential candidates are typically chosen by the presidential nominee at the national party convention.[16] Except for presidents running for reelection, the choice is often made in haste—something like twenty-four hours—and in a climate of excitement and celebration. There is usually too little time to check the records and the qualifications (or disqualifications) of various possible vice-presidential nominees. That the results of such a process can be unhappy for the presidential candidate, his party, and the country has been demonstrated in Nixon's designation of Spiro Agnew in 1968 and 1972 and George McGovern's of Thomas Eagleton in 1972.

As long as the office of vice-president exists, there is probably no ideal way to resolve the problems of succession in the event of a presidential vacancy. But those who would improve our governmental system should consider better ways of screening and choosing vice-presidential candidates. They should consider also the possibility of establishing a new permanent position, with appropriate staff, in the office of vice-president, with continuing responsibility for transition planning and with authority and responsibility to attend all meetings with the vice-president, to maintain relations with the president's assistants and personnel advisers, and to develop and continuously maintain contingency plans in the event of the president's departure. This position and its responsibilities could properly be legislated by Congress and thus avoid any implications about the president's survival.

## Suggested Changes in the Government Structure and Calendar

Until 1933 the schedule for elections and related matters was extremely awkward and cumbersome. Elections were held early in November; the old lame-duck Congress convened early in December and usually completed its business while the incumbent president, also a lame duck, was still in office. About four months after the election, on March 4, the new president would be inaugurated, but he would not even see the new Congress assembled until the follow-

16. Except when the office becomes vacant during a presidential term. In that case, a candidate is nominated by the president, subject to confirmation by both houses of Congress.

ing December unless he called a special session. In 1933 the Twentieth Amendment to the Constitution was ratified, but it had no influence on any interparty transition until that of Truman to Eisenhower in 1952–1953. It provided that the presidential inauguration be moved up to January 20, thus shortening the temporal distance between election and inauguration by about six weeks. It provided that the regular annual sessions of Congress begin on January 3 so that a new president would find the new Congress in session when he took office. Special sessions of lame-duck Congresses can be called by the president after the fall election—as in 1980. These provisions, which remain today the law of the land, have shortened and somewhat ameliorated the disjointed situation that pertained before, but there remains considerable awkwardness in the timing of the legislative program, the budget, and other matters.

A number of further changes in our governmental system have recently been proposed and are currently under study and discussion. The majority of them aim in various ways to bridge the separation of powers and to move our system in the direction of parliamentary government. Others would change methods whereby presidents and other officials are nominated and elected, with the objective, among others, of shortening the process. Most of the proposals would inescapably modify the transitions from one president to another, though that is not their primary purpose.

One suggestion of immediate relevance to unscheduled transitions is that in the event of vacancies in both the presidency and the vice-presidency, succession should go to members of the cabinet in the order of the seniority of cabinet positions, *i.e.,* secretary of state, secretary of the treasury, secretary of defense, and so forth. The argument underlying this proposal is that, under current law, in such a contingency, succession to the presidency would go first to the Speaker of the House, second to the president *pro tempore* of the Senate. Either or both of these offices might be held by the opposition party and the transition would create a politically grotesque situation.[17]

17. The possibility of such an event is not as remote as it first appears. In 1973–1974, in the months between the resignation of Vice-President Agnew and

Another proposal for change is that the presidential term be extended from four to six years. Like the suggestion on the vice-presidency, this would require a constitutional amendment. It might reduce the frequency of interparty transitions and their accompanying dissonances and periods of international uncertainty between elections and inaugurations. Probably the most telling argument for this change in the field of foreign affairs is that major undertakings, such as a SALT treaty or a Panama Canal treaty, often require more than four years to develop, negotiate, and ratify. A new president must first learn the ropes and the people with whom he must deal, develop strategies, and then use all his persuasive powers both abroad and at home. His last year in office is likely to be of limited use because of the long reelection campaign. If he is defeated, the new president may have to start all over again. It seems quite possible that President Carter might have obtained ratification of SALT II, in spite of Afghanistan, had he had a six-year term. It may be noted that the Panama Canal negotiations stretched over fourteen years and were probably possible only because of the continuity of the leadership of the negotiating team and the general agreement on objectives by four successive presidents.

Against the six-year term is the argument that it stretches out the period before an incompetent or unpopular president can be held accountable and replaced. The six-year proposal is usually accompanied by a proviso forbidding a president from serving two successive terms. Critics of the idea allege that this would seriously reduce the president's influence as leader, as well as his accountability. Furthermore, the recent record suggests that a six-year term would not greatly increase the average lengths of presidents' continuous span in office. Assuming that President Reagan completes his second term, eight presidents will have served an average of five and one-half years each in the forty-four years after World War II. But

---

the confirmation of Vice-President Ford, had President Nixon died, resigned, or been impeached, the Democratic speaker of the House, Carl Albert, would have become President of the United States with a totally Republican staff, cabinet, and administration. The same danger occurred between Ford's assumption of the presidency and the confirmation of Nelson Rockefeller as vice-president later in 1974.

the mean would have been considerably longer—more than seven years—were it not for the assassination of Kennedy and the resignation of Nixon. Those events of course could have occurred regardless of the length of the president's constitutional term.

Most immediately relevant to the transition calendar are two directly opposing possibilities—one to lengthen and the other to shorten the period between election and inauguration. The first is predicated on the argument that eleven weeks is simply too short a period for a new president to develop a workable approach and series of strategies and programs for governing the nation, to select and appoint several hundred new officials, and to mobilize and organize an effective and coherent administration. It may be noted that many private organizations now select their principal officers as presidents-elect more than a year in advance of their assumption of responsibilities. But in the governmental realm, it is doubtful that such an arrangement would ever be acceptable to the people, impatient that a new administration be more immediately responsive to their votes. And from the standpoint of the incumbent president and his appointees, it might magnify and lengthen a lame-duck period, already difficult, past the limits of toleration.

Probably the more realistic suggestion is that the interregnum be shortened to a very few weeks, thus diminishing the period of ambiguity over who makes decisions and speaks for the United States at home and abroad. This would of course quicken the response to the election, and it would probably reduce the possibilities and incentives for political byplay during the interregnum. The arguments against it are about the same as the claims in favor of lengthening the period—the difficulties of forming an effective and responsible government in a very short period.

The most dramatic expression for shortening the interregnum was confidentially proposed by President Woodrow Wilson during the election campaign of 1916. He apparently intended, in the event of his defeat by opponent Charles Evans Hughes—which he expected—to reduce the interregnum to almost zero. His proposal was to have the vice-president and the secretary of state, who was then next in line to succeed to the presidency, resign, after which he would appoint his opponent, Hughes, as secretary of state. Then he would himself resign, and Hughes would succeed to the presidency.

But the plan was never tried, for the simple reason that Wilson won the election.

During the spring of 1984, the Senate Judiciary Committee held hearings on a Senate joint resolution introduced by Senators Claiborne Pell and Charles Mathias, which would have moved the beginning of congressional terms back to November 15 and shifted the presidential inauguration to November 20. This would have provided only about two weeks for the formation of a new government. At those hearings an alternative was offered that seems at once more comprehensive and more workable. It would have continued the nominating convention in the summer as at present, condensed the political campaigns essentially to the month of September, held elections of both the president and Congress the first Tuesday in October, and provided for the convening of Congress on the first Monday in November and the inauguration of the president on Friday of that same week. The major annual messages, including the president's budget, would become the responsibilities of the new president.[18]

There are practical difficulties to all of these proposals that may be forbidding, at least for the near future. To move the date of inauguration either forward or backward would require a constitutional amendment and would probably also entail a change in the time of organizing the new Congress. The other alternative, changing the date of the presidential elections, could be done by statute but would require enormous changes in the habits and customs of voters. It would also involve disturbance of the laws and practices of the states and local governments and of a considerable number of state constitutions. Moving election day forward into December or January would entangle the election campaign with the Christmas holidays. Moving it back into October or September might entail another change in the timing of the fiscal year and of the elaborate congressional procedures for reviewing and acting on the budget—not necessarily an undesirable outcome. If the inauguration were moved back into December, the frantic preparations that accompany the

18. *Commencement of Terms of Office of the President and Members of Congress: Hearing Before the Subcommittee on the Constitution of the Committee on the Judiciary, United States Senate, 98th Cong., 2nd Sess.*

opening of Congress and organizing of the new administration would overlap the buying sprees and the celebration of Christmas, and of course in November there is Thanksgiving.

All in all, it appears doubtful that the punctuation points of presidential transitions will be changed in the near future, even if they should be. This book has been written on the assumption that the existing calendar will continue.

CHAPTER 3

# The American Experience

The orderly transfer of power as called for in the Constitution takes place as it has for almost two centuries and few of us stop to think how unique we really are. In the eyes of many in the world, this every-four-year ceremony we accept as normal is nothing less than a miracle.

—Ronald Reagan

The whole process has gotten out of proportion. The transition has become a summer camp, a reward for people who helped you get elected and want jobs in the new administration. Eighty per cent of their work may wind up on the shelf, but that doesn't matter. What counts is that they get a taste of the spoils.

—Unidentified aide to former
President Carter

Almost every president and president-elect in the past forty years has attested, after the election, to his intent to make the transition cooperative and smooth. Like the customary preinaugural meeting between president and president-elect and the joint statement that follows it, this act is meant to assure the public and the world, allies and adversaries alike, of the continuity of authority. Indeed, the official transition proceedings are only a part of an important set of rituals, customs, and activities that have grown up around transitions, intended in one way or another to address the problems and issues of changing the guard without upsetting the course of government. Most of these measures have little or no grounding in law, and yet a general expectation has developed that they will take place at every transition. Attempts to circumvent them would be politically costly.

## The First Century and a Half

The efforts to make transitions orderly are almost exclusively confined to the period since World War II. Although assurances of active cooperation now seem commonplace, in 1952 they marked a striking departure from earlier practice. Previous incumbent presidents and presidents-elect of the opposite party usually ignored and avoided each other. Outgoing President John Adams, for example, did not even attend the inauguration of his successor, Thomas Jefferson, but left for his home in Quincy, Massachusetts, early in that inaugural morning. Most later interparty transitions have been less bitter, but until 1952, a century and a half later, they were no more systematic.

This was not for lack of opportunity. Until the election of 1826, presidents usually served two full terms; after President Andrew Jackson's administration the rule was reversed. For the balance of the nineteenth century only one president served two full consecutive terms: Ulysses S. Grant (1869–1877). Another, Grover Cleveland, served two divided terms (1885–1889 and 1893–1897); two others, Abraham Lincoln and William McKinley, were reelected to a second term but were assassinated soon after their second inaugurals. All of the rest of the elected presidents served one term or less, and the majority were not even renominated by their parties. Moreover, four nineteenth-century presidents died in office (not including McKinley, who was assassinated in 1901) and were succeeded by a vice-president, but not a single one of these vice-presidents was later elected to the presidency in his own right.

Thus, during the last two-thirds of the nineteenth century the single-term presidency became the rule: Horace Greeley labeled it "the salutary one-term principle" in his opposition to a second term for Lincoln in 1864.[1] Further, from 1840 through 1896, nine of the fifteen presidential elections were won by candidates of parties in opposition to that of the incumbent president. In other words, presidential transitions were frequent and were accompanied by interparty turnovers more often than not.

Presidential elections during the first third of the twentieth century moved away from this pattern. Of the eight presidential election years between 1901 and 1932 only two resulted in an interparty transition. Only one president in that period, Woodrow Wilson (1913–1921), served out two full terms; two died in office. This assured

1. Stefan Lorant, *The Presidency: A Pictorial History of Presidential Elections from Washington to Truman* (New York, 1952), 256.

greater continuity but, of course, did little to arouse concern about orderliness during interparty transitions.

The rarity of full two-term presidents after Franklin Roosevelt, coupled with the failure of any candidate to succeed a president of the same party in an election, has given rise to relatively frequent interparty transitions—a reversion to the experience of the last two-thirds of the nineteenth century. There have been five such party turnovers since World War II. In foreign affairs (as indeed in domestic affairs) these recent transitions are unquestionably far more difficult, significant, and dangerous than were most of those in the nineteenth century. American presidents had from the beginning admonished the nation to avoid foreign entanglements; most of the time the army was mainly a token guard and a police force for suppressing the Indians, and the navy was not much more. We basked in the presumed protection provided by two oceans. We could enjoy leisurely and casual transitions and takeovers of the administration by men with little background for it. Alexis de Tocqueville, the keenest observer of American government in the nineteenth (or any) century, declared that this country could afford its conduct of the election and transition of presidents because the office was relatively weak in our system and because the country itself was so constituted and situated that the dangers of a hiatus during an election and changeover were minimized.

> In America the President exercises a certain influence on state affairs, but he does not conduct them; the preponderating power is invested in the representatives of the people, not in the President alone; and consequently in America the elective system has no very prejudicial influence on the fixity of the government. . . .
>
> The policy of the Americans in relation to the whole world is exceedingly simple; and it may almost be said that nobody stands in need of them, nor do they stand in need of anybody. . . . Few of the nations of Europe could escape the calamities of anarchy or of conquest every time they might have to elect a new sovereign. In America society is so constituted that it can stand without assistance upon its own basis; nothing is to be feared from the pressure of external dangers; and the election of a President is a cause of agitation, but not of ruin.[2]

2. Alexis de Tocqueville, *Democracy in America* (2 vols.; New York, 1945), I, 135–36.

In this regard, Tocqueville was echoing many others, including Americans, who would have considered a strong elective chief executive and the accompanying transfer of power suicidal except in the unusually insulated circumstances of the United States.

It appears true that the central political issues of most of the presidential campaigns during the first 150 years of our history as a nation were not foreign affairs. But this argument can be overplayed. From the beginning, our Presidents were heavily involved in external questions. The first three narrowly avoided major wars, and the fourth, James Madison, presided during a disastrous war with Great Britain. His successor, James Monroe, pronounced the doctrine that bears his name and has ever since provided us a justification and warrant for interventions in Latin America. Successors to these early presidents up to our entry into World War I participated in negotiations with, or warred upon, a great variety of foreign countries, including Mexico, Canada, Britain, France, Russia, and Spain. The chief of American negotiators was always the president, and foreign affairs must often have been near the top of his agenda. In general, one must marvel, and be thankful, that electoral campaigns and transitions did not invite repeated disasters. Tocqueville almost certainly understated the importance and centrality of presidents in foreign and defense matters, even when he wrote a century and a half ago.

The presidents in the early decades were distinguished from most of their successors in ways significant for a study of transition and foreign affairs. All had abundant experience in foreign policy prior to their presidencies. Washington, of course, had been a commanding officer in British and colonial contests with the French and Indians, as well as the American Revolution against the British, and he had managed our military relationship with our French ally during the revolution. Those who followed him had all dealt with foreign countries as responsible representatives, ambassadors, and ministers; four had been secretaries of state (Jefferson, Madison, Monroe, and John Quincy Adams). In fact, high-level diplomatic experience seems almost to have been a prerequisite for election to the presidency. But the tide turned. After 1828 the only former secretaries of state to become president were Martin Van Buren in 1836 and James Buchanan in 1856. Thus, in the last 130 years no former secretary of state has become president. Few of those who have been elected have had any responsible experience in foreign affairs. One of the most notable exceptions was Herbert Hoover, who supervised American relief efforts in Belgium, Poland, and elsewhere in Europe during and following the First World War and who organized the foreign commerce service during the 1920s when he was secretary of commerce. It should be noted, however, that during the last two-thirds of the nineteenth century the nation had a number of strong and effective secretaries of state, *e.g.*, Daniel Webster, William H. Seward, Hamilton Fish, James G. Blaine, and John Hay, though many of these lacked any prior experience in foreign affairs.

A number of presidents have had high-level military experience: George Washington, Andrew Jackson, William Henry Harrison, Zachary Taylor, Ulysses S. Grant, and, most recently, Dwight Eisenhower, whose work as commanding officer of the allied forces in Europe during World War II and as the first commander of NATO after the war certainly qualified him as diplomatist as well as soldier. William Howard Taft had been governor of the Philippines and secretary of war, and both Roosevelts had served as assistant secretaries of the navy. Most recent presidents have held commissions during wartime, and several had experience in Congress and/or as vice-president, which brought them in contact with foreign and national security problems. But on the whole, prior experience and responsibility in external affairs during the current century have been thin.

It is probably more than coincidental that two of the greatest calamities in American history ripened and exploded during or soon after presidential transitions, though their immediate origins—but not their implications or the later involvements they led to—were primarily domestic rather than international. First was the Civil War. The election of Lincoln in 1860 sparked the secession of South Carolina and other southern states. Between the election in early November of 1860 and the inauguration the following March 4, seven southern states seceded and formed a provisional Confederate government in Montgomery, Alabama. Four others joined soon after the inauguration. During the four months that then separated the election from the inauguration, there was almost no communication between the incumbent president and the president-elect, who bided his time until mid-February in Springfield, Illinois, receiving hundreds of callers and exchanging an abundance of correspondence. President James Buchanan sought at one point indirectly to enlist Lincoln's support for a compromise advanced by the Democrats, but he was unsuccessful, and Buchanan's influence, never very strong, declined to the vanishing point as the end of his term approached. Lincoln meanwhile said and did rather little publicly, though his general position was stated in his speeches on his circuitous route from Springfield to Washington. There was still hope after Lincoln's inauguration that Virginia would choose to stick with the union and that without Virginia the rebellion would collapse. Lincoln's efforts to dissuade Virginia failed, and for most of the southern states, the die was already cast. Five weeks after his inauguration, Lincoln dispatched an expedition to resupply the federal garrison at Fort Sumter in Charleston's harbor. This provoked the Confederate attack that started the Civil War. In short, here was a classic and disastrous example of the dangers of leaderlessness during a presidential transition.[3]

The second calamity occurred during the Great Depression of the 1930s and involved the transition from President Hoover to President Franklin D. Roosevelt. According to Laurin L. Henry, the preeminent authority on presidential transitions, Hoover and Roosevelt, through their correspondence and personal conferences, ended a "long-decaying convention that Presidents and presidents-elect of different parties should overlook each other's existence until inauguration day."[4] But these contacts were not effectual in producing cooperative action, because of the differing philosophies of the two men, their antagonistic postures as a result of the election campaign, and the intrinsic problems of an interregnum period in which the president was unable or unwilling to take decisive action involving future commitments and the president-elect refused to accept any responsibility. Their difficulties began almost immediately after the election when Hoover unsuccessfully sought Roosevelt's agree-

3. These summary remarks are drawn principally from Roy Franklin Nichols, *The Disruption of American Democracy* (New York, 1948), and Philip Van Doren Stern, *Prologue to Sumter* (Bloomington, 1961).

4. Laurin L. Henry, *Presidential Transitions* (Washington, D.C., 1960), 446. Much of this paragraph is summarized from Henry's extensive description of the Hoover-Roosevelt transition.

ment to join with him on the pressing problem of adjusting the foreign payments on war debts. The deepening economic and financial crisis reached its desperate nadir during the month immediately preceding the inauguration of Roosevelt, with a widening wave of bank and business failures and a growing threat of total collapse of the economic system. Even under these circumstances, collaborative efforts failed. Hoover was requesting Roosevelt's support on undertakings that the latter felt would be a repudiation of the New Deal he would propose and a compromising of his freedom of action. The nation's paralysis was as complete as it had been in 1861. In the words of Arthur M. Schlesinger, Jr.: "This was hiatus, the great void. The old regime's writ had run, while the new had no power to break through the stagnation. Hoover was a discredited failure, Roosevelt a vague and now fading hope; and, suspended between past and future, the nation drifted as on dark seas of unreality."[5]

On the day following his inauguration, a Sunday, Roosevelt assembled a meeting of the new cabinet and at one o'clock the following morning issued the proclamation closing all the banks that were not already closed. The first and almost the only example of collaboration between the incoming and the outgoing officials occurred during that first week of Roosevelt's term when they jointly drafted the bank proclamation and a banking reform bill. Thus began "The Hundred Days"—the most feverish policy-making activity in American history, the first phase of the New Deal.

It may be hoped that the transition to Lincoln that preceded the Civil War and that to Roosevelt that preceded the New Deal were not precedents for the future. But they are vivid illustrations of the problems and the dangers of interparty transitions in times of crisis. And although much has been done to lessen and ameliorate those problems and dangers since 1932, one cannot assert with any confidence that they have been eliminated.

---

5. Arthur M. Schlesinger, Jr., *The Crisis of the Old Order, 1919–1933* (Boston, 1957), 456. For an account of the interregnum maneuvering between the incoming and outgoing administrations over the upcoming World Economic Conference and American policy toward the Japanese incursion into Manchuria, see Robert H. Ferrell, *American Diplomacy in the Great Depression: Hoover-Stimson Foreign Policy, 1929–1933* (New York, 1957), 231–77.

## Institutionalization of the
## Transition Process, 1948–1984

Apart from the reporting and counting of the electoral vote and the accouterments accompanying the inauguration—the administration of the oath, the address, the parade, and the balls—there was little systematic process attached to presidential transitions until the end of World War II. Presidents-elect usually took vacations after their election, and then considered, negotiated, and announced their top-level appointments, talked with their immediate aides and advisers as well as with party leaders, and received hundreds of visitors. They seldom communicated with the incumbent president, who simply minded the store until the inauguration. Contacts between the two were infrequent, formal, and cool.

Credit for the first step is due President Franklin D. Roosevelt, who arranged briefings on the international situation and the conduct of World War II for candidate Thomas E. Dewey in 1944. But his intent was probably more to prevent Dewey from making false or embarrassing statements in the campaign than to prepare him for a transition. Nonetheless he established a precedent that every president since that war has honored.

Four years later, the same candidate, Dewey, and President Truman prepared themselves and their staffs much more comprehensively for the "transition that didn't happen" in 1948. The overconfident Dewey, then governor of New York, was far advanced well before the election in his plans for taking over the national administration. Development of a legislative program was under way; officials of his New York state budget staff visited Washington and conferred with leaders in the Bureau of the Budget; other of his representatives were in frequent touch with Republican members of Congress as well as some Democratic officers in the administration; some of his choices for the cabinet were designated and were shopping for houses in Washington—an error that some still think was disastrous politically. For his part, Truman was reluctant to take any public action that might suggest that he did not expect to win the election. But he was acutely conscious of his own miserable unpreparedness when Roosevelt died, and he sought assurance that would not happen again. He quietly designated a transition representative who had talks with a counterpart representative of Dewey, sometimes in Truman's presence. On foreign policy, Dewey's principal adviser, John Foster Dulles, was briefed by the State Department and, with the approval of the secretary of state, conversed informally with European foreign ministers. The Truman administration provided Dewey with weekly intelligence briefings, following the example of 1944. Of course, all of this effort appeared to be wasted when the election results were in; there was no interregnum. But it provided useful precedents for the future.

The first full transition after World War II was that of 1952–1953, when Truman passed the baton to Eisenhower. It was different from many of its predecessors in several respects. First, the incumbent president had not been a contender in the election; he and his top people were not losers, though they had of course supported the losing candidate, Adlai Stevenson. Second, the winning candidate was a military hero whose experience and interests were primarily in foreign and defense policy. He had little background in domestic policy or politics. Third, the victorious Republican party had not been in power for twenty years, and almost none of its leaders had had prior experience in governing the country. Likewise, there were very few in the incumbent Democratic administration who had experience in transitions. And in the interim the government's size, scope, and responsibilities in both international and domestic affairs had multiplied many times. Experience from the 1920s and early 1930s could not be of much help to either side.

Most of the activities conducted in 1948 were repeated: the designation of transition representatives, intelligence briefings, planning of legislative programs, and others. However, the preparations for transition by Truman and his administration began earlier and were more thorough than ever before. Immediately after Truman's announcement on March 29, 1952 that he would not run, officials in the Bureau of the Budget and elsewhere in the administration, as well as a good many outside it, initiated studies and papers preparatory to transition. At that time no one knew who the candidate of either party would be, but all knew the next president would not be Harry Truman. One observer later wrote that "the writings of reports had reached epidemic proportions, and a respectable civil servant, college professor, or civic reformer would have been less embarrassed to appear in public without his trousers than without his proposal for the consideration of the new administration." [6]

Most of the elements of subsequent presidential transitions were in fact extensions and elaborations of activities undertaken by Truman with Dewey in 1948 and with Eisenhower in 1952–1953. In general but without slavish consistency, the numbers employed or assigned and the costs of transition have increased with each successive turnover, to the point that managing the transition personnel adds greatly to the complexity and confusion normally expected in any interparty transition. There are several major activities that have been involved in the transitions since 1952–1953.

1. *Organizing and Staffing for Transition.* Both the incumbent president and the aspiring candidates must develop resources for handling transitions. If the incumbent president is not a candidate for reelection, as in the cases of Truman in 1952, Eisenhower in 1960, and Johnson in 1968, he normally orders that steps be taken before the election to prepare for the transition, as Truman did in 1952. Presidents Eisenhower and Johnson generally followed this precedent. Eisenhower in 1960 somewhat reluctantly also allowed White House staff to assist the Brookings Institution in its series of advisory reports to candidates Nixon and Kennedy on transition planning. President Johnson in September, 1968, asked all three candidates (Humphrey, Nixon, and George Wallace) to select transition representatives who were to work with his own representative, Charles Murphy. Nixon made some of the most extensive preparations for assuming power of any of the candidates, and his representative, Franklin Lincoln, held preelection meetings with Murphy and with Clark Clifford—then secretary of defense—who made available to Lincoln his files on the Eisenhower-Kennedy turnover.

When an incumbent president is also a candidate for reelection, as has been the case in every election after 1968, he is predictably reluctant to prepare publicly for relinquishing power until after his election, but work on transition materials usually proceeds quietly in the departments and agencies. The coordinating agent for the development of internal materials for the incoming administration has

6. Rowland Egger, in a paper delivered at a meeting of the American Society for Public Administration, as quoted in Henry, *Presidential Transitions*, 471.

long been the Bureau of the Budget—since 1970, the Office of Management and Budget. But top leadership of the transition team is normally vested in a designee of the president on the White House staff. Other officers at lower levels—departments, agencies, bureaus, and divisions throughout the administration—are named as transition officers.

It has become standard practice for a presidential candidate, who hopes to become the president-elect, to designate one of his advisers to plan and handle his transition. This designation is often made long before the election. Jimmy Carter asked Jack Watson to prepare plans for transition in April, 1976, more than two months before the nominating convention. Some optimistic candidates have named transition directors even before the spring primaries.

Transition organizations usually begin informally and modestly; then they grow and grow and grow. A winning election in November provides a new burst of enthusiasm, growth, and funds, but finally and quite suddenly, they die at the time of inauguration or soon thereafter. They are customarily loose, even chaotic. And they add new dimensions to the disorder that can be almost routinely expected in a change of government. Consider first that the transitionists come from a variety of backgrounds, perspectives, and ambitions. Some are experienced political operators, initially skilled in the politics of getting the candidate elected; others, often the majority, are volunteers, most often with an ideological bent. A dominant objective of many in both categories is to win an influential position in a new administration. A few represent special interests, and some (at least in 1980–1981) were on detail from congressional staffs seeking information unavailable to them as employees of the Congress. During the election campaign there is the danger that those who are planning the transition may not be "in sync" with those conducting the campaign itself, and this may be a source of jealousy and bitterness when permanent positions and allocations of power are assigned after the election. This was the unhappy experience of the leaders of the Carter campaign and transition groups in 1976–1977. It was largely avoided in the Reagan organization of 1980–1981 when the direction of the transition activities was handled by Edwin Meese, a high official in the campaign organization.

2. *The Financing of Transitions,* like that of political campaigns,

has long been a problem. From the beginning of concern about the transition process, a substantial part of the services of people, from the candidates and the president-elect on down, has been contributed gratis by volunteers. Such voluntarism is often offered in the expectation of an influential job in the hoped-for new administration. Some personal services must obviously be paid for, as well as such costs as office space, equipment, supplies, communications, and travel. The expenses of the Eisenhower transition in 1952–1953 were around $385,000, paid for by donations from individuals and corporations supplemented by a subsidy from the Republican National Committee.[7] The total costs of the Kennedy transition, including the various task-force studies, were on the order of $1.3 million—about $1 million supplied by contributions and $360,000 from the Democratic National Committee. In the fall of 1961, President Kennedy created a Commission on Campaign Costs, which subsequently recommended among other things that the government itself should appropriate funds to cover the costs of transitions, on the grounds that this was properly a public expense, not a partisan one. A major outcome of that report was the Presidential Transition Act of 1963, which authorized the administrator of General Services to provide office space and pay transition-related expenses, including salaries, to both the outgoing and the incoming presidents and vice-presidents after an election. The amounts initially authorized were subsequently increased to $2 million for the incoming administration and $1 million for the incumbents. But the significance of the law lay not only in acknowledging public responsibility for financing transitions but also, in the words of Laurin Henry, in "providing a statutory obligation of cooperation between incoming and outgoing administrations" and in "legitimizing access by representatives of the President-elect."[8]

7. Interview with former Senator Hugh Scott (who handled the financing of the Eisenhower transition) by Frederick C. Mosher, Kenneth W. Thompson, and W. David Clinton, December 3, 1982.

8. Stephanie Smith, *Presidential Transitions and the Presidential Transition Act of 1963* (Washington, D.C., 1980), 6–7; P.L. 88-277 (1964); Laurin Henry, "The Transition: From Nomination to Inauguration," in Paul T. David and David H. Everson (eds.), *The Presidential Election and Transition, 1980–1981* (Carbondale, Ill., 1983), 195–218.

The Reagan transition of 1980–1981 was by far the most elaborate and expensive of all. Beginning in April of 1980, four months before the Republican convention and more than half a year before the election, his campaign associates began building a large transition-planning organization that was financed by private contributions to a "Presidential Transition Trust." After the successful election, they built a new transition organization that included about 1,550 people, more than half of whom were volunteers. The federal funds provided for this operation were augmented by about $1 million in private contributions to the "Presidential Transition Foundation."

The transition organization has seemed almost to have become an impermanent but nonetheless active new branch of government, difficult to control and hold accountable. In view of the fact that many transition expenditures are incurred months before public financing is authorized, it has been proposed that the applicability of the Transition Act be extended back to the nominating convention. But opponents hold that this would encourage premature and irresponsible behavior prior to the election. The question remains moot.

3. *Intelligence Briefings.* The longest continuing practice in the preparation for presidential successions is the provision of current and up-to-date information about national security and other foreign affairs to aspiring candidates and, later, to presidents-elect. This practice, which can by now legitimately be termed a tradition, was begun in 1944 and has been repeated in every succeeding presidential election year. The briefings are initiated soon after the nominating conventions, though some (notably by the Johnson administration) were begun even earlier. They are usually conducted by officials of the CIA, often supplemented by representatives of the State Department, the Defense Department, and the White House. In 1960, for example, candidate Kennedy and his aides received several briefings from CIA director Allen Dulles. And Chester Bowles, one of Kennedy's foreign policy advisers, arranged to be briefed every two or three weeks by Secretary of State Christian Herter in Herter's home. This precedent has proved sufficiently strong to survive the most ideological of campaigns: in 1984 the Reagan administration offered and the Mondale campaign accepted such briefings.

Until the election is over, these briefings provide the candidate only with information about the current state of world affairs without elaboration on current or proposed policy. There have been a few exceptions, such as President Johnson's frequent briefings about Vietnam in the fall of 1968. After the election the incumbent administration provides fuller briefings to the president-elect and his representatives, covering the current agenda, contemplated policies and programs, and outstanding commitments. In 1960, CIA officials briefed President-elect Kennedy, including information on the preparations for the invasion of Cuba that became the Bay of Pigs fiasco. In 1968, after the election of Richard Nixon, President Johnson dispatched Cyrus Vance, Dean Rusk, and Richard Helms to conduct a "no holds barred" briefing for Nixon and Agnew. But in the briefings, an incoming administration may see an attempt to commit the president-elect to the policy of the outgoing administration. In 1980 Carter officials who sought to provide Reagan officials with information about the Iranian hostage negotiations were sometimes frustrated by the apparent reluctance of the incoming administration to be briefed.

Perhaps the most sensitive information that could be made available is that describing informal commitments or semicommitments that the outgoing administration has made to other governments. This problem is explored further in Chapter 4.

4. *Educating, Learning, and Planning.* Ever since Truman's presidency, incumbent administrations have recognized a basic duty to prepare their successors for an orderly transition. This practice was given legal sanction by the Presidential Transition Act of 1963. Since so many of the political appointees have had little or no experience in the federal government relevant to their new jobs, their preparation must include as its largest component information about the organization, programs, policies, and problems with which they will have to deal. When the incumbent is running for reelection, he does not publicly begin transition preparations until after the election.

Transition organizations of incoming administrations have followed no set pattern, and each president-elect has introduced innovations. Eisenhower and his immediate associates built a group of more than one hundred persons in the Commodore Hotel in New York City, and it was augmented by a great many others who were stationed elsewhere. They contracted with a private consulting firm to survey all of the titles and qualification requirements of all positions to be filled by the president, and to make this information available to the incoming administration. Both undertakings, the transition headquarters and the position survey, were firsts in American history.

Kennedy in 1960–1961 introduced the expression, if not the idea, of transition task forces, consisting of knowledgeable persons and experts in various fields of government activity, to study and make recommendations to him on questions of policy and program that the new administration would face. The use of task forces more or less akin to those set up by candidate, President-elect and then President Kennedy has been standard practice ever since for aspiring candidates. Their reports are normally written by persons *outside* the government who have had prior experience most relevant to the subject under study. Some of the authors are designated later on for appropriate appointments in the new administration.

The most recent and the most ambitious use of task forces was that of Ronald Reagan in 1980–1981. In April, 1980, Reagan met with about 70 defense and foreign policy advisers and asked them to develop specific recommendations on the budget and foreign policy for the first one hundred days of his administration. The number swelled to 132. They were directed by Richard Allen, who would become Reagan's first national security adviser.

Such task forces should be distinguished from departmental and agency study teams that enter and work in government offices with counterpart incumbents who brief them on the activities, relationships, problems, and files. These study teams, which are not ordinarily formed until after the election, are organized and coordinated hierarchically within the agencies and up to the heads of the transition effort for the incoming president. At upper levels, they are related to counterpart officials in the incumbent administration and may be given offices near theirs. It may be noted that unless many or most of the study-team members are subsequently hired in the new administration, most of their work and findings will have to be transmitted twice: from the incumbents and their files to the transition teams and then by the latter to the new permanent appointees.

One other device to help prepare incoming administrations for their work has been the use of outside organizations, "think tanks," to study and write papers on different problem areas. One such effort was carried out before the election of 1960. On its own initiative and with the support of a foundation grant, the Brookings Institution produced a book on the American transition experience in the twentieth century (Laurin Henry's *Presidential Transitions*) and a number of reports on the problems and alternatives any new administration would have to face in 1961. Representatives of the candidates of both parties were kept informed of this work, and copies of the reports were released to John Kennedy, the winning candidate, the day after the election. Brookings' approach was intended to be bipartisan and strictly neutral.

In contrast, in 1980 another think tank, the Heritage Foundation, with a frankly conservative bent, undertook to prepare a comprehensive and fairly detailed monograph, replete with recommendations for the benefit of the Reagan administration on almost every policy issue it could conceive of. Some have said that this three-thousand-page opus has been followed in the main and that the majority of its recommendations have been carried out.[9]

Possibly, the point of diminishing returns has been reached in attempts to prepare incoming administrators more fully. To the confusion already attending changes of government have been added reports and advice, verbal and nonverbal, of dozens of task forces, agency transition teams, consultants, and think tanks. In 1980–1981, soon after their designation as heads of two of the most important departments, the incoming secretaries of state and defense simply dismissed their agencies' transition teams. The accumulation and absorption of enormous amounts of ill-digested data leave little time for orderly and responsible planning, for assessments of advantages and disadvantages, or for the anticipation of unintended costs and benefits.

5. *Recruiting, Selecting, and Nominating Political Appointees.* There is no task that is more demanding and urgent for presidential candidates and incoming presidents than the recruitment, choice, and preparation of nominees who will fill the crucial posts in the new administration. In the transitions since World War II, there has

---

9. Charles Heatherly (ed.), *Mandate for Leadership: Policy Management in a Conservative Administration* (Washington, D.C., 1981).

been a tendency toward greater systematization of the recruitment and selection process in the White House and even in the election campaign. There has been a White House personnel officer in each administration since Roosevelt's, and these officials, normally professionals in the personnel field, have been supported by growing numbers of assistants.

Despite efforts at systematization, the personnel operation of a new president must be described as frantic and chaotic. And despite the efforts to start the recruitment earlier—during and even before the nominating conventions—the actual designations of appointees have been coming later and later. (These and other personnel problems associated with transitions are discussed in greater depth in Chapter 6.)

6. *Development of Program and of Basic Documents.* There are a number of actions that a new administration must take early in its term—usually in January or February. The most important are the inaugural address; a legislative program, including priorities and methods; changes in the budget, which will just have been transmitted by the outgoing administration; and normally an address to the Congress comprehending the major elements of the president's program. All of these should reflect and to some extent grow out of the election campaign and the various transition studies, and work on some of them often starts well before the election. The task of coordinating them, making sure that they are consistent internally and with one another and with the objectives and commitments of the incoming president, is a challenging one, especially given the relatively short time the interregnum allows. This is one reason why it is so desirable that persons be named for certain positions soon after the election: the president's immediate advisers in the White House, the national security adviser, the director of legislative liaison, the principal cabinet officers, the chairman of the Council of Economic Advisers, and the director of the Office of Management and Budget, which prepares the budget and has been responsible for putting together the legislative program.

7. *Establishing and Maintaining Relationships with Other Leaders.* Obviously, the effectiveness of a transition and subsequently the character of the new administration will depend heavily upon the interpersonal connections of the incoming appointees with a

great number of individuals: their predecessors in office; the career officials with and through whom they will work; the legislative leaders and members in committees relevant to their work; political and professional leaders in relevant fields outside of the federal government; and, not least, one another, especially those in agencies closely related in purpose and function and those in staff agencies, such as the Office of Management and Budget, the Office of Personnel Management, and the General Services Administration. Such relationships begin with the conversations of the incoming president with the outgoing president and with congressional leaders and continue down the echelons of responsibility as soon as the new officials are named. Occasionally the lame-duck officer is asked to stay on the job in an advisory capacity until the newcomer is fully prepared to take over his duties.

Thus, it is evident that the tasks involved in transitions from one party to another are many and difficult, especially given the temporal constraints of election and inauguration dates. The temporary organizations and other devices instituted to handle them have been unsteadily growing since World War II—to the point that managing them has become a major part of the problem. Of course, the nation and the world have become increasingly complex, and America's role as leader of the Free World is more demanding. Nonetheless, one sometimes cannot help sighing for the simplicity of earlier times, when incoming and outgoing presidents had virtually no paid staff to help (or hinder) the transfer of authority.

# CHAPTER 4

# Preparation for Power
## Information, Communication, and Learning

◆•◆

> We need the perspective, missing from recent administrations,
> that our interests are permanent, that each team must pass the
> baton in a marathon relay race.
>
> —Winston Lord

> We need to popularize the idea that a learning process is at once
> inevitable and legitimate, that ignorance in some significant re-
> spects is every new man's fate . . . bound to produce adjust-
> ments, disappointments, changes, and reversals both in policy
> and personnel.
>
> —Richard E. Neustadt

Some of the transition activities summarized in the last chapter are
intended principally to educate the top officials of the incoming administration for their new positions. This is not easy. The preparation of the "black books" by the incumbents, explaining the objectives of their organizations, their current and anticipated problems,
their priorities, and the pros and cons of various proposed solutions,
is a demanding task. It requires grasp, selectivity, and objectivity,
lest the successor suspect he is being given a "snow job." Conversation among the incoming and outgoing people and the top career
officials is also important—if indeed the new designees are ready to
participate before the incumbents leave. If the parties are friends,
acquainted over a period longer than a day or two, that is a plus. The
task forces studying and reporting on the new administration's policies as well as the transition teams can be effective tools for preparing its incoming executives. But they are most useful if these future
officials serve on them, get the information firsthand, and participate or lead in the development of plans and priorities.

   The business of learning one's job would be simpler if one could
observe how his predecessor performed over a period of time and

then gradually assume responsibilities as he became ready for them. Unfortunately, this is often not a possibility in transitions except at the highest levels. Too frequently the successor is not even designated before the incumbent leaves office. The new appointee's assumption of office is sudden, with little time for learning the job, let alone for seasoning. Furthermore, the nature of the work in the front line of foreign affairs leaves insufficient time for learning and for long-range thinking and planning. The agenda is to a considerable extent controlled by events abroad and actions of foreign countries, and the so-called policy positions are heavily occupied with day-to-day emergencies and fire-fighting.

## The Problems of Secrecy and Compartmentalism

As suggested in Chapter 1, the problems of communications from a dying to a fetal administration are exacerbated by the pervasiveness of secrecy. Most policy-oriented documents, prior to their public announcement, are classified for national security reasons, and of course the clearance of new appointees is a routine requirement. It is doubtful that candidate Kennedy would have charged the incumbent administration with allowing a "missile gap" to develop if the CIA had been able to brief him during the campaign on its then incomplete evidence that, if any gap existed, it was to the Soviets' disadvantage.

But secrecy is invoked for other reasons. One is to protect recent and ongoing negotiations with other nations, whether in bilateral talks, at international conferences, or within international organizations. Woodrow Wilson learned—and since his time, many others have relearned—that the open diplomacy he espoused does not always work. One must also protect friendly nations and their representatives from offense and embarrassment, and these are subtle concerns to pass along to newcomers. So are questions of business and trade secrets and violations of personal privacy as they apply not only to colleagues and predecessors in the government but also to representatives of foreign governments.

Secrecy also blocks communication within the government itself—among departments and other agencies and among offices and divisions within individual agencies. This *compartmentalism* is an aggravating factor in transitions. An incumbent official can hardly give a complete and rounded account of any situation or problem if he is not aware of relevant activities and information of other concerned agencies. Compartmentalism is a government-wide problem but is especially difficult in foreign affairs because so many different agencies, foreign and domestic, have international business, because agencies have differing loyalties and constituencies, and because great geographic or organizational distances can separate agencies and their outposts from one another. New ambassadors to the United States can be—and some have been—severely embarrassed because they were not advised of decisions or agreements made in Washington. A new ambassador, or an old one, to a foreign government can be embarrassed if he learns from a newspaper that representatives of the Department of Agriculture have negotiated an agreement involving several hundred million dollars with that government or if he learns of certain activities of the CIA of which he was not aware. Compartmentalism was a major contributor to the disastrous Bay of Pigs invasion of Cuba in 1961. Shortly after he was sworn in as secretary of state, Dean Rusk was enjoined from consulting his department's intelligence group about the likelihood of a Cuban uprising after the projected invasion force had landed, and the Joint Chiefs of Staff were similarly instructed not to consult their planning staff on the military feasibility of the invasion.

Communications from old to new administrations in foreign affairs have been helped in the past by a relatively high degree of bipartisanship on foreign policy matters and by a core of foreign affairs people of both parties who move in and out of public office, share philosophies and general views on American objectives, and enjoy mutual respect and friendship. Most of our secretaries of state since Dean Acheson have been members of the so-called foreign policy elite. Until Carter broke the precedent in 1977, CIA directors survived political changes (though it could be argued that the real break came when Ford appointed a former chairman of the Republican National Committee to the post). And while the same cannot be said of most of the other foreign affairs policy leaders at the second and third levels of administration, there has generally been a greater degree of continuity than in the domestic sphere, because of the existence of strong and knowledgeable career services that customarily survive partisan change.

## The Problem of Attitudes

There are probably no greater obstacles to effective communication than the attitudes the members of the incoming and outgoing administrations and the career people have toward one another and the resultant social and interpersonal relations of the three groups. This is not primarily a matter of incompatible personalities. Nor is its source only ideological or philosophical. In the largest sense, it is built into our political system. We are structured along two sides of the aisle, two parties in a nearly continuous opposition that comes into its sharpest national focus every fourth November. Ours is a competitive society, and most of our favorite spectator sports are between two teams or two individuals. There are winners and losers who do not particularly care for each other as the contest heats up and, perhaps least of all, immediately after its end. Our biggest game is politics, and for many of us it is not just a spectator sport. We participate in it as well as watch it, following the results on TV much as we watch the Superbowl. But American national politics is more than a football game. It begins as a many-sided competition that is gradually reduced through processes of elimination in trial runs and coalitions to a contest between two sides. These survivors fight it out to the end, when one or the other wins. The governing rules of conduct are few and are seldom enforceable until after the contest is over, except through allegations in the press and their impact on the voters. There are few who might qualify as authoritative umpires and referees.

Little wonder that, when the final results are in, the winners are exhilarated, the losers unhappy; both are bloodied and spent. The time is not propitious for the winners, if they are newcomers, to undertake an entirely new type of game that nevertheless carries no less urgency—indeed more, in terms of the welfare of the nation— and in which there are only vague indicators of winning and losing. Nor is it an auspicious time for the incumbents to remain on the field after the election and carry on with appropriate enthusiasm the task of running the nation for the eleven weeks, more or less, before they will leave their jobs.

Regardless of other factors, the very nature of the contest militates against friendly and constructive relationships between the two sides. But there are other factors, most of which are built into the system, to aggravate these tensions. Each side represents one or the other of the two political parties, which have, for more than a century, survived by opposing each other. Each party represents some general, even if vague, principles, ideologies, slogans, and policies at least in part opposed to those of the other. Further, each major candidate, supported by his principal spokesmen, has brought his own slant to the issues of the day. The differences between the parties and between the candidates—seldom their agreements—are the foci of political campaigns. The party out of power is usually the more aggressive, attacking the policies, the alleged inefficiencies, at times even the character, of those currently in power. In recent years these attacks have increasingly extended to the whole government— the bureaucracy, the Congress, and even the judiciary. Incumbents are normally on the defensive against such aggression, though they, too, sometimes attack parts of their own government, including the bureaucracy. They challenge as well the views and the records of the opposing candidate and his followers, charging them with being un- informed, reckless, dangerous, irresponsible, and inexperienced. When to these factors are added perhaps long-standing personal dis- likes between the candidates or their followers, the problems of transitions are further aggravated. Even when president and presi- dent-elect have had a prior mutually respectful acquaintance, as Truman and Eisenhower did, the stresses of the campaign can result in abiding hostility that impedes cooperation.

The attitudes of some incoming electoral victors are not condu- cive to good listening or thoughtful consideration and discussion of problems. They can be an unsavory mix of exuberance and conceit, of arrogance and suspicion. On the other hand, the existence of such attitudes should not be overemphasized. They are not universal, and except for the true believers of the right or left, they tend to mellow— they have to mellow—as the realities of governance begin to sink in soon after the election: the enormity and the intransigence of the problems, the importance of background in terms of knowledge and experience, the dependence on those in the Congress, in the bu- reaucracies, and on the outside for information and advice and support.

But at the start some newcomers find little in the government of which they approve—even if they are not clear about how they would change it. They are to some extent prisoners of their own campaign rhetoric. There is little acknowledgment that the outgoing administration has done much right or, in some areas, that it has done anything at all. And there is often little understanding of the enduring bedrock of government and its commitments and problems both at home and abroad—the situation that the incumbent administration discovered when it arrived and that is unlikely to be changed drastically by the newcomers. More than one incumbent has complained that newcomers refuse to accept the facts unless they conform to and support their predetermined ideology.

The common criticisms of career personnel seem to be especially virulent among new appointees of an incoming administration. They are that the careerists have narrow vision and little imagination, are overly concerned about the security of their jobs, fear and therefore resist change, and obstruct and even sabotage the efforts of their political superiors. Such charges are no doubt justified for some upper-level federal personnel—as in other large organizations. But that they are exaggerated is suggested by the frequent favorable evaluations by political appointees for their career subordinates when they leave. In fact, a recent questionnaire study of more than five hundred presidentially appointed executives in administrations from Presidents Johnson through Reagan indicated that most of them had deep admiration of career executives. A total of 84 percent of them ranked the competence of senior career officials high or very high, and 83 percent ranked their responsiveness high or very high. These percentages varied little from one administration to the next.[1]

The attitudes of the election losers, nevertheless, are not always conducive to effective transitions. In the first place, many of the incumbents are anxious to protect the policies and programs they have been superintending and, in some cases, have introduced. And they would like to protect, if not themselves, at least others in their agencies, career and noncareer, who are allies in those programs. Second, they are necessarily concerned about their own futures. For some, the conduct of their public jobs becomes secondary almost immediately after the election to finding appropriate new opportunities, usually outside the government. Third, they generally feel that

1. National Academy of Public Administration, *Leadership in Jeopardy: The Fraying of the Presidential Appointments System* (Washington, D.C., 1985), 29.

they were unfairly attacked by their victorious opponents in the recent campaign.

Yet, it is our observation that the outgoing president and administrative leaders are usually more anxious to help educate their successors for their new jobs—their dimensions, importance, problems, contingencies, and relationships—than the newcomers are to learn them. The latter are suspicious of what they are told if they listen at all. They feel themselves to be part of a new wave that will learn soon enough (if they do not already know) how to do the job and do it better. If this means, as it often does, that they must reinvent the wheel, they are confident that their wheel will roll with less friction than the older one. The memoirs of few presidents acknowledge advice given by their predecessors, but all are replete with suggestions for their successors. These generalizations are probably less applicable for officials at the lower reaches of the executive branch than the upper; indeed, in recent years transition teams representing the incoming administration have conducted studies in some detail of the work under way, usually adorned with proposals on how it can be improved.

Outgoing presidents, their top assistants, and other administrative leaders usually take a more cooperative approach to the effective passing on of the baton to their successors. It has become established practice for them to set up official machinery at the top and within all agencies to facilitate transitions and to direct (or have the Office of Management and Budget direct and supervise) the preparation of detailed materials on the activities and problems of virtually every office. One senses that those leaving feel a responsibility that things progress and not halt—especially the things that they have started. Beginning with Truman, every outgoing president has issued instructions to his staff to make special efforts to cooperate with the newcomers, regardless of whether they are of his party. In every case they were to make information accessible and prepare appropriate briefing materials. Such preparation began well before the election except when the incumbent president was running for reelection, and even then some planning went on behind the scenes.

Another resource that is available to an incipient new administration consists of the members and staff of the relevant committees and subcommittees of Congress. Here incoming executive branch officers can learn a great deal about the arguments pro and con on major issues, the political, legislative, and interpersonal backgrounds of the people involved, and the probable responses in Congress on different types of proposals. The points of view will differ from those of the incumbents, who are of the opposite political party, and from those of the career officers, who are presumably neutral.

Finally, organized efforts at training designated appointees are also useful. Seminars to help new officials learn the folkways of Washington have been conducted by the Brookings Institution, the John F. Kennedy School of Government at Harvard, and the Federal Executive Institute, among others. A White House staff orientation program in 1976–1977, intended to give members of the incoming Carter staff suggestions on their effectiveness and to allow them to develop a sense of camaraderie, included sessions chaired by outgoing cabinet officers, members of Congress, and Ford's press secretary, OMB director, and national security adviser.

## Political Constraints on Communication

One might conjecture that in an ideal society coherence and continuity from one administration to another would require that all information and ideas should be passed along or at least made readily accessible to the incoming group. But it must be borne in mind that the two political parties, as well as their representatives in office, or soon to be in office, are adversaries. If the incoming group finds information that could prove damaging or embarrassing to the other party or its prominent members, it will be tempted to use this knowledge in the manner most advantageous to itself, subject only to such constraints as it may recognize for the national interest, personal privacy, and fairness.

The background materials on most sensitive issues, especially in the areas of international relations and national security, normally include some information (and perhaps a great deal) that could be selectively leaked or otherwise made public, to the detriment of the administration and the political party that are about to depart office or have just left it. It includes memoranda of advice and argument on policy questions and on their domestic political ramifications; records and descriptions of discussions with, and informal assurances to, representatives of foreign powers, members of Congress, and others; and remarks about the personalities, integrity, and other characteristics of officials, both foreign and domestic. Most of this kind of information is protected from public access for at least a period of years by the Freedom of Information Act, the Privacy Act, the Presidential Records Act, and the generally respected, though still debated, doctrine of executive privilege. But there is little to protect an outgoing administration (and its party) from its successors if it leaves all its papers behind and tells everything it knows. This means that some persons must draw the thousands of lines between what information should, can, and must be passed along by mouth or pen and what can ethically and prudently be withheld.

It is our impression that most outgoing presidents since Truman have taken steps to assure that as much of the relevant information as possible be assembled and passed along to the successor administration, including information about confidential commitments and semicommitments. But how much background information of a potentially damaging political or personal nature was omitted and to what degree such information deprived the recipient of a full understanding of a situation one can only guess.

Except in those areas and to the extent that American policies are truly bipartisan, this problem of interadministration communication is built into the system as in any democratic government. The British, we are advised, have sought with some success to overcome the dilemma by entrusting the senior civil servant in each ministry, usually the permanent undersecretary, with the responsibility for briefing incoming political officers on both the substance and the background of all matters that are currently active; he also retains the records of the deliberations of the outgoing administration, which are not made available to the newcomers.[2] It is doubtful that such a

2. William P. Bundy, "Presidential Transition Problems," in Kenneth W. Thompson (ed.), *Problems and Prospects* (Lanham, Md., 1986), 21–27. Such procedures are of comparatively recent vintage. As late as the turn of the century, Lord Salisbury, serving as both prime minister and foreign secretary, "never consulted his Permanent Under-Secretary . . . on any matter of importance, did much of his work at home, and on occasion kept his transactions with other Governments completely secret from the Foreign Office." Upon his retirement, he "took all his private letters with him down to Hatfield and considerable confusion was thereafter occasioned by gaps in correspondence." See Lord Strang, *The Foreign Office* (New York, 1955), 147; Harold Nicolson, *Diplomacy* (New York, 1939), 195. On the painfully slow development of continuing state diplomatic archives in Europe, see Garrett Mattingly, *Renaissance Diplomacy* (Boston, 1955), 146–47, 229–31, 241;

scheme could work across the board in this country, mainly because so few of our top career public servants enjoy any such esteem as they do in Britain—or such a reputation for political neutrality.[3] Outgoing officials would be reluctant to leave papers that might be used to damage them; newcomers—at least some of them—would be reluctant to hear, absorb, and trust such messages from public servants who had served the other party with distinction, loyalty, and perhaps enthusiasm.

## The President's Written Record

A particular problem for the transfer of information from an old administration to a new one lies in the confidentiality and accessibility of the president's papers, which include documentary materials created or received not only by the president but also by his immediate staff and other units and individuals in the Executive Office of the President who are called upon to advise and assist him. Documentary materials are broadly defined to include correspondence, memoranda, papers, pamphlets, pictures, tapes, movies, recordings, and virtually anything else useful for the storage of information except the human brain. After George Washington removed his own papers from the President's House in 1797, the presidential papers, as they are generally labeled, were considered to be the president's personal property to be disposed of as he (or his estate) wished—until the 1970s. And since Herbert Hoover's presidency, it has become customary, and authorized but not required by law, for every departing president to remove his papers to a presidential library usually lo-

---

William James Roosen, *The Age of Louis XIV: The Rise of Modern Diplomacy* (Cambridge, Mass., 1976), 47–49.

3. Actually, our national government as a whole tried a somewhat comparable system in pursuit of recommendations made by the first Hoover commission in 1949. All the departments and most of the larger agencies established offices of assistant secretary for administration (or a similar title) to be filled by career civil servants who would survive political transitions. They were envisioned, at least by some, as America's version of the British permanent undersecretaries. But it is doubtful that many, if any, of them ever had the keys to departmental policy. Most of these offices remain (like the under secretary for management in the State Department), but one by one they have lost their career protections, in practice if not always in law.

cated near his home, where most of them are cared for in perpetuity by the National Archives and are available to the public, including representatives of the press, historians, and other scholars.

This has meant that outgoing presidents could examine, sort out, and destroy any materials that might prove embarrassing or might tarnish their reputations or those of others in their administration, regardless of the value of the information for coping with ongoing policies and for the understanding of history. It has also meant that every new president and his staff find that the White House "cupboards are bare"—bare of the back-up records on foreign and national security affairs as well as on other matters. One former member of the national security staff remarked, with some exaggeration, that the only paper left for the newcomers was toilet paper. Of course, they have access to the official documentary records in the various agencies concerned—the State and Defense departments, the CIA, and others. But the less formal materials and records on negotiations, conversations, explanations, and arguments in which the president or members of his staff were involved, including some materials that may be secret, even to the rest of the government, are often more significant than the official documents themselves. The absence of such documentation would seem on its face a severe handicap to the continuity of defense and foreign policy from one administration to the next.

Most of this changed as a consequence of Watergate. In the fall of 1974, former President Nixon signed an agreement with the administrator of general services (whose jurisdiction then included the National Archives) that among other provisions would have ensured the eventual destruction of the famous tapes. This action enraged a majority in Congress, which promptly passed a bill that abrogated the agreement, gave custody of the Nixon tapes and other materials to the General Services Administration, and banned their destruction, an act later upheld by the Supreme Court.[4] That act applied only to the Nixon materials, but Congress was soon at work drafting a permanent bill to govern the ownership, disposition, and ac-

4. The act was the Presidential Recordings and Materials Preservation Act of 1974 (P.L. 93-526). The court decision was *Nixon* v. *Administrator of General Services*, 97 S. Ct. 2795 (1977).

cessibility of presidential papers. The product, the Presidential Records Act of 1978, went into effect in 1981 and is still the law of the land.[5] That act declares that presidential records, which do not include personal records not developed for or used in the transaction of government business, are the property of the government. On the termination of a president's tenure, the records immediately come under the custody of the archivist of the United States. This means of course that they are immediately removed from the White House and other executive offices, as they were before. The archivist is given up to five years to process the material and then is instructed to place it, and manage it, in a presidential library or other suitable facility. Outgoing presidents can place mandatory restrictions on public access to certain materials for up to twelve years; these protected categories are comparable to the exceptions in the Freedom of Information Act and include classified material, material on presidential appointments, trade secrets, confidential communications between the president and his advisers, and material that would threaten personal privacy.

Although the documents are not immediately available in the White House offices, a succeeding president and members of Congress can gain access to any materials from the archivist that are not elsewhere available and are necessary to conduct the public business, as long as they know what to request. This is a distinct improvement on the earlier process, under which access to presidential records was completely controlled by the former president. But the procedure as defined in the law is certainly more awkward than it would be were the materials filed in one of the executive office buildings, especially when one is on an uncertain search and is not familiar with the kinds of materials that exist and how they are indexed. It is too early to discover evidence of how the prescribed system has worked—how frequently, how promptly, with what impediments and delays. It is also too early for an accurate assessment of the extent and kinds of materials retiring presidents have been able to exclude on the grounds that they are personal records, including diaries, journals, and materials relating to "private political asso-

5. P.L. 95-591 (1978).

ciations" that do not bear upon the carrying out of official presidential duties.

## International Commitments

The transfer of information, including the supporting documentation of decisions that have been reached, can be most significant if the subject matter involves a commitment, promise, or threat to a representative of a foreign government that may or may not have been made in writing or in a recorded conversation.[6] Such pledges have not always been known to new presidents and their administrations. Truman—perhaps the least prepared for his unexpected accession of any of the recent presidents—was reduced to sending a special representative to London in May of 1945 to assure Prime Minister Churchill that Truman "would definitely fulfill every engagement made by President Roosevelt"—and to ask "exactly what the engagements and agreements with the Soviets were."[7] More recently, the new Carter administration was apparently surprised to find in February of 1977 that for twenty years the United States had been paying King Hussein of Jordan an average of twenty million dollars annually in return for intelligence information. The administration halted the payments immediately, but Carter reportedly learned of them only when the Washington *Post* began investigating them.[8]

6. We are indebted for much of the information and analysis in this section to "Executive Non-Agreements" (1984), a paper by Ryan J. Barrilleaux of the University of Texas at El Paso; to Daniel Franklin of Colgate University for his Ph.D. dissertation, "Departure or Debacle: Congressional Resurgence in the Aftermath of Watergate and Vietnam" (University of Texas, 1984); to the comments of Inis L. Claude, Jr., of the University of Virginia; and to the Legal Adviser's Office of the Department of State.

7. U.S. Department of State, *Foreign Relations of the United States: The Conference of Berlin (The Potsdam Conference), 1945* (2 vols.; Washington, D.C., 1960), I, 71.

8. Washington *Post,* February 18, 1977, p. 5, February 19, 1977, p. 1, February 22, 1977, p. 31, February 24, 1977, pp. 1, 22, March 5, 1977, p. 44. It is unclear whether the payments appeared on a list of private undertakings to other countries prepared during the 1976–1977 interregnum by a member of the NSC staff and given to Carter immediately after his inauguration.

Presidents and others in the executive branch make foreign policy commitments in great numbers, ranging from informal statements by American representatives at the UN in the course of bargaining over the wording of resolutions, on one hand, to public declarations by chief executives pledging the good faith of the United States, on the other. If they take the form of executive agreements, other states are entitled under international law to regard them as equally binding as treaties, and they continue in force after the departure of the administration under which they were concluded.[9] How are these promises passed along from one administration to another so that new presidents are neither left in the dark (as Truman was) nor confronted with surprises (as happened to Carter)?

In the case of executive agreements, the chances that commitments will not be communicated have been reduced since the early 1970s for reasons that have nothing to do with transitions. Senate hearings in 1969 unearthed a number of significant commitments, of which Congress knew nothing, made over many years by representatives of the executive branch. As part of the general resurgence of congressional power brought on by the Vietnam War (which, of course, congressional critics believed to be the most egregious example of an executive commitment made without proper congressional authorization), Congress in 1972 approved the Case-Zablocki Act.[10] It required the State Department to submit to Congress, within sixty days of their execution, the texts of all agreements other than treaties concluded between the United States and other nations. Sensitive agreements are held by the Senate Foreign Relations Committee and the House Foreign Affairs Committee under an injunction of secrecy; all others are published in the *Treaty and Inter-*

9. Martin Feinrider, "America's Oil Pledges to Israel: Illegal but Binding Executive Agreements," *New York Journal of International Law and Politics,* XIII (Winter, 1981), 525–68; O. J. Lissitzyn, "Duration of Executive Agreements," *American Journal of International Law,* LIV (October, 1960), 869–73. Had an early variant of the Bricker Amendment of the 1950s been approved, all executive agreements would today automatically lose validity one year after the expiration of the presidential term in which they were negotiated unless the succeeding administration reaffirmed them.

10. P.L. 92-403, 1 USC 1126.

*national Agreement Series.* Subsequent amendments closed a potential loophole by mandating deadlines for the transmission to the State Department of all agreements negotiated by other executive-branch agencies and departments—a step that incidentally aided State by making it aware of what other agencies were doing overseas.

For the first time, then, there exists, at the Office of Treaty Affairs within the Legal Adviser's Office at the State Department, a comprehensive record of all the executive agreements presently binding on the United States. Persons with proper security clearance on transition study teams or in incoming administrations can find at a single location all operative agreements, both confidential and nonconfidential. Availability of the records on the background of these commitments and on the negotiations that preceded them, of course, remains subject to the Presidential Records Act and the actions of the outgoing administration, but at least the final text can be examined.

Two problems remain, however. First, what constitutes an "executive agreement"? Not until 1981, in response to a congressional directive, did the State Department issue a regulation setting forth standards distinguishing this from other types of commitments.[11] This rule includes the requirements that executive agreements be "of political significance," that they not be made up simply of "vague commitments" that lack "objective criteria for determining enforceability," and—perhaps most important for our purposes—that "two or more parties must be involved—unilateral declarations do not constitute an international agreement in the meaning of the law."

The exclusion of unilateral declarations raises the possibility that important commitments will remain unnoticed. Two cases illustrate the point.

In 1967 Secretary of State Dean Rusk was confronted by the Israeli ambassador, Abba Eban, with a letter from 1957 signed by one of Rusk's predecessors, John Foster Dulles, pledging that in the event of any threat to freedom of navigation in the Gulf of Aqaba, the United States would act to ensure or restore that freedom. The ambassador, in effect, was demanding that the United States live up

11. *Federal Register,* XLVI (July 13, 1981), 35917–921.

to its word when President Nasser of Egypt mounted just such a threat. Neither Rusk nor President Johnson knew of the letter's existence, and both were shocked and embarrassed by that fact. Despite ascertaining that Eisenhower agreed with the Israeli interpretation of the 1957 note, Johnson argued that an inherited commitment, in and of itself, would not guarantee American action. "I am fully aware of what three past Presidents have said," he told Eban on May 26, "but that is not worth five cents if the people and the Congress do not support the President." Nevertheless, Johnson began working to honor Eisenhower's pledge and had secured agreement from Great Britain, the Netherlands, and Australia on a joint naval task force to open the Gulf when the Israelis moved unilaterally and the Six-Day War broke out on June 5.[12]

In 1970, when the United States detected Soviet construction of a submarine base at Cienfuegos, Cuba, National Security Adviser Henry Kissinger called for the records of the Kennedy-Khrushchev understanding that ended the Cuban missile crisis of 1962. He expected to find confirmation of the generally accepted interpretation that America had pledged not to invade Cuba in return for the Soviet Union's removal of the missiles under UN inspection, and its promise never to reintroduce such offensive weapons systems into Cuba. He learned that "there was no formal understanding in the sense of an agreement, either oral or in writing"; rather, there were "mutual assurances," "implicit" and "never formally buttoned down."[13]

It seems unlikely that either of these pledges, unilateral statements that they were, would meet the standards for classification as executive agreements, and therefore they could be elusive to a new President and his subordinates who did not already know of their existence. If they were not defined as executive agreements, the State Department would not be bound to report them to Congress; nor, presumably, would other agencies be bound to report them to the State Department. To the extent that knowledge of these commitments remains scattered throughout the executive branch (par-

---

12. Bundy, "Presidential Transition Problems"; Lyndon B. Johnson, *The Vantage Point: Perspectives of the Presidency, 1963–1969* (New York, 1971), 291–97.
13. Henry Kissinger, *White House Years* (Boston, 1979), 633.

ticularly as increasing numbers of "domestic" agencies become involved in some aspect of foreign affairs), an incoming administration cannot know where to look to inform itself. That large category of pledges that are not termed executive agreements may still escape its attention.

A second problem, beyond the mechanics of the transfer of agreements and the requirements of legislation, is the profound tension between democracy and international law. Democratic regimes have many advantages in confronting the universal issue of the transfer of power, including most particularly the legitimacy that success in a free election gives to its winner and the felt obligation among incoming and outgoing officials in a constitutional government to respect the rights of their fellow representatives of the people. Indeed, it might be remembered that George F. Kennan, in his influential 1947 article, "The Sources of Soviet Conduct," emphasized that one of the Soviet Union's major weaknesses was the "great uncertainty" of the transfer of power among the rulers of a totalitarian regime: "That they can keep power themselves, they have demonstrated. That they can quietly and easily turn it over to others remains to be proved." [14]

Nevertheless, democracy requires deference to the right of a majority to change its mind and have that reconsideration respected by the state, while international law, if it is to attain any of the stability and predictability implied in the phrase "the rule of law," requires that a state assume and honor obligations for the indefinite future unless the other party or parties to the accord agree to change them. As Johnson implied in his conversation with Eban in 1967, democracies institutionalize the principle that the people may change governments and thereby government policy, but the basic principle of international law is that commitments (including treaties, executive agreements, and some other pledges) bind the *state*, which is to say that they do bind successor governments.

It is clear that no political leader can literally compel his successor; any new government can choose to disavow existing inter-

14. George Kennan, "The Sources of Soviet Conduct," *Foreign Affairs*, XXV (July, 1947), 578, 580.

national commitments if it is willing to pay the costs—including the cost to its reputation for good faith. But this should be an informed choice, with the possible disadvantages and benefits clearly understood. Along with the experience of career officials and its own appointees, a knowledge of current commitments gives to incoming administrations some of the necessary information.

# CHAPTER 5

# The Translation of Intent into Action

New brooms sweep clean; and official new brooms, I think, sweep cleaner than any other. Who has not watched at the commencement of a Ministry some Secretary, some Lord, or some Commissioner, who intends by fresh Herculean labours to cleanse the Augean stables just committed to his care? Who does not know the gentleman at the Home Office, who means to reform the police and put an end to malefactors; or the new Minister at the Board of Works, who is to make London beautiful as by a magician's stroke,—or, above all, the new First Lord, who is resolved that he will really build us a fleet, purge the dockyards, and save us half a million a year at the same time?

—Anthony Trollope

The contrast between the high hopes of the campaign and the functions of office is never more vividly illustrated and more painfully experienced than during a presidential transition, perhaps especially in foreign affairs. The incumbents have long been immured in the realities of responsible decisions and often at the time of the interregnum are suffering from delay and frustration—at or about Panmunjom or Paris, Tehran or Beirut, and a good many other places. The victorious newcomers may or may not be inspired by a different ideology, but they are almost certain to bring with them different notions about the actions they should take to achieve their objectives. The newcomers are usually encumbered with a variety of sincere beliefs, statements made before and during their campaigns, party platforms, campaign promises, and other commitments.

There are a number of constraints that impede the translation of these intentions into feasible programs. Parts of the agenda and the priorities of American actions in the international field are beyond the direct control of the president or indeed of Congress. They can and should develop plans and programs but with anticipation that

other nations and international organizations may initiate actions—
or respond to actions the United States has taken—that negate, delay, or otherwise modify our own plans. Foreign relations are a complex game of interactions among a large and varied number of players, most of whom can take many different moves. The United
States is a very important and powerful participant in this sometimes deadly game. But it is only one. Any of the other players can
interfere with our agenda.

Here at home there are further limitations on presidential power.
The presidency of the United States is the most majestic office in the
land and probably the most powerful in the world. But it is not om-
nipotent—a fact that often escapes the notice of new occupants of
the Oval Office and their staffs. Even new presidents who are experienced in Washington sometimes hold exaggerated ideas of what a
chief executive can accomplish alone without relying on, or against
the wishes of, other actors in the policy process, and the seduc-
tiveness of the notion is even harder to resist when a new president
has had little contact with the capital. An incoming president is usually prone to overestimate his influence.

The difficulties associated with the mistaken assessment of presidential power are the greater because new presidents are not anxious
to be told that the reach they aspired to in the campaign exceeds the
grasp they can manage after the inauguration. Richard Neustadt,
having observed the initiations of several presidents at first hand,
has attested that for incoming presidents,

> unconcern is usual. The very changeover conduces to it. New re-
> places old, and vigor tiredness; sharp exhilaration drowns out dull ex-
> perience. The White House shines with fresh paint and the West
> Wing with fresh faces. Possibilities seem, for the moment, infinite
> because so many personalities are still unknown, relations still poten-
> tial. All is heightened by the fact that for [new presidents] and their
> aides, arrival at the White House after years of hard campaigning is
> like reaching an oasis in the desert: faultless air conditioning, match-
> less switchboard, superb secretaries, visitors by appointment only
> (press included), cars on call, along with tennis, saunas, helicopters
> for the President and even, if he wishes (LBJ did), instant Fresca.[1]

1. Richard E. Neustadt, *Presidential Power: The Politics of Leadership from
FDR to Carter* (New York, 1980), 224.

The perquisites of life in the White House only increase the "heady quality" that accompanies any candidate's accession to the presidency, making him reluctant to heed counsels that say not everything is possible, especially when those counsels come from people associated with the departing (and partially discredited) administration or from high-level career officials. It becomes the frequent and unpleasant task of the latter group to advise the new president and his political appointees why he cannot or should not do many of the things he wants and perhaps has promised to do. This is no doubt one reason why so many new political officers, including presidents, criticize the perversity of some members of Congress and the alleged negativism and conservatism of the bureaucracy.

Even in foreign affairs, the realm of the president's broadest constitutional authority, there are many pledges that the chief executive cannot redeem by himself; they require actions by or through other institutions, both at home and abroad. It therefore behooves a new president to gain a thorough understanding of the manner in which these other power groups operate. The most important of them is Congress. In pressing for the transformation of his campaign promises into government action, he needs to know the rhythms of the legislative branch as well as its partisan and ideological makeup. He must have the respect and preferably the friendship of many members in both houses and both parties.

As one aide to President Kennedy said after encountering these frustrations, "Everybody believes in democracy until he gets to the White House and then you begin to believe in dictatorship, because it's so hard to get things done. Every time you turn around, people just resist you, and even resist their own job." [2]

This chapter discusses three interrelated elements involved in making a new administration's intent operational: new or changed policies and programs, organization and reorganization, and the budget. A fourth element, the appointments of new personnel, is treated in Chapter 6.

2. Thomas R. Cronin, "Everybody Believes in Democracy Until He Gets to the White House: An Examination of White House–Departmental Relations," *Law and Contemporary Problems,* XXXV (Summer, 1970), special issue titled "Papers on the Institutionalized Presidency," 574.

## Policies, Programs, and Priorities

The birth and nurture of a new president's foreign policies derive from a variety of sources, some going back well before his nomination for president. They include his previous record in office to the extent it brought him in contact with international affairs; his speeches and other statements made before and during the primary campaign, the election campaign, and the interregnum; the platform of his party; and statements of party leaders and other prominent supporters that are believed to be accurate reflections of his own position. More immediate are the analyses of issues and recommendations on them provided by designated experts in various fields and by task forces and transition teams before the election or between the election and the inauguration. For the Reagan transition, there were some twenty-four preelection policy task forces (only two of which dealt directly with foreign affairs) consisting of more than three hundred persons, most of whom were volunteers. Their reports, together with those of the various departmental transition teams and a transitional congressional advisory committee, were presented shortly after the election to an office of policy coordination that reviewed, analyzed, and synthesized them. The ultimate product was a set of policy guidelines to cover the first hundred days of the new administration.

Despite such Herculean efforts, it is doubtful that any new administration can be fully prepared with solutions to all the problems facing it in foreign policy. And it is doubtful that it should even try to do so on those many issues for which the responsible officers who will have to carry out the solutions are not yet on the job. In cases in which it is feasible, the best answer may be to delay. But for some, the international situation and the calendar impose certain time constraints that can hardly be avoided (see Chapter 2).

A major set of decisions for an incoming president concerns how many and which of his proposed initiatives he will transmit to the Congress after his inauguration. It is a hard judgment. If he advances very few, he may upset many of his backers who had supported him partly or completely for the measures he originally proposed and now passes over. Such an action may provoke complaints from Congress and elsewhere that he is not doing his job.[3] If he submits a full agenda, he is likely to overload his own staff as well as Congress, which may balk, deny his requests, and thus injure his reputation as a leader. This latter course is a heady temptation, particularly if his election margin was substantial or of landslide proportions. The new president is likely to be vulnerable to the "hundred-day syndrome," the feeling that he must seek all he can get while he is at the peak of his popularity and influence.

The experiences of Jimmy Carter in 1977 and Ronald Reagan in 1981 offer interesting contrasts in this regard. Carter has often been criticized for seeking a great deal of new legislation near the start of his term. This "shopping list" of legislative proposals allegedly inundated certain committees of the Congress with more than they could handle and probably damaged his relations with the Congress in future years. Reagan, on the other hand, focused his popular strength and his effort mainly on one thing—his economic program as set forth in his radically revised budget and his tax plan. A considerable list of social measures were delayed or passed over to the indefinite future, much to the distress of some of his most ardent supporters. His successful proposals included large increases in appropriations for arms over several years, but also major reductions in domestic programs, foreign aid, and subsidies and loans for international trade and investment.

As foreign and domestic policies have become ever more inextricably intermixed and Congress has asserted its prerogative to be consulted on a variety of issues once left to executive discretion, incoming presidents wishing to take new steps in foreign affairs have found themselves required to secure Congress' approval on a lengthening list of items. A lack of selectivity on the president's part, however, can sour legislative-executive relations at the outset and endanger future diplomatic initiatives as well.

3. For example, in 1953 the chairman of the House Foreign Affairs Committee told a witness discussing the new administration's view on an extension of certain foreign-aid legislation: "Don't expect us to start from scratch on what you people want. That's not the way we do things here—*you* draft the bills and we work them over." Richard E. Neustadt, "Presidency and Legislation: Planning the President's Program," *American Political Science Review*, XLIX (December, 1955), 1015.

Whether he has presented few or many proposals, no incoming president's first months in office have been unmarked by complaints that he and his staff did not know how to work with Congress. Even Reagan, whose administration displayed a masterful touch in securing passage of his economic program in 1981, was embarrassed by the congressional uproar over two other issues that year—Social Security and the sale of AWACS aircraft to Saudi Arabia. In both cases the administration was charged with not consulting Congress early and fully enough. Managing relations with 535 members of Congress and key members of their staffs is a difficult and demanding art, especially for a new presidential team with little or no experience in the Senate or the House. And the penalties for errors may be high in terms of future congressional and popular support.

## Promises and Performance

In the enthusiasm of political campaigning, candidates for the presidency commonly promise things that are simply beyond the realm of possibility or would have unhappy effects or seem silly if honest efforts were exerted to carry them out. These situations often develop simply through lack of knowledge of the relevant facts, lack of understanding of the full ramifications of an issue, or partisan disparagement of the achievements of the predecessor administration. Examples of these are replete in all the recent transitions: Eisenhower's promise to "unleash" Taiwan and his implied promise to free the "enslaved" (communist satellite) nations of the world; Kennedy's promise to correct an alleged "missile gap" (which did not exist) and his allegations that the Eisenhower administration had not been sufficiently aggressive against Cuba; Nixon's secret "plan" to end the war in Vietnam "with honor"; Carter's promises to reduce nuclear armaments far below the previous SALT I understandings and not to give up practical control of the Panama Canal Zone; Reagan's promise to reestablish official relations with Taiwan and his attacks on the Panama Canal treaty. All of them promised a balanced budget, if not during their first year, then in the near future.[4]

4. Arthur M. Schlesinger, Jr., and Fred L. Israel (eds.), *History of American Presidential Elections, 1789–1968* (4 vols.; New York, 1971), IV, 3300, 3834–35;

Among the most annoying problems of a new president is what to do about his campaign promises: which to try honestly to honor, which to ignore, which to acknowledge publicly were made in error, which to hedge or delay. A mistaken course of action, promised with the best of intentions but with inadequate knowledge, can have heavy costs if honored. Of course, it would be best that such promises not be made or be sufficiently qualified as not to damage the new presidency. But short of that, the most prudent course would be to delay action until the likely consequences are fully understood, assuming that such a course is possible.

Another potential source of embarrassment for a successful presidential candidate is the platform his party adopted the previous summer. He or his representatives may or may not have had a major hand in drafting its key provisions, but presumably they are sympathetic with it. In either case, it does not seem to have been a source of serious difficulty for most presidents, and some feel that it does not carry much weight in the development of policy. For example, former Secretary of State Dean Rusk has contrasted "the world of opinion," where the "primary purpose is to solicit votes," with the "vastly different . . . world of decisions," where there are "real problems . . . which have dozens and dozens of secondary and tertiary problems surrounding them." He recalled "sitting in hundreds of meetings in the government where decisions were made in both Democratic and Republican administrations, and I've never heard anybody say, 'let's get out the party platform and see what it has to say about this.' These are quadrennial wonders and that's the end of it as far as policy is concerned." Yet, recent empirical studies indicate that, regardless of whether the decision makers look at the platforms when the decisions are made, there has been substantial conformity between administration decisions and proposals on one hand and platform positions on the other. The levels of agreement between decisions and platforms have been rising in both parties

---

Sidney Kraus (ed.), *The Great Debates: Kennedy vs. Nixon, 1960* (1962; rpr. Bloomington, 1977), 371–72; George F. Bishop *et al.* (eds.), *The Presidential Debates: Media, Electoral, and Policy Perspective* (New York, 1980), 255; Jack W. Germond and Jules Witcover, *Blue Smoke and Mirrors: How Reagan Won and Why Carter Lost the Election of 1980* (New York, 1981), 216.

over the last three decades and, according to Paul T. David, rising remarkably during the 1970s.[5]

There have been many examples of elected or reelected presidents quietly forgetting or completely ignoring pledges in party platforms or in campaign oratory—as Presidents Woodrow Wilson, Franklin D. Roosevelt, and Lyndon Johnson did when the nation entered upon overseas wars. But few new presidents are cynical enough to dismiss entirely what they or their platforms have been telling the voters, and many feel an obligation—because of the impact on their possible campaign for reelection, if nothing else—to make some effort to move United States foreign policy in the directions sketched in those statements. As the primary campaigns have lengthened, political aspirants must deliver their stump speeches more often, and this repetition may make them more convinced that their pledges to the electorate do indeed contain the answers to the problems facing the nation. An extended election season also encourages candidates to make more promises to the various audiences their pollsters tell them they must convince in order to win. The increased number of promises by candidates is matched by the increased length of party platforms, which are often veritably filled with such hostages to fortune.[6] Moreover, if with the breakdown of the foreign policy consensus, candidates are becoming more ideological, they are also becoming more reliant on the uncompromising notes struck in campaign rhetoric and more determined to act on those sentiments once in office.

## Organization for Decision Making

Many incoming presidents have said unkind things about the "bloated" federal bureaucracy, but few offer many constructive proposals to

5. Dean Rusk, "At the Pleasure of the President," Washington *Post*, July 18, 1982, p. B8; Dean Rusk, "The President and the Secretary of State: Leadership and Organizing Policymaking," in Kenneth W. Thompson (ed.), *The Virginia Papers on the Presidency*, Vol. III (Washington, D.C., 1980), 16; Paul T. David, "The APSA Committee on Political Parties: Some Reconsiderations of Its Work and Significance" (Unpublished paper, 1983).

6. A rough estimate of the 1952 Democratic platform puts it at fewer than ten

improve or reorganize it. President Carter, it is true, complained that there were too many agencies and vowed that he would reduce their number from 1,900 to 200, but the origins and meaning of those figures remain a mystery. He established a large staff in the Office of Management and Budget to plan and oversee reorganizations, mainly in the domestic agencies. Among his achievements were a minor re-shaping of the White House staff, a major reform of the civil service and the organization managing it, and the establishment of two new departments—Education and Energy. Before his election in 1980, candidate Reagan vigorously attacked those same departments, but at least for the first five years of his presidency he did not squander much of his political resources in efforts to abolish them.

New presidents have not typically made promises about how they would organize for the conduct of foreign affairs; indeed few of them have given the matter much thought before their election. But once elected, they are soon confronted with the problem of how to mobilize their advisers and their subordinate organizations to reach and effectuate policy decisions in foreign and national security af-fairs. The basic positions and structures are there, established by statute: the Departments of State and Defense, the National Security Council, the CIA, and others. But the interests of these agencies overlap with each other and also with the concerns of the other do-mestic departments and many other federal agencies. All agree that, within the constraints of the Constitution and the laws, the president makes foreign policy. But who keeps the president informed? Who presents him with recommendations and options? By what proce-dure do they reach him? How are the multifarious concerns of the various agencies admitted to the consideration of different policy problems? Who handles or coordinates crises? Who has the presi-dent's ear? Who negotiates with foreign countries on what matters? And who can speak for the administration?

These questions are particularly important and difficult at the out-set of a new administration. The agencies concerned, the Congress, the media, private pressure groups, and many of the American people are watching and pressing for their particular interests. So

---

thousand words, as compared with over thirty-seven thousand words in the party's 1980 platform.

are other nations of the world, both friends and rivals. At no time is it more nearly essential that an administration speak with one voice or not speak at all until it is confident in what it wants to say.

Until the 1930s the problems of many voices and confused responsibility were minor. The secretary of state was the president's adviser and spokesman in foreign affairs. Few other federal agencies were interested, not even the military departments. The New Deal and World War II changed all that, and as our international responsibilities broadened, other federal agencies became involved, and foreign policy and defense policy became increasingly interlocked. After the war the National Security Act of 1947 created the National Security Council (NSC) as a coordinating body and adviser to the president, with an executive secretary and staff to assist it.[7]

The office of assistant to the president for national security, generally known as national security adviser, was established originally as just that, not as an operator or a public spokesman. Presidents Truman and Eisenhower kept the staffing for the coordinating activity separate from the advisory activity in two different offices, both inconspicuous. Subsequent presidents combined the two activities in a single office and gave the adviser a larger staff.

The extent of presidential discretion in organizing for foreign affairs is indicated by the wide variations in style and in practice of presidents since Truman. Eisenhower, pursuing the order and structure taught by his military experience, established two boards, one to plan policy and one to see that the various concerned agencies carried it out. Kennedy, who preferred informal and interpersonal arrangements, promptly abolished both of Eisenhower's boards. He assigned foreign policy problems to *ad hoc* task forces and individuals he trusted, and he conducted much of his foreign affairs business at lunches. Overseas he directed that ambassadors be in charge of all United States activities in their countries except military operations and instituted the concept of "country teams," which consisted of the heads of the federal agencies operating in each country.

7. 61 Stat. 496. The statutory members of the National Security Council are the president, vice-president and secretaries of state and defense. The chairman of the Joint Chiefs of Staff and the director of the CIA are statutory advisers.

President Johnson was congenial with his secretary of state, Dean Rusk, and had high respect for his judgment and competence. At first Johnson relied heavily on Rusk and the State Department. But as the Vietnam War grew to overwhelming significance, his reliance for help and advice beyond himself fell increasingly upon his national security adviser, Walt Rostow. Before Vietnam absorbed nearly all of his attention, Johnson established in Washington the so-called Interdepartmental Groups (IGs) to develop plans and foreign policies. These included at first a Senior Interdepartmental Group (SIG) consisting of the top officer, or the one next to the top, of each agency significantly involved in foreign affairs. It was chaired by the under (later the deputy) secretary of state. The Interdepartmental Regional Groups (IRGs) for each of the various regions of the world were composed of officials at the assistant secretary level and were chaired by the assistant secretary of state for each region.[8]

The first task President-elect Richard Nixon assigned to his designated national security adviser, Henry Kissinger, during the 1968–1969 interregnum was to draft a plan of organization and procedure for handling foreign policy. Following a bitter struggle with senior officials of the State Department, Kissinger's plan was approved and announced immediately following the inauguration. It abolished the SIG and replaced it with a Review Group that would review and revise papers prepared by the IGs before they were presented to the full NSC. The State Department continued to chair the Interdepartmental Groups (at least in the early days of the administration), but Kissinger chaired the Review Group and thus gained substantial control over foreign policy.

Wishing, like Kennedy, to simplify the organization of the NSC staff, President Carter on his inauguration day approved a plan devised primarily by his national security adviser, Zbigniew Brzezinski. A Policy Review Committee would deal with issues of general foreign, defense, and international economic policy; it would be chaired by the appropriate secretary for the subject at hand, most

8. The membership of all the groups included representatives of the Defense Department, AID, CIA, the Joint Chiefs of Staff, the USIA, and the national security adviser or staff.

frequently the secretary of state. A Special Coordinating Committee, chaired by Brzezinski, would handle intelligence policy, arms control, and crisis management. For issues of less immediate importance, the IGs, chaired now by senior officials in several departments, continued to function. This plan, too, provoked disagreement among the president's advisers, primarily between Brzezinski and the affected cabinet officers.

In early January, 1981, President-elect Reagan agreed that his designated secretary of state, Alexander Haig, should negotiate and draft a plan of organization comparable to that of Kissinger but with a nearly opposite effect: in Haig's expression, it would make the secretary the president's "vicar" of foreign policy. Such a document was then prepared with inputs from the future heads of Defense, the CIA, and other agencies *and* from the president's adviser-to-be on national security, Richard V. Allen. A document agreed on by these officials was submitted and discussed at the White House in a meeting of the principal drafters and the new president's three top advisers within hours after the inauguration on January 20. (All the participants were still in their dress clothes.) At the close of the meeting, the president's counselor, Edwin M. Meese III, put the draft in his briefcase. Despite later efforts by Haig and his colleagues, neither that document nor any substitute was signed by the president for at least a year.[9] The early rivalries, distrust, and uncoordinated public statements on foreign policy of the Reagan administration might have been lessened had this not been the case. These may have contributed to the later resignation of Allen and still later of Haig himself. The coordinating structure eventually adopted by the Reagan administration included the regional groups and four senior interdepartmental groups, each chaired by a representative of the department or agency that had primary interest in its subject matter.

The National Security staff in the White House has had an interesting history since its establishment in 1947. It began as a relatively small group of about eight civil servants, coordinating and processing

9. Alexander M. Haig, Jr., *Caveat: Realism, Reagan, and Foreign Policy* (New York, 1984), 58. We have relied upon Haig's book for much of the information in this paragraph.

papers from the agencies for the president and the National Security Council. It was nonpolitical and nonpartisan, distinctly subordinate to the Department of State in authority and prestige. This situation pertained under both the Truman and Eisenhower administrations. It changed under Presidents Kennedy and Johnson. They relied much more on noncareer, foreign policy experts from the universities and professional organizations, the so-called "in-and-outers." They viewed themselves, and were viewed, as advisers to the president with personal rather than partisan loyalty, coexistent but not coequal with the State Department, more visible than their predecessors but still unknown to a large part of the public.

President Nixon and his first national security adviser changed the picture substantially. The staff grew to over forty professionals and came to have strong political loyalties. It worked on day-to-day issues and became a major competitor of the State Department in decision making, influence, and prestige. Since the Nixon-Kissinger era, its posture has fluctuated with different presidents and national security advisers, but in general it has become much more activist, more polarizing in its influence on foreign policy, and more politically oriented than it was in its earlier years.

A new president has a great deal of latitude in determining how his administration will operate in the area of foreign affairs. Some of his approach is expressed in the kinds of people he designates for top posts in the White House and to head key departments and agencies. And a great deal of the administration's *modus operandi* is developed through experience and trial and error during the months and years of its life. This seems inevitable. But most administrations have found it desirable to issue a basic charter of responsibilities, relationships, and procedures for handling foreign and national security policy at or near the beginning.

It would be a mistake to try to prescribe any one, best way for a president to organize for his handling of foreign affairs. Each president has his own style of operating and making decisions and his own friends and acquaintances in whose views he puts trust. Obviously, he can shape and reshape the structures he has inherited, perhaps eliminating some and adding others. And this process goes on for many months after he is inaugurated. But it is desirable that basic organizational issues be confronted and that the framework be laid early, preferably by or near the date of inauguration. A central issue for many years and a repeated bone of contention has been the role of the president's national security adviser and his relationship to the secretary of state and also to other agency heads such as the secretary of defense. Bound up with this issue is the procedure by which foreign and defense policies are initiated, studied, drafted, processed, and cleared on their way to the National Security Council and the president. It seems desirable that a new president should, well before his inauguration, be presented an impartial and analytic paper showing his major options and the probable features and consequences of each. This would enable him to make his choice and issue it soon after his inauguration.

## The Budget

Ever since the passage of the Budget and Accounting Act of 1921,[10] the executive budget process has been a source of difficulties of procedure and timing in its relation to presidential elections, the convening of Congress, the president's inauguration, and the fiscal year. Under that law, a new president had in effect to operate under budgets prepared by his predecessor for the first sixteen months of his administration. Until ratification of the Twentieth Amendment of the Constitution in 1933—too late to affect the inauguration that year of Franklin D. Roosevelt—the outgoing president had to prepare and submit a budget for the fiscal year that would not begin until July 1, nearly four months after he had left office. Both the president who prepared the budget and the Congress that passed the appropriations were lame ducks throughout the interregnum, which was then four months long. The new Congress would not even convene until the following December unless called into special session by the president. Actually, only two newly elected presidents, Hoover in 1929 and Roosevelt in 1933, were inaugurated under those budgetary provisions. Roosevelt's main New Deal programs in 1933 and later years were initially financed outside of the regular budgetary process.

Under the Twentieth Amendment, which is of course still in

10. 42 Stat. 18 (1921).

force, Congress convenes on the third of January, and a new president is inaugurated on January 20. The budget has still to be prepared and transmitted to the Congress by the outgoing president. The procedure was further modified by passage of the Congressional Budget and Impoundment Control Act of 1974, which moved the beginning of the fiscal year from July 1 to October 1.[11] This gave Congress more time for its vastly more complex review and action on the budget but did not materially modify the deadline for presidential transmission, which remained in mid-January. In transition years, the outgoing president must prepare the budget and, a few days before the inauguration, send it to Congress. The incoming president has several weeks in which he may propose changes in time for appropriate congressional consideration within the new budget calendar. In fact every incoming transition president since Truman has taken advantage of the opportunity to recommend changes in the budget previously submitted by his predecessor. Some have also initiated changes in the budget for the fiscal year during which they were inaugurated.

During the New Deal of the 1930s and the war and postwar era of the 1940s it became generally accepted that the federal government had an important if not primary responsibility for the health of the American economy and, to a lesser extent, of the world economy. It had long been accepted that the initiative for federal action should come from the president. During those years the United States also assumed—or simply accepted—the principal leadership role in international, defense, and economic affairs for the entire Free World; in these areas as well, and to an even greater extent, the president was the central figure. In both the domestic and international realms, the president's budget, its totals and its major elements, has been significant, partly as an expression of the president's policy directions and priorities, partly as an essential practical tool to make his policies and programs operational. The proportion of the budget that is truly discretionary on a year-to-year basis has declined over the last thirty years because of the growth of entitlement programs and of prior year commitments. But as President Reagan demonstrated in 1981, even some entitlements can be

11. P.L. 93-344 (1974).

changed. The largest part of the budget that still contains substantial discretionary elements is in fact national defense.

A new president's proposed changes in his predecessor's budget during a transition year are very significant: They are signals of the nature and degree of change in the posture and direction of the federal government under the new administration. They are, in part, real and factual expressions of intent and predictions of the future— far more solid than the rhetoric of campaign speeches, debates, and the inaugural address. The groundwork for the budget will largely have been completed in the months preceding the election under the direction of the outgoing president, before he knows whether he or another candidate of his party will continue in office. But the most important decisions and changes are made during the two months following the election. With the knowledge that he will not have to defend his budget in the Congress and in public, the outgoing incumbent always faces the temptation to make himself and his party look good, to make things easier or more difficult for his successor, and to give an added push for his policy objectives. There are many devices at hand if he succumbs to temptation: overestimates of revenues or of the speed with which popular programs can be carried out; underestimates of new obligations and outlays or of inflation and unemployment; optimistic projections on business activity, the balance of trade, price levels, and the federal deficit; and predictions of doom if measures he desires are not taken. It is not unknown for an outgoing administration to pad certain desired items to permit its successor to make substantial cuts without seriously damaging the program. One cannot say to what extent such distortions might have been in the budgets anyway. It may be noted that economic and programmatic assumptions and predictions cover a wide range of possibilities. One may estimate an extreme of optimism or of pessimism with legitimacy—even though it has little probability of coming to pass.

The Congress may never enact some of the budgetary proposals of a new president, but if it is ever to do so, it is most likely to give them a chance at this time. His situation in the executive branch is even more favorable. During the months immediately following election, he is surrounded by a number of eager and loyal friends and colleagues in the White House and the Executive Office. His cabinet and principal agency heads are newly appointed and relatively unfamiliar with the new responsibilities, people, organizations, operations, problems, clientele, and pressure groups with which they will have to deal. Most of the intermediate political positions between those agency heads and the career staffs are still vacant, and this means that effective communications between the political appointees and the permanent executives of the operating agencies (and their clientele and interest groups) are rare. Never will the White House and its Office of Management and Budget (OMB) be in a position to make more centralized, uncompromised decisions. The career staff of OMB, probably still the richest lode of knowledge and information in the executive branch, will have just completed the regular budget under the outgoing president. Many of them are anxious, in accord with their professional standards, to demonstrate their allegiance to their new political bosses and to the newly elected administration. Those not so disposed can leave, and some do leave.

But an incoming president has handicaps, too, and some of them may be forbidding. One is the shortness of time and the need for speed. This is coupled with lack of knowledge of, and familiarity with, the operations and problems of the government, the budget process itself, and the people involved both in the executive branch and in Congress. Immediately after learning of the election of General Eisenhower in 1952, President Truman wrote the president-elect inviting him to send immediately two representatives, one on the budget, one on foreign affairs. Within a week, Eisenhower's budget representative, Joseph M. Dodge, was there, sitting in on Budget Bureau meetings, reading the files, talking to its officials. He was later named Eisenhower's first budget director.[12] Since then, incoming budget directors have been among the first designees of every new president.

The present calendar and practice in times of transition are awkward and wasteful of the time of staffs and of the president and president-elect themselves. They invite gaming by the incumbent

12. Eisenhower also quickly named Dodge's foreign policy counterpart, Senator Henry Cabot Lodge, who had just been defeated for reelection. Lodge became United States ambassador to the United Nations in the new administration.

administration and are potentially damaging to the budgetary product. Hugh Heclo has recently written: "The outgoing President's budget has become a pernicious influence. It creates the wrong structure of incentives for both old and new Presidents. For the old President, it encourages the striking of a budgetary posture without responsibility for execution. For the new, it becomes a target against which one has to bid. Comparing numbers and percentage changes takes the place of analyzing policies." [13]

The outgoing president is responsible for preparing and transmitting a budget for the fiscal year that will not begin until eight and a half months after he has left office, an even longer lapse than under the old calendar. The incoming president may be able to change some of the numbers, but there is not time to go through another budget cycle, and usually he and his staff are not knowledgeable enough to make many changes. (The Reagan administration was an exception in this regard.) The process invites hasty, flashy, but ill-considered proposals. Nonetheless, a new administration normally has to operate its first twenty months with budget appropriations largely built by its predecessor and passed by the last Congress.

An outgoing administration can make it difficult for its successor during the interregnum by denying the latter access to its files, its current hearings, and its career staff. Thus, the Ford administration in 1976–1977 refused access to the incoming Carter people until after the New Year. Four years later the Carter administration provided access to the Reagan representatives on a few parts of the budget, mainly regulatory agencies, in December. Just before Christmas it furnished a budget of "current services"—i.e., a budget for the following year based upon existing programs without any changes in policy but taking into account assumptions on inflation, unemployment, and other factors. [14] Access to the OMB budget examiners was not permitted until after New Year's Day, less than three weeks before the inauguration. Delays like these aggravate the pressure, especially for new OMB appointees who are unfamiliar with the

13. Hugh Heclo to David Bell, February 24, 1984 (Copy in Miller Center files).

14. The budget for current services is already prepared every year pursuant to the Congressional Budget and Impoundment Control Act of 1974.

federal budget process and the major program issues confronting budget makers for the next fiscal year.

The rationale for this restraining of information derives in part from the increasingly political nature of the budget. There is fear that the newcomers will take political advantage of sensitive data and recommendations before the incumbent president has made his decisions on them. Furthermore, the period between November and early January is the busiest period of the year for OMB personnel, and helping and talking with newcomers would be a major distraction.

A number of suggestions have been offered to alleviate these difficulties. One is to move inauguration day back so that it falls immediately or soon after the election. This would make it possible for the president-elect to superintend the final months of the budget process and make the crucial decisions on the budget for the next fiscal year. It would require a constitutional amendment, which does not seem likely (see Chapter 3), and it would thrust onto the new administration responsibilities for which it would be almost totally unprepared. A somewhat comparable result might be achieved without constitutional amendment by a system wherein the president-elect designates his budget director soon after the election and the incumbent budget director then informally details all or most of his existing budget staff to him. He would then superintend the making of the budget, which would be transmitted to Congress a month or so *after* the inauguration. Such a system, we are told, has been used successfully in California. Like the earlier suggestion, it would have the flaw of imposing responsibilities upon a new administration before it was ready to handle them. It also might create a situation of total confusion and conflict arising from divided authority and responsibility during the interregnum.

A more modest proposal would retain the present practice but take steps to improve the capability and understanding of the new team before it assumed office. Soon after the November election, the incoming president would designate his new budget director and authorize him to appoint at once a small, high-level staff of persons who would later become senior officers in the Office of Management and Budget. The incumbent president would be required soon after the election to issue a budget of current services showing the estimates of federal costs, during the budget year, for programs and activities already mandated by law. He would not have to submit a regular budget, though he could of course include his basic recommendations for change in a message to the Congress. The incoming group could use the current-services budget as its base from the outset. Its work would be more effective if it were given access to OMB files, could attend OMB hearings, and could talk with OMB budgeteers. And the date of the new president's transmittal of the budget might be delayed until May, thus allowing the executive branch more time for budget preparation.

Another suggestion, also intended to prepare the incoming budget people, would extend the learning and planning back into the pre-election months and provide public funds to be spent for this and other purposes during the election campaign. In the last two transitions the new president's aides actually began work on the budget well before the election, but expenses were met from private contributions.

A final suggestion goes in almost exactly the opposite direction from the others. Its basic premise is that an incoming administration is ill-equipped to make important budgetary decisions until it is settled in office with a staff and with knowledgeable executives in the various agencies. This means that the new president should be discouraged as far as possible from making significant budgetary decisions for a good many months after he is in office; otherwise, the argument goes, his decisions on the budget may be wrong, perhaps disastrous.

The Office of Management and Budget (OMB) is the agency most involved on a continuing basis with putting into practice a new president's intent. Since 1939, that office, then known as the Bureau of the Budget, has been the central agent of the president not only for putting together the annual budget but also for overseeing the organization and management of the rest of the executive branch and the coordination and clearance of all proposed legislation.

In these capacities the Bureau of the Budget became a critical element in interparty transitions, and its position was a difficult one. It was first a coordinator of transition activities and preparer of the budget for the outgoing president. Then, quite suddenly, it had to move to the opposite pole—to educating and assisting the new president's team in the White House as well as the agencies, and to being the critic and modifier of the budget it had just created. President-elect Eisenhower's choice to become budget director, Joseph M. Dodge, was so impressed with the competence and evenhandedness of the Bureau of the Budget staff that he chose not to replace any of them, even though virtually all were appointed in Democratic administrations. But since 1970, when the agency was given its present name, it has gradually moved in the direction of greater political responsiveness and loyalty, and away from its traditional aspiration to be neutral in the political sphere. In 1974 appointments to the top two positions in OMB, till then considered an exclusive presidential prerogative, were made subject to senatorial confirmation. And beginning with the Nixon administration, an increasing number of positions were created that were outside the civil service. During the Carter and Reagan administrations, all but one of the highest posts in OMB—a total of about fifteen positions—have been political, filled by appointees of each new administration who replaced the incumbents. This is not to cast aspersions on these appointees, who have included many able people and were not party hacks. But the instability of the agency's leadership at a time of transition, when stability is most needed, can be a major difficulty. OMB's civil service personnel are now three or more echelons down in the organization. It is now more difficult to take advantage of their knowledge, memory, and analytic experience than was true in earlier transitions.

# CHAPTER 6

# The People
# and Their Relationships

These considerations [voters' reasons for throwing out an incumbent president, including "dislike of his measures"], and the influence of personal confidences and attachments, would be likely to induce every new President to promote a change of men to fill the subordinate stations; and these causes together could not fail to occasion a disgraceful and ruinous mutability in the administration of the government.

> —Alexander Hamilton
> *The Federalist*

I want the best man for the job possible. If I know the best man and he is loyal to me, that is the fundamental consideration. If I don't know the man and he's the best for the job, by God, there ought to be somebody I know who is as good for the job. So, go back, find me somebody else who is equally good, but who is equally loyal, who is *indisputably* loyal.

> —Bill Moyers, summarizing
> the position of Lyndon
> Johnson

Substantial policy knowledge and administrative experience are not incompatible with political qualifications and should be the primary criteria in the selection of presidential appointees.

> —National Academy of Public
> Administration

After the last hurrah has been shouted and the returns are in, five clusters of people who will be directly involved in the transition are roughly discernible. One of them is the incumbent president (whether he has sought reelection or not) and his political appointees, who feel the dejection if not repudiation of defeat and whose continued federal employment is numbered within eighty days.[1] A second is the president-elect and his vice-president-elect and their immediate coteries—exhilarated, ecstatic, nearly exhausted, largely innocent of governmental responsibilities, and not quite ready to face up to their next challenge—the forming of a government. Many of these will people the White House staff. A third cluster is the several cadres of senior career personnel, whether civil service, military, Foreign Service, or other, who will find the election results happy or sad, relevant or irrelevant, promising or depressing, perhaps a source of nervous uncertainty if not a threat. There is also a fourth category known as the transition teams, which include ardent advocates of the successful presidential candidate and his programs, many of whom have hopes—and some have promises—of high posts in the new administration.

Finally, there is the fifth cluster, which, starting from near zero, will rapidly grow to several hundred. It comprises the designated political appointees of the new administration other than the immediate advisers and aides. They will, one by one, be designated and later nominated by the incoming president and by other appointive politicos responsible to him. The more important of them must be confirmed by the Senate. The identity of the leading figures of this cluster will be widely advertised in the press, but almost none of them will assume any legal position or have any legitimate power until January 20 at the earliest.

The number and proportion of leadership posts that are reserved for political (or simply noncareer) appointments in the United States are high compared with other democratic and developed countries, and they have been sporadically growing over the last thirty years.[2]

1. *Political appointments,* as used in this volume, are those made by the president, with or without consent of the Senate, and those appointments to second-level positions whose occupants may be removed at the will of the appointing officer. Most of the top-level appointments made by the president require senatorial approval, which is normally given after a brief investigation and hearing. In transition years the Senate committees may conduct their inquiries of a few of the topmost nominees even before the inauguration.

2. In Britain, Canada, France, and Germany the noncareer positions number fewer or a little more than one hundred. The American states, all of which have a

In the same period, the size of the federal work force, despite fluctuations in time of war, has been slowly declining in relation to the total labor force. The growth of political appointees has typically occurred after the inauguration of new presidents as part of their efforts to gain control of the executive branch and also with the establishment of new programs.

The five clusters constitute a melange of friends, enemies, but mostly strangers; of sophisticates and innocents; of idealistic reformers and persons simply seeking or holding onto a job; of professionals—mainly lawyers, bankers, businessmen, professors, military officers, and civil servants; of males and females, blacks and whites, from every region of the country. The interregnum is a phenomenon that could occur only in America, but here it is recurrent on a calendared basis whenever a presidential election is decided in favor of a challenger from the party out of power.

In terms of numbers, based principally on the 1980–1981 transition, the president's entourage consists of between twenty and forty persons. Recent transition teams have had more than a thousand. Of the noncareer appointees under the incumbent president, there are over three thousand, but only a fraction of these, roughly between four hundred and six hundred, are politically crucial. The bulk of the new president's appointees are not named and nominated until after the inauguration. Those designated before then are the cabinet secretaries, principal agency heads, and a few officials at a lower level. The career executives who will remain on the rolls are probably in excess of ten thousand. They include the upper ranges of the civil service, the military services, the Foreign Service, and others.

The various clusters share only a single mission during a transition: to transfer the baton of governmental power from one party to the other within the time frame set by the Constitution and the laws. All generally agree that the fundamental structures, processes, and safety of American government be upheld. And in those pockets of policy in which there still exists genuine bipartisan agreement, the new relationship may be friendly and accommodating despite the

---

three-branch government similar to the federal government, vary widely in their numbers of noncareer positions. Some, like California, have few in the line departments; others have more than the national government.

opposing political affiliations. Above and beyond all of these are the normal manners of civility and courtesy that persons of dignity accord others whom they respect, regardless of the depth of their disagreements.

Still, the differences among the various clusters are hard to bridge. Each group has its own views, perspectives, expectations, ambitions, and fears. Excepting most of those in the career services and some in the other groups, each cluster has just emerged from a winner-take-all clash in which it has both thrown and received brickbats. One side is anxious to establish that its policies and methods are superior; the other, to vindicate and maintain its achievements. The incumbents find it increasingly difficult to hold an administration together, given its declining influence at home and abroad and the growing anxiety and efforts of its members to find new jobs and attend to personal and family problems. But if there is a glue to bind them together in those trying weeks, it is to defend and protect what they have wrought and to push forward with the unfinished enterprises they have begun.

The new president-elect and his entourage have sprinkled, even engulfed, their campaigning months with criticisms of the actions and efforts of their predecessors and with promises to undo or replace what has been done. They seek quick nostrums and preferably spectacular demonstrations of change. Some receive the information given them by the incumbents and the career officials with skepticism if not distrust and disdain.

The president-elect's own small cluster will soon be augmented through the designation of future political appointees, a majority of whom will at the start be strangers to the president's group and to each other. Some of them share the ignorance, the innocence, and the distrust of the winning team, though probably to a lesser extent; they will soon be scattered among the various departments and agencies. Their relations with the president-elect's entourage are not generally close or loving, and some are likely, if recent experience is indicative, to become increasingly distant or even hostile toward the White House staff. Almost every president-elect since World War II has promised heavy reliance upon, and delegation to, his cabinet if not outright cabinet government. But sooner or later, mostly sooner, all but Eisenhower have reneged on the promise, often following a running series of battles between the White House and the political appointees "out there" in the executive branch. The seeds of these battles are sown in the appointments and assurances of the interregnum and the weeks following it.

Meanwhile, another series of skirmishes may have arisen between the incoming group and another cluster—the transition teams. They are partly paid, partly volunteer, and always very temporary. Their cores are frequently organized by aspiring candidates well before the election, in one case (Carter's) even before the nominating conventions. Their mission is to obtain information and to project plans for the new administration, preparing books of facts and options and recommendations for the president-elect and his appointees. As noted earlier, the incumbent president establishes a matching transition team, headed by a top White House official and working through a designee of the Office of Management and Budget and assigned officials of each department and agency. The two teams, one representing the incumbents and the other the newcomers, usually work to alleviate misunderstandings and to ameliorate (or sometimes sharpen) differences on policy questions. The transition teams for the president-elect can be useful intermediaries between the officials currently in power and the newcomers with their variant aspirations and ideas. Some of them may be chosen to fill positions relevant to what they have just studied in depth on a transition team. This is in fact the optimal outcome in the use of transition teams: the designation of members to appropriate positions in the incoming administration wherein they may directly utilize the information and perspectives they have gained in their transition studies in a responsible administrative position. In other cases, transition teams involve double transmissions of information and advice: from the incumbent administrators to the transition team and from the latter to the incoming administrators. The possibilities of error and of misinterpretations are doubled. Transition teams always entail some disappointments and recriminations on the part of "transitioners" who do not get jobs. At worst, they may create outright hostility, even in the public arena, as when the Carter transition group in 1976–1977 fought for control over appointments—and lost to those in his campaign organization.

## The Career Services

Another significant cluster consists of the upper ranks of the various career services—military, Foreign Service, civil service, and others. In most of the agencies concerned with foreign affairs, they are the most numerous in their assigned fields, the most knowledgeable, and the most permanent of all. Collectively, they have major advantages over all the others. They know, or have access to, the backgrounds of American officials at home and abroad, and are familiar with the issues with which the new administration will be concerned. They are the ones who search for, sort, sift, and draft most of the documents and oral information on which future decisions and actions will be based. They know where the bodies are buried. And they know how to manipulate the throttles for action or for delay or inaction. Through many years of association, they have developed interpersonal networks built around policy issues that cross organizational, congressional-executive, and even international lines. The outgoing administrators will likewise have built networks, which are dissolving during the interregnum, but the newcomers will be just beginning to build theirs and will be hardly able to match the cohesiveness and communications of the career servants.

The potential influence of the top career personnel grows as that of the outgoing administration winds down to zero on the day it leaves office. The new administration at the top—both in the White House and in the agencies—is often inexperienced and only partially briefed. Most of the intermediate positions, such as assistant secretaries and assistant administrators, are vacant or are temporarily filled by career persons on an acting basis. Indeed, the acting secretary of state on a number of days in January, 1981, was a Foreign Service officer. This increased power of the career personnel may or may not be beneficial to the smoothness of the transition.

Not all factors work in favor of the upper echelons of career personnel during transitions—far from it. Most career officials in acting political positions are reluctant to make aggressive or innovative decisions except in the most compelling circumstances. In general, they feel wanting in the power, the confidence, or the access to superiors that are requisite to positive action. It has become typical in recent elections for aspiring presidential candidates of both parties to attack "the bureaucracy" as the source of many or most evils. Not all incumbent presidents have resisted such attacks; in fact, they have sometimes echoed them.

They suffer other disadvantages as well. Those who have served the outgoing administration are automatically suspect among the newcomers. They are known to have supported and helped carry out—perhaps initiated and openly advocated—policies that are now bad words. In fact, effectiveness for the previous administration can be a black mark in the minds of the new political appointees and may be a signal for reassignment or early retirement. Likewise, support for a predecessor's foreign policy in one or another area may be a signal for both a radical change in policy and the reassignment or retirement of the career officers involved.

Even the alleged permanence of career personnel is not assured. Favorable provisions for retirement are available and are often encouraged for senior career officers. Beyond that, after 120 days a new administration has powers to assign and transfer the senior executives of the civil service as it wishes. The reassignments may of course be so unfavorable as to induce early retirement.

The posture of a career official during a transition is a difficult one. He is expected to educate, help, and take orders from new bosses who are usually junior to him in age and experience and relatively unversed in the situations and problems to which he has been exposed much of his life. Very likely they distrust him as much as he distrusts them, and sometimes both have good cause. He is enmeshed in a tangle of conflicting loyalties: to the departing administration, to the new one, to his colleagues and the permanent organization that he serves, to his profession and its standards, and to his own convictions about the national interest. He regards himself properly as a professional. But in what ways is he a professional? As a supporter and advocate of the positions of his superiors, whatever they may be and even if they require a 180-degree turnaround in his position? As a professional neutral who scrupulously avoids expressing any position? As an objective expert who, on the basis of his own studies of issues, assumes and pushes for positions he believes in the best interest of the United States? The questions are not easy; nor is any answer likely to be generally and durably popular.

The career services in the foreign affairs agencies are particularly strong. They thus constitute major forces for continuity and stability—or, to put it more negatively, they are resisters of change. The Foreign Service occupies about half of the influential posts in the State Department, both domestic and overseas, but not all those at the top. Comparable corps operate in the Agency for International Development and the International Communications Administration as well as in the more domestically oriented departments like Agriculture and Commerce. The Central Intelligence Agency has its own career system. The military departments of course have their officer corps, largely immune from day-to-day politics and the vicissitudes of political transition. Near the top of the Office of the Secretary of Defense and most of these other agencies (not including the CIA) are career civil servants, some of whom survive presidential changes.

In the State Department the office of under secretary for political affairs has, by custom, become a career position for a ranking Foreign Service officer. The incumbent usually survives presidential transitions but may be transferred soon after inauguration. The effectiveness of this office in smoothing transitions is diminished when the incoming White House team distrusts the Foreign Service generally. The CIA up to and including its director seems to have been immune to transition politics for its first thirty years. But President Carter in 1977 removed the incumbent director, George Bush, who had been chairman of the Republican National Committee. He sought unsuccessfully to replace him with Ted Sorensen, who had been a Kennedy White House aide and director of Kennedy's election campaign, and then appointed Stansfield Turner, a navy officer. At the next transition, President Reagan appointed his own campaign director, William J. Casey, to the post; the days of political immunity for the post appear to be over. It should be noted, however, that Casey had rich experience in intelligence work in the Office of Strategic Services (OSS) and in the military during World War II. He subsequently served in several other important governmental posts. There has long been partisanship at the top and in the upper reaches of the civilian posts in the Office of the Secretary of Defense and the assistant secretary of defense's Office of International Security Policy. The same is true of the heads of the Agency for International Development, the International Communications Agency, and others, though the bulk of their upper-level personnel are in a career service.

Finally and most important, there is the White House itself. It has no career service, and few of its professional and clerical people survive transitions. President Reagan's "new broom" brushed away even the secretaries. In an interparty transition, the incoming president designates a new national security adviser well before he is inaugurated. Presidents Kennedy, Johnson, Nixon, and Carter built what seemed to be a firm tradition of appointing as their national security advisers professors of political science who had specialized in international relations. But President Ford interrupted the practice, and President Reagan has apparently terminated it in appointing persons with military and political careers. The national security staffs at first were principally civil servants with tenure. When Eisenhower succeeded Truman, all but one member stayed on. During the 1960s McGeorge Bundy brought in a new team, principally recruited from campuses and research groups. Henry Kissinger and most of his successors relied heavily on career officers from the State and Defense departments, with a few from the CIA. This means that the majority (like those brought in from outside) depend for their careers and their promotions on their "home" agencies, not the White House. At the time of transition, turnover is typically high, but a few stay on at least until their successors have become acclimated. In other words there is rather little continuity of individual people but considerable reliance on the career services to detail their personnel for White House assignments.

## Political Appointments and Assignments

Ultimately, the success of every president depends upon the officers whom he appoints, the career public servants whom he inherits, *and* the effectiveness with which they work with one another. The transition personnel who are not appointed to positions after the inauguration vanish from the scene, as do the outgoing political appointees. In point of time, political appointments are an incoming president's first concern. In recent election years the building of systematic machinery for seeking out and winnowing potential appointees has begun soon after, or even before, the nominating conventions.

The first question that is applicable to each of the considerable number of positions where the option exists is whether to bring in a new person from the outside, to retain a holdover political appointee from the previous administration, or to fill the job by assigning (or keeping) a career official. One of the most repeatedly controversial issues is the choice between career Foreign Service officers and political appointees for top positions in the United States and abroad. It is a standard complaint in the State Department that too many unqualified amateurs are appointed to significant ambassadorships and to high or intermediate positions in the State Department. This allegedly results in a dilution of American effectiveness in diplomacy as well as damage to the morale of the career contingent in the department. After the Foreign Service was established as a career system in 1924, the proportion of ambassadors drawn from the career service rose sporadically to a high of 78 percent under President Carter in 1978. But more than half of President Reagan's appointments in his first year were noncareer. It should be pointed out, however, that the proportion of noncareer ambassadorial appointments is normally highest immediately following a new president's inauguration, when the pressure for political rewards and the distrust by political officials of the career personnel are most virulent. But it should also be noted that the politically appointed amateurs are often assigned to the most prestigious and desirable capitals, which include those of the greatest diplomatic importance: London, Bonn, Paris, Rome, Tokyo, Mexico City, Rio de Janeiro, Peking, Moscow et al.[3]

The statistical evidence does not confirm that there has been significant overall increase in the proportion of noncareer officers filling top positions in the State Department at home in the last twenty-five years (assistant secretaries and their equivalents, and deputy assistant secretaries). On the domestic front about half of the assistant

---

3. See Senator Charles McC. Mathias, Jr., "Politics or Merit?" *Foreign Service Journal*, LIX (April, 1982), 28–32, 36. Mathias was writing in support of a bill he had introduced in the Senate in 1981 (S. 1886) requiring that at least 85 percent of all ambassadors be career FSOs.

secretaries and others of equivalent rank are and have been career, while roughly two-thirds at the rank of deputy assistant secretary are career.[4] The statistics tell nothing, of course, about the relative quality and experience of either the career or the noncareer appointees, about the assignments and reassignments of the career officers and the reasons for them, or about the political "litmus test" applied to these officers and those below them to make sure they are of the "right" political party and in sympathy with the president and his goals.

Political appointees share one attribute: they have no assurance and, in most cases, no expectation, of a career in their posts or in the government. They view themselves and are viewed by others as temporary and expendable. Their loyalties, aspirations, fears, values, working and behavioral standards, and criteria of success or failure—all are different from those of the career people with whom they work. And they differ widely among themselves. It is useful to consider them as falling into four fairly discrete categories, here listed not in order of prestige, legal standing, and responsibility—in which the second category would surely head the list—but of immediacy to the president.

First are the immediate friends and aides of the president—his entourage. Most of them were leaders in the victorious presidential campaign. They are typically loyal to the president, young, smart, and expert in politics but not in governance. Most are appointed to offices in the White House or elsewhere in the Executive Office of the President. They are appointed by the president without Senate confirmation and are the first-named appointees.

Second are members of the cabinet, some deputy and undersecretaries, heads of major agencies, and ambassadors to major countries overseas and to major international organizations. They are appointed after broad political and representational consideration but are not potential partisan competitors with the president. The majority are not close confidants; some have never met him until a day or two before their appointment. These selections are particularly important because they are widely viewed as indicators of presidential

4. These data are based upon statistics furnished by the Department of State in February, 1984.

intentions and directions. Such personnel decisions are also key policy decisions.

Third are officers at the subcabinet level: assistant secretaries, assistant administrators of major noncabinet agencies, and administrators of smaller agencies. A minority have been politically active, and most are loyal to the party, the president, and his goals. They are occupationally mobile but likely to be more specialized than their superiors. Most of those in the foreign affairs agencies have had prior experience or study in that field.

The fourth group are deputy assistant secretaries and assistants to secretaries; heads of bureaus, administrations, and offices within departments; and regional and overseas representatives. They are likely to be occupationally professionalized in a specialty appropriate to their governmental responsibility, and some are distinguished leaders in their professions. However, some of these appointments are patronage rewards for political work and contributions.

Viewed as a whole, the four groups constitute the central nervous system of the executive branch. They form the communications network from the president to the operators of government who make up its various career services; they range along the continuum from the purely "political" (concerned with winning elections, public opinion, and relations with Congress) to the solely "governmental"; they are responsible for the translation of broad lines of policy preference into specific deeds; and they report back on those deeds and their effects from the operators to the policy leaders. The categories are a four-level bridge from general to specific, from politics to professionalism.

In each group people are sought and chosen according to different considerations and by different methods. Many of the top-level people in the first category are known even before the election, though their specific assignments are frequently uncertain and may be the source of bitter competition. The president makes the crucial choices, and his appointees have a good deal to say about who will work under them. The second category becomes a primary concern for a new president-elect before or immediately after his election. The determinations usually follow extensive consideration by him and his most trusted advisers, both within and outside of the government. The nominees are announced seriatim or in clusters beginning in late November and running into January. The third and fourth groups follow later. A few are designated before the inauguration, but some are not approved for many months. A few holdovers from the previous administration are invited to stay until their replacements are installed, but in many agencies there exists a vacuum between the secretaries and their operative staffs during many weeks of policy making and budget revision in the winter and spring of the year of inauguration. This situation may invite stability and conservatism on one hand or a high degree of centralized decision making in the Executive Office of the President on the other.

Some of the old considerations associated with the spoils system are less significant than they were, though they are by no means absent. The national party machinery—and those on the state and local levels—have lost some of their clout. Congressmen still nominate appointees and clear others from their states. But the main initiative lies in the executive branch, principally in the White House. Agreement with the incoming president's ideology has become a dominant criterion for appointment. The best demonstrator of such agreement is early support of the future president's candidacy, preferably by the time of the presidential primaries. General managerial considerations are more important than they once were for appointments at the top levels, as are professional competence and reputation at the levels of program and bureau management. Interest groups are far more influential than they used to be.

Beyond the general considerations, the attributes sought in candidates for these positions vary widely, but they are almost always a mix of most of the following qualities:

1.  Political value
    A.  Political strength the nominee may contribute to the administration
    B.  The nominee's contributions in terms of work, time, money, and support for the new president (especially how early in the campaign that support began)
    C.  The nominee's acceptability to the national party, the local party, the Senate committee reviewing the nomination, the congressmen (and some of their staffs) in the nominee's home state, and the president's own team
    D.  The nominee's acceptability to, and influence on, the appropriate interest groups

2.  Loyalty
    A.  To the party and its general ideology
    B.  To the president and his objectives and ideology
    C.  To the public interest as defined by the incoming administration
    D.  To the agency head and other superiors to whom he or she will report
3.  Representativeness and balance in region and state, occupation, income, age, sex, and race
4.  Compatibility with the national security
    A.  Loyalty to the nation
    B.  Lack of habits and a life-style likely to endanger the national security
5.  Specialism or generalism, as appropriate
6.  Managerial competence
7.  Education, experience, and reputation
8.  Freedom from conflicts of interest
9.  Ethics, including no past behavior that might be embarrassing to the administration
10. Reputation as a team player, meaning the ability to get along with the political officials in the White House, the executive branch, and the committees and staffs of Congress
11. Family relationship or personal friendship with member(s) of the administration or its political party

## The Appointment Processes

Those in the world of big business know the arduous and prolonged procedures and clearances normally required for the appointment of a new executive, and those in academia are familiar with the careful scrutiny and negotiation that precede appointments of professors. Executive appointments in the federal government are at least as significant, and the processes are far more arduous.[5] Furthermore, they must be performed with extraordinary speed.

5.  Efforts to reform the appointments process are currently being pressed by the National Academy of Public Administration, which has coordinated major studies and published two reports on the subject. The first, by John W. Macy, Bruce Adams, and J. Jackson Walter, was *America's Unelected Government: Appointing the President's Team* (Cambridge, Mass., 1983). The second was *Leadership in Jeopardy: The Fraying of the Presidential Appointments System* (Washington, D.C., 1985). The studies leading to the latter report were coordinated under the

Methods for recruiting and selecting incoming political executives have been developing sporadically since World War II. Both Truman and Eisenhower used private consultants to seek candidates for political jobs, but in neither case does it appear that the consultants' proposals had a significant impact upon the outcomes. Kennedy and particularly Johnson went beyond their predecessors in setting up organizations within the White House for recruiting and reviewing candidates on a positive basis, *i.e.*, going out and finding and promoting candidates rather than simply receiving and negotiating voluntary applications and nominations of friends, politicos, interest groups, and others. Since the 1960s every administration has established an office in the White House and some sort of system, usually computerized, for developing, maintaining, and using a file of potential political appointees. The Reagan campaign team enlisted the services of a professional executive recruiter in the summer of 1980 to devise a plan for political appointments, and the development of a system was well under way many weeks before his election. Typically, after the inauguration, the system and the people managing it move into the White House and become a continuing presidential personnel office.

There are three enormous difficulties in the process of appointing political officers at the time of party transition. The first is that every incoming administration of a different party starts almost from scratch. Most of the recruiters—whether in the transition organization, the White House, or the agencies—are new and inexperienced. The system of the prior administration is largely scrapped, and its records having to do with candidates of the outgoing party are nearly worthless. Until recently, there has been virtually no attempt to capitalize on the experience of previous administrations; each must invent the wheel again.[6] The result has been delays in filling executive positions in the executive branch and probably the appointment of some mediocre, even embarrassing, candidates. This situation has been deplored by presidents from Reagan at least as far back as Abraham Lincoln. The practice of many of our recent presidential

---

leadership of G. Calvin MacKenzie. Further reports and essays on the subject are now being published.

6. Macy, Adams, and Walker, *America's Unelected Government*, 31–32.

candidates of beginning to establish a system many weeks before election day seems desirable, however one may feel about other pre-election transition activities. Indeed, a veteran in this field, in a newspaper article even before the 1984 primaries, urged the candidates to begin considering their possible appointees.[7] He also suggested that the national committees of the major parties maintain up-to-date files of qualified people for federal jobs that could be drawn upon by winning candidates, but there is some question whether such a system would be practicable.

A second serious difficulty is the sheer volume of the task. In the latter part of President Johnson's administration, his personnel operation, headed by John W. Macy, who was also chairman of the Civil Service Commission, had built a computerized talent bank of 30,000 names, cross-referenced by skills and background characteristics. But the hardest part comes at the beginning, when there is no talent bank. In those weeks just before and after the inauguration, incoming mail runs as high as 1,500 pieces a day, almost all of it letters of application, résumés, recommendations, and patronage requests. They come from campaign workers, from congressmen, from state and local officials, and from party headquarters—federal, state, and local.[8] Relatively few of these applicants will actually be appointed, but the letters must be handled courteously, and some require a good deal of political sensitivity.

The third difficulty is the complexity of selection and clearance. The traditional method of political recruitment has been labeled BOGSAT—"A bunch of guys sitting around a table," asking each other, "Whom do you know?" And probably this description sometimes still applies, especially for positions at the very top. But today, the volume of applications and vacancies and the variety of considerations require a more systematic method. The main steps involved are not too different from, but are far more extensive than, those in executive and professional recruitment elsewhere: identification of positions and the qualifications desired for each; a search for candidates throughout the country, using other channels than just

7. John W. Macy, "Candidates, Discuss Appointees Now," New York *Times*, February 9, 1984, A31.
8. Macy, Adams, and Walker, *America's Unelected Government*, 31–32.

political ones; evaluation of candidates, involving negotiations with the agency concerned, the White House staff, sometimes the president himself, the party, the appropriate congressmen, and interest groups; selection of the best candidate and negotiation with him or her; and finally, clearances involving the same people and organizations, followed by a full field investigation by the FBI.

A great many noncareer appointments, including most of the White House staff, are made by the president without confirmation by the Senate, and the heads of most agencies have a good deal of noncareer hiring authority (though the president may require that their appointments be approved in the White House). But in the great majority of top-level appointments, the executive part of the process culminates, if all goes well, in a presidential nomination to the Senate. Each candidate is there referred to the Senate committee responsible for overseeing the agency concerned. In the case of appointments to the State and Defense departments and related agencies, this means either the Foreign Affairs or the Armed Services Committee. There is no standard procedure for the different Senate committees, but there are normally a brief investigation and review of the documents submitted by the executive branch, which is conducted by committee staff; a hearing; a committee review and discussion; and a vote of the whole committee. If it is favorable, the matter is then submitted to the full Senate, which may have a brief debate and normally votes to confirm.

In the Carter and Reagan transitions the time taken for Senate confirmation greatly increased over earlier ones. Confirmation of more than half of their appointments in the State Department took longer than two months, and in the Defense Department, about one month. But some cases required three months or more, some were delayed by a half year, and a few were held up by an individual senator indefinitely.

The recruitment of political appointees in foreign policy and national security posts has been simpler than in the rest of the executive branch, at least until the Reagan transition. In the first place, the pool from which choices are made is typically much smaller. There have been a few exceptions, but for the most part appointees in these fields have come from that coterie of the American intelligentsia that has had significant teaching, writing, or direct experience in or closely related to foreign affairs—or some combination of the three. Until quite recently, this meant that persons with generally compatible understandings of American problems and objectives could be chosen by and from either party—a basis of consensus existed that now seems to be splintering.

There is normally a contest over influence in the initiating, reviewing, and "signing off" of individual nominees between the heads of the departments and agencies, on one hand, and the leaders of the White House staff, on the other. The former seek persons whose competence and wisdom they trust, often on the basis of prior acquaintance, and who they think will be loyal to the agency and their superiors in the agency in which they may be appointed. The White House officials seek unswerving ideological and personal loyalty to the president and often suspect that appointees may be swayed too far by the "natives" in the agencies and by interest groups. The Carter administration is said to have swung far in the direction of delegation of initiative and influence to the agencies; the Reagan administration, like Nixon's, endeavored to retain central control in the White House, or return it there, after brave pronouncements about decentralization.

The initiative for appointments to the positions of undersecretary and assistant secretary may be delegated to the top appointees in the particular agencies before or after they take office, and this is usually the case in the Department of State. The division of responsibilities for the nominations of candidates has become a source of confusion and conflict in several administrations. Designated cabinet secretaries are not well equipped to carry through the various steps either before or soon after they are in office, and so a substantial share of the responsibility rests in the White House. And the clearance process during the interregnum and after the inauguration within the White House is arduous indeed, as indicated by the chart on the following page showing that process in the Reagan White House in 1981.

The candidate must undergo an FBI investigation that will produce a report of facts, allegations, and rumors about his and his family's life-style, political and social beliefs and activities, financial integrity, sexual behavior, criminal record (if any), medical history, and any other matters that might be a source of embarrass-

## Clearance Process for Reagan Appointments, July, 1981

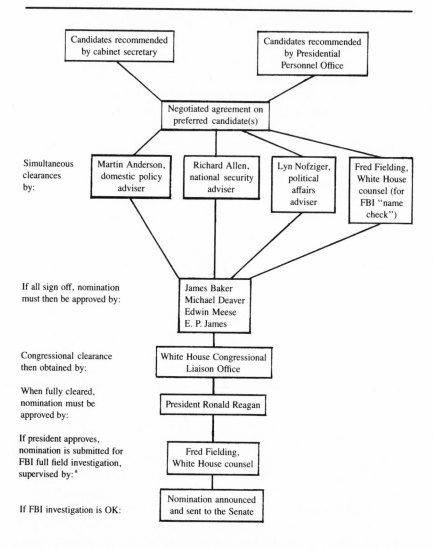

Candidates recommended by cabinet secretary

Candidates recommended by Presidential Personnel Office

Negotiated agreement on preferred candidate(s)

Simultaneous clearances by:

Martin Anderson, domestic policy adviser

Richard Allen, national security adviser

Lyn Nofziger, political affairs adviser

Fred Fielding, White House counsel (for FBI "name check")

If all sign off, nomination must then be approved by:

James Baker
Michael Deaver
Edwin Meese
E. P. James

Congressional clearance then obtained by:

White House Congressional Liaison Office

When fully cleared, nomination must be approved by:

President Ronald Reagan

If president approves, nomination is submitted for FBI full field investigation, supervised by:[a]

Fred Fielding, White House counsel

If FBI investigation is OK:

Nomination announced and sent to the Senate

*Source:* John W. Macy, Bruce Adams, and J. Jackson Walter, *America's Unelected Government: Appointing the President's Team* (Cambridge, Mass., 1983), 62.

a. Simultaneously, the Office of Government Ethics informally reviews financial-disclosure statements with the White House counsel. Usually, fifteen days before the nomination goes to the Senate, OGE formally reviews and begins preparation of the report to the Senate committee.

ment. He must also prepare a detailed questionnaire about his financial record and condition, which will be reviewed by the Office of Government Ethics. If any potential conflict of interest exists, he may have to set up a blind trust or divest some of his holdings. He must also prepare himself for a grilling in a Senate committee hearing that may or may not be friendly. If he does not live in Washington or whatever the city of his future headquarters might be, he will have to find and acquire lodging and move or arrange to move his family.

Assuming that all goes well, the candidate takes the oath of office on, or some time after, January 20. But the roads to presidential appointments are tortuous, and a few are almost certain to strike a land mine along the way—in the agency of assignment, the White House, the FBI, the Office of Government Ethics, or the Senate.

## The Slow Start

The consequence of the numerous stages of this process is delay. The slow leak in effectiveness that crippled the outgoing administration is succeeded by a sluggish start of the incoming one. In the two departments of most concern to foreign affairs, State and Defense, the secretaries are typically designated by the president well before his inauguration—in December or even November. They and their deputies can usually be sworn into office on January 20, the day of inauguration, or soon thereafter. But they are almost the only ones. Some other officials near the top trail along in late January and February: the undersecretaries, the heads of the Agency for International Development, the International Communications Agency, the Arms Control and Disarmament Agency, and the service secretaries of the army, the navy and the air force. The intermediate level officers are far behind. In 1981, only one of Reagan's eleven appointees as assistant secretaries of state was ready to take his oath of office before May. Two of those posts were not filled by the Reagan White House until July and August respectively. The record of the Carter administration was somewhat better, but both were far slower than their predecessor transition presidents Eisenhower, Kennedy, and Nixon. Under Carter, half of the senior positions remained unfilled until near the end of March. Under Eisenhower, Kennedy, and

Nixon, the comparable median was in February. It is paradoxical that the two transition presidencies that made the most preparations before election were the slowest to get their full team aboard, and it is not altogether clear why.

The degree to which these delays must have hurt the nation in the continuity of the nation's policies and the development of new ones to handle new conditions and emergencies is inestimable. Some of the most significant offices for the coordination of foreign affairs are the five regional assistant secretaries of state for Europe, Latin America, the Near East, Africa, and the Far East. In the Reagan transition all of the appointees to these posts were confirmed in May or June of 1981, from four to five months after inauguration. One of the most important positions for national security policy is that of assistant secretary for international security planning in the Defense Department. The Reagan appointee to that post was not confirmed until August, 1981, six and a half months after the inauguration. It must be kept in mind, too, that when these appointees assume office, they are not yet fully prepared for their new responsibilities; indeed some are far from it. They will still need training, indoctrination, and on-the-job experience.

It is little wonder that most former secretaries of state agree that the first six to nine months of their terms were "a wasteland period."[9] If to these months are added the three months of declining influence of the outgoing administration, there is a total period of nearly a year—one quarter of a presidential term—when the United States is running at half throttle or less in its conduct of foreign affairs.

The alleged reasons for the delays in appointments include slowness in the FBI checks and in the investigation and correction of potential conflicts of interest, and cumbersome procedures in the White House and elsewhere. Certainly a major factor has been political considerations and delays in the departments, the White House, and the Senate. A variety of steps could be taken to alleviate these matters: earlier consideration of possible appointments, earlier designation of future agency heads, streamlining procedures, talent banks maintained by the political parties, simplification of

9. White Burkett Miller Center *Report,* No. 4 (Fall, 1983), 1.

FBI checks and Senate reviews, and others. But the basic problem is beyond perfect solution; the job is simply too big. Only the most fortunate organization could recruit and hire so many persons of superior quality to such levels of responsibility under so many different pressures in so short a time. This would be true even of organizations with skillful and experienced recruiting personnel and with large computerized files of potential applicants.

Perhaps it would be wiser for an incoming administration to acknowledge (to itself at least) that it cannot "hit the ground running," as the saying goes, in every area and that it is preferable to be selective and to go slow in order to minimize mistakes both in taking actions and in making appointments. It might also be wise to give more respect to, and place more reliance upon, career personnel and holdovers from the previous administration.

# PART II

# Transitions Since
# World War II

# One President at a Time?
# Or Two? Or None?

I am now so near the moment of retiring, that I take no part in affairs beyond the expression of an opinion. I think it fair that my successor should now originate those measures of which he will be charged the execution and responsibility and that it is my duty to clothe them with the forms of authority.

> —President Thomas Jefferson
> January 21, 1809 (six weeks
> before the end of his term)

He [President-elect Ronald Reagan] and I understand very well that I will be the President in the fullest sense of the word until Inauguration Day, and then instantly at the time he takes the oath of office, he will have the full responsibilities.

> —President Jimmy Carter
> November 20, 1980

Presidential transitions would probably be a good deal less difficult if either of these antipodal declarations were, or could be made, completely realistic. Most modern presidents would consider Jefferson's prescription a "cop-out." Indeed, it is unlikely that Jefferson would have written it if Aaron Burr or Alexander Hamilton had been succeeding him rather than James Madison, his close friend and political disciple. Carter's words echo the sentiments of other recent presidents and are legally correct. The responsibility of the office rests with the incumbent until the day and minute he is succeeded. Our government is not a dyarchy; we can have only one president at a time. The proposition is clear enough in the Constitution. But in practice, it is frayed at the edges, and sometimes the fraying penetrates much deeper than the edges. This is partly because developments in our society, in the economy, and in international relations do not have clear-cut beginning and ending dates. Most of them are ongoing, as is most of American government. Some are touched off by other nations beyond our control. Even those that the United States initiates normally take time to plan and negotiate and put into operation. This means that a great many decisions made by or under one president will have an impact, often their dominant impact, upon successor administrations. Many issues, though raised long before, will not be fully resolved and negotiated by January 20. During a transition, when the influence of an incumbent administration is waning and when its successor might either carry on or change course, the maintenance of completely separated jurisdiction can be largely fictional—and dysfunctional.

Nonetheless, most observers and former participants would agree that generally the rule of law should be the rule of thumb. Ultimate accountability rests with the incumbent. When in operational terms it becomes desirable to bend or depart from the rule, either side or both sides should anticipate as nearly as possible the consequences to their own future and to the national interest. There are several potential kinds of relationships between the two sides of a transition and between each of them, on one hand, and foreign governments and international organizations, on the other. These relationships range all the way from unilateral actions by either side without consulting or notifying the other to collaborative decisions that both sides participate in reaching (though the incumbents normally assume primary responsibility in accord with the Constitution). Action by one side may be taken to help or embarrass the other, to expedite or obstruct its work. And such actions raise all kinds of questions: of tactics, of politics, of constitutionality, of ethics. The various kinds of relationships are described in the following paragraphs, and there are many examples of them in the five succeeding chapters.

*Unilateral actions on the part of an incumbent administration* may extend from "midnight appointments" to changes in major offensive or defensive deployments, possibly even military offensives, or the signing of treaties and executive agreements with foreign governments. Along the way are a variety of intermediate devices that may commit or at least strongly induce successors: completing or canceling contracts for military procurement or construction; making agreements for economic or military assistance to foreign countries; establishing or breaking relations with foreign governments; transferring political appointees to career jobs or making their jobs career; introducing artificial or unlikely items and predictions into budgets and other official documents of the government. There are any number of ways that an incumbent administration can freeze existing policies and programs it favors, or can otherwise make it difficult for its successor to change them. One member of an outgoing administration informed us that his president ruled against any new unilateral initiatives that were not absolutely essential and ordered that current undertakings as far as possible be cleaned up before inauguration, so that the new administration could come in with a slate that was as clear as possible of unresolved questions.

The wisdom and propriety of *unilateral actions of an incoming administration* during an interregnum raise different problems, but some of them, too, may be sensitive ones. There are no questions about some of these actions: the announcement of prospective appointments to top posts, the advocacy of positions previously proposed, the exhaustive search for information, the criticism of current policies and actions of the incumbent administration. But it is hard for an incoming administration to refrain from seeking to influence policy or delay actions it does not like, even though it has neither legal authority nor political responsibility to do so. Should it declare that it will cancel a policy or program recently announced by the incumbents? Or urge friends in Congress to delay action on measures it doesn't like? Or deal secretly with friends in the incumbent administration to promote changes it desires?

An intermediate kind of relationship occurs when one side, usually the incumbents, *informs* the other of its plans and intentions concerning an issue in advance of public announcement. This provides the latter the opportunity to endorse or question an action if it wishes, but there is no demand that it do so. It is one step short of the incumbents' *consulting with and seeking the advice of* the incoming administration before taking or publicly announcing an action. Consultation of this kind is commonly a quest for agreement and public support to strengthen the position of an administration whose days are numbered. It may also signal a willingness to discuss, compromise, and *come into agreement* on an issue of concern to both sides.

Whether the agreement or the advice—or, equally important, the refusal to reach agreement or give advice—is made public openly or through planned or unplanned leaks, of course, makes a great deal of difference. When publicly announced, it is usually construed as a *commitment* on the part of the incoming administration to actions proposed by (or agreed to with) the incumbents. And surely support and commitment are the purposes of the exercise on the part of the latter. There have been well-known examples of such quests for support in almost every transition we have studied. The incumbents need endorsement to strengthen their hand; the newcomers are usually cautious about giving it until they have had a chance to study the issue and reach their own conclusions. Furthermore, they seek to establish their independence and their separateness from what has gone before. Against these feelings are the dangers that the United States might appear as a divided country before the world. There are benefits to the nation when both sides in a transition can present a united front on vital issues—like peace in Korea or Vietnam or freedom for hostages in Iran.

The most extreme form of sharing responsibility occurs when the incoming group actually *participates* in planning, negotiating, and announcing a joint decision. This has been understandably rare, at least on major issues. For example, newcomers are reluctant to participate in overseas conferences during interregnum periods. Incumbents often prefer passing difficult problems along to their successors rather than working out joint solutions. A consequence is that new administrations seem always to be confronted with a substantial number of difficult, unresolved issues when they assume office.

Relationships between incoming and outgoing administrations are further complicated by the presence and the frequent involvement of foreign countries in American affairs. They are always part of the interested, expectant, worried audience of American politics and transitions. Some have an immediate concern in issues current at the time of transition and seek to deal with the side that offers results more favorable to their interests. After an election, foreign governments quickly shift their focus and their contacts to the winners, and this of course is a reason why the incumbent administration rapidly loses its "clout."

Foreign governments and their representatives offer both opportunities and problems to newly elected, but not yet inaugurated, administrations. The latter are suddenly the targets of attention and cordial welcome in international society. Their views—and their favors—are eagerly sought. But what they do and what they say before they have assumed legal responsibility can undercut the still incumbent administration, nourish an overseas perception of American division and confusion, and ultimately embarrass and weaken them.

The problems that incoming administrations must confront during an interregnum range all the way from diplomatic etiquette— such as when a secretary of state–designate receives and converses with foreign emissaries—to major national issues—scuttling an international arms conference or planning the overthrow of a government. Should a fetal administration respond to a request from another government even while knowing that the incumbent administration has refused the same request?

The simple answer is that suggested by the phrase "one president at a time": avoid representations and proposals to foreign governments until in office. But if applied literally, this dictum would be dysfunctional. The interregnum is a period for preparing and learning. In foreign affairs, that surely includes getting acquainted with the people with whom one must later deal. And learning should include acquiring information about how others perceive situations and issues, not just about the views of one's predecessors. In addition, when an incoming official considers that the incumbent administration is taking actions that will reduce or eliminate his options, can he not properly take steps to counter or delay such actions?

In the foregoing discussion, the incoming administration has been treated as though it were a single entity. In fact, however, the first representatives of the new president-elect are the small army of transition personnel, of whom none have designated appointments in the future administration, few will get such appointments, and half are unpaid. The lines of responsibility are at best tenuous, and the temptations to say important things to the press, to foreign leaders, and to officials at home are inviting. Some transition personnel have been sent abroad to talk with the political leaders of other countries, presumably to make acquaintances and gather information. But some at least have gone beyond that in stating views, intended actions, and assurances of the president-elect. President Sadat of Egypt asked whether all or any of the three representatives who visited him separately in 1980–1981 were actually authorized to speak for the American president-elect. Obviously, the problems of interadministration relations during transitions would be eased if those purporting to represent the president-elect were in fact responsible to him.

The five chapters that follow concern the five interparty transitions that have occurred since World War II. Each consists of a discussion of the transition's main features and of two abbreviated case studies of major problems that attended the transition period. We have not attempted a comprehensive treatment of any of the topics, for reasons of space if nothing else. Instead, we have concentrated on those phases and features most illustrative of the issues of transitions themselves. They are intended to illuminate how the different presidents and presidents-elect handled their interrelationships and their relations with foreign powers and to illuminate some of the general problems that were sketched in Part I.

# CHAPTER 7

# From Truman
# to Eisenhower

General Eisenhower was overwhelmed when he found what he faced.

> —Harry S. Truman, on his
> interregnum meeting with
> President-elect Eisenhower

[My meeting with Truman] added little to my knowledge, nor did it affect my planning for the new administration, but I did thank the President sincerely for his cooperation.

> —Dwight D. Eisenhower

As the first interparty transition in twenty years and the first to take place after the Second World War had made the United States one of the world's two preeminent powers, the transition of 1952–1953 was one in which the major participants were necessarily feeling their way. Yet an extensive series of precedents was set. No transfer of power before or since has had a greater impact on the expectations of the actors involved in all transitions than the one from Truman to Eisenhower.

This record is all the more remarkable given that the transfer took place under the shadow of the country's frustrating and bitterly controversial war in Korea. The conflict was perhaps the central issue in the campaign, it figured prominently in the events of the interregnum between the election and the inauguration, and it constituted the primary preoccupation of the new administration once it had assumed office. Indeed, this transition cannot be said to have ended fully until the Korean armistice was agreed to in June of 1953. From beginning to end, the war hung over events in Washington, impeding cooperation between the arriving administration and the departing one and posing unforeseen challenges to the country's ability to carry out the succession smoothly and safely. The fact that sensitive negotiations aimed at ending the fighting were going on concurrently with the transition caused added difficulties.

However, Korea was not the only foreign policy issue facing the United States at that time. A simmering dispute between Great Britain and Iran over the holdings of the Anglo-Iranian Oil Company, which the Iranian government had nationalized, threatened to estrange the United States from both countries. Washington was also encountering resistance from its West European allies to fulfilling the goals previously laid out for NATO's conventional-force levels. Although the Americans could not know it, Stalin was approaching the end of his life, and his passing in March, 1953, would force the recently arrived Eisenhower administration to consider anew the type of relationship it would seek to establish with the Soviet Union. Foreign reverses had created within this country a widespread fear of domestic communist subversion, which would be turned first against the old administration and then against the new, as Senator Joseph McCarthy and others accused both of ignoring threats to internal security.

Faced with these difficulties, those on all sides who were responsible for the conduct of the transition produced a remarkable number of innovations in the effort to manage the transfer of power. As the retiring chief executive, Truman offered intelligence briefings to both Eisenhower and Adlai Stevenson during the campaign. However, the value of the gesture was diminished in Eisenhower's case by the bad feelings that had developed between the general and the president over campaign charges and also by a mix-up in scheduling that made it appear the briefings were being used for partisan political purposes. Truman and Eisenhower met at the White House during the interregnum and issued a joint statement pledging cooperation. At the initiative of the president and the Policy Planning Staff of the State Department, all departments and agencies drew up reports designed to acquaint the appointees of the incoming administration with their duties and with ongoing policies. Eisenhower named his transition liaison chiefs quickly after the election and appointed his entire cabinet soon enough that he could hold group meetings with it twice before the inauguration. A number of advisers with foreign policy responsibilities accompanied Eisenhower on his journey to Korea in December, and others joined them aboard the cruiser *Helena* for extended consultations on the return trip.

Despite these efforts, the transition of 1952–1953 displayed shortcomings that hampered not only the turnover of power but also the effective conduct of American foreign policy. In general, the changeover from Truman to Eisenhower was marred most by the cool relations between the two principals and by the pervasive climate of suspicion toward, and the weariness with, the departing administration. The debate over charges made by Senator McCarthy and others that there was widespread disloyalty in the government, especially in the foreign affairs and national security agencies, had poisoned the atmosphere between the newcomers and the outgoers and also between the newcomers and the career services. Some Eisenhower appointees suspected that civil servants employed during the preceding long Democratic reign were at best covert partisans and at worst security risks. Although the effects of this distrust were felt throughout the government, the heaviest price was paid by the foreign affairs agencies. Badgered by departmental and congressional loyalty investigations, career diplomats—including Charles Bohlen, Eisenhower's appointee as ambassador to Moscow—found it impossible to contribute as much as they might have to the education of the new political team, which was itself distracted from settling in by the need to demonstrate its own anticommunist vigor.

The McCarthyite challenge also substantially weakened the Foreign Service over the long term. By creating an atmosphere of fear and suspicion, loyalty investigations by the new administration and by members of Congress encouraged career officers to avoid controversy, even at the cost of watering down their reports from the field and declining to pass along unpleasant information. The ruining of the careers and reputations of most of the State Department's China watchers was a particularly potent example of the harm done the Foreign Service. In part, such apprehensions stemmed from FSOs' concerns over transitions: would some future administration reexamine the files and use them to attack the trustworthiness of their authors? Some felt that fears left by this episode hampered the work and credibility of the State Department for years to come.[1]

Beyond the distrust and animosity that characterized much of this transition, two quite different influences should be cited. One was Truman's decision not to run for another term in 1952. The president's announcement in March of that year that he would not be a candidate for reelection made him a lame duck for his last ten months in office and contributed to what his secretary of state called a "virtual interregnum of more than a year" in which "our nation's effectiveness in the international community . . . slowly declined as the administration's tenure ran out and only slowly picked up again as its successor gained the experience and confidence necessary to effectiveness."[2] At the same time, the fact that Truman was not himself defeated by Eisenhower may have made cooperation between the two and their subordinates easier than if the turnover had been one from vanquished to victor. Relations between the two camps were strained enough without adding the animosity that sometimes develops in head-to-head combat.

The second influence was the existence of broad areas of policy agreement between the two major-party candidates. In selecting Governor Adlai E. Stevenson as their nominee, the Democrats chose a champion who fully supported the Truman administration's handling of foreign policy in general and the Korean War in particular, while in giving their nomination to Eisenhower, the Republicans selected an internationalist candidate whose experience as Supreme Allied Commander in Europe (Eisenhower having been chosen for that post by Truman in 1950) had associated him with the policies of the incumbent administration as well. Despite their differences over the relative merits of containment and liberation, the candidates set the pattern for bipartisan consensus on foreign policy themes that would help to ease transitions for nearly two decades.

General assessments of the success of the transition as a whole,

1. Henry, *Presidential Transitions,* 662–72.
2. Acheson, *Present at the Creation,* 632–33. For documents relating to the administrative aspects of the transition, see U.S. Department of State, *Foreign Relations of the United States, 1952–1954* (Washington, D.C., 1983), Vol. I, Part 1, pp. 1–44.

though useful in comparing one transition with another, can provide little information on the relationships between individuals, the course of events in particular agencies, or the effect of transitions on specific areas of policy. For no transition are these all of a piece. Therefore, it is useful to examine somewhat more closely two cases in the Truman-Eisenhower transition: the negotiations over prisoners of war in Korea and the American effort to settle the Anglo-Iranian oil dispute.

## The Korean Prisoners of War

Differences over Korea inserted a sour note into the transition at the very beginning of the interregnum. Trouble began the morning after Election Day, when from his campaign train Truman sent a curt telegram of congratulations to the president-elect, ending with the sardonic comment "The *Independence* [the presidential plane] will be at your disposal if you still desire to go to Korea."[3] The implication that this sentence carried—that Eisenhower's pledge in late October to go to Korea was merely a campaign ploy to be discarded once the election was over—may have added a touch of sarcasm to his reply thanking Truman for his "courteous and generous" message and saying that, for the trip to the battlefront, "any suitable transport plane" would do.

Upon his return to Washington and after conferring with Secretary of State Acheson, Truman sent Eisenhower a second, more conciliatory telegram pointing to the need for an orderly transfer of power, "particularly in view of the international dangers and problems that confront this country and the whole free world," and inviting the president-elect to the White House "to discuss the problem of this transition period, so that it may be clear to all the world that this nation is united in its struggle for freedom and peace." In a public statement issued the same day, the president emphasized these sentiments and called for public backing of the new admin-

3. The texts of almost all the messages between Truman and Eisenhower during this period are reprinted in Harry S. Truman, *Years of Trial and Hope* (New York, 1956), 576–87, *passim.* Vol. II of Truman, *Memoirs,* 2 vols. See also Henry, *Presidential Transitions,* 478–85.

istration and Congress in the face of the difficult problems they would face, particularly in foreign affairs: "The proper solution of these problems may determine whether we shall have a third world war—and, indeed, whether we shall survive as a free and democratic nation." Eisenhower's reply on November 6 accepted the White House invitation and told the president, "I share your hope that we may present to the world an American unity in basic issues."

Truman's change in tone was prompted partly by the calming passage of time between his first and second telegram. As befitted a professional politician, he was always ready to hit hard during a campaign and then forgive and forget afterward. A more significant explanation, however, lay in the president's realization that, now that his successor had been chosen, his own authority might decline even more rapidly than it had been shrinking since his renunciation of another term in March. If American policy was not to drift leaderless until Inauguration Day, Truman might need to draw on the popular support just demonstrated for the man elected as his successor. Left on its own, the Truman administration could suffer the withdrawal of the rest of its effective power.

On no issue were the dangers of this possibility greater than on the war in Korea. By the early fall of 1952, after months of talks, it seemed that the primary obstacle to achieving an armistice at last in Korea was the contentious issue of the disposition of prisoners of war. The North Koreans demanded that all prisoners on both sides be returned, regardless of their expressed wishes (a position consistent with traditional international law, but tainted by its application after World War II to unwilling Soviet and East European prisoners who were sent back to face imprisonment or death). The Americans, who were conducting the armistice negotiations for the United Nations forces, refused to accept anything other than the principle of voluntary repatriation only. In taking this stand, they were acting both for humanitarian reasons and in the belief that the prospect of large-scale defection-through-surrender would deter the Soviet Union and its allies from future military adventures.[4]

4. For a fuller record of the sequence of events, at least as they appeared inside the Truman administration, see U.S. Department of State, *Foreign Relations of the United States, 1952–1954*, Vol. XV, Part-1, pp. 558–721 *passim*.

Acheson was, he later wrote, "fully persuaded that the Communists would not reach final agreement with our dying administration, especially since General Eisenhower, who was highly critical of our management of the war, was going to Korea to form his own views."[5] Nevertheless, the secretary of state felt it was important to obtain a UN General Assembly resolution endorsing the American negotiating position (including its stand on POW repatriation), "thus leaving our position with strong international support for our successors in office when they took over on January 20, 1953." The difficulty for Acheson was that India, supported by Canada and Great Britain, had put forward a "compromise" proposal that would repatriate all prisoners who would not forcibly resist being returned and continue to hold the others indefinitely. This approach, in the Americans' view, retained the form but surrendered the substance of nonforcible repatriation.

Acheson himself went to New York to lobby for defeat of the Indian plan, but found his efforts greatly hampered by uncertainty among other delegations over the possibility that American policy would shift after the changeover of administrations. British Foreign Secretary Anthony Eden, then in New York for the debate, found that "the American delegation were in the unenviable position of caretaker," that Eisenhower's attitude was guarded, and that among other delegations there was "irritation at the American constitution, which compelled the interregnum."[6] Some Republican spokesmen, in their frustration over a war that never seemed to end, had called for the return of all prisoners, regardless of their wishes; Eisenhower's impending trip to Korea might portend fundamental alterations in the American stance, including the prospect of much bolder military measures. In such a fluid situation, many delegations that Washington had counted on for support were reluctant to put themselves on record. Acheson ended a November 6 memorandum to Truman on the UN debate with a suggestion: "If General Eisenhower feels that it were possible for him to do so, a statement by him setting forth the purposes of his trip to Korea and his support for the efforts now being made by the U.S. Government in the Gen-

5. Acheson, *Present at the Creation*, 701.
6. Anthony Eden, *Full Circle* (Boston, 1960), 23–26.

eral Assembly, would be of the greatest assistance in meeting this critical situation."[7] Truman agreed and directed that the matter be taken up with Eisenhower when the latter visited the White House on November 18.

The president, however, was reluctant to leave the matter here. His meeting with the president-elect was more than a week away, and action in the General Assembly was imminent. Even if he was able to persuade Eisenhower at their face-to-face meeting to endorse Acheson's efforts, such support might come too late to affect the vote in New York. In an effort to gain the incoming administration's backing immediately, Truman sent a letter to Eisenhower on the same day as his second telegram, listing several matters then pending that required rapid decisions. One of them was the repatriation issue. The president's list—composed entirely of issues of foreign policy—illustrates that it is in this realm that many of the major difficulties of presidential transitions lie. But it also shows how vexing is the dilemma of deciding who actually exercises authority in this stage of the transition—the old president or the new. "All these things are vital policy matters which can only be decided by the President of the United States," Truman wrote, "but I would prefer not to make firm decisions on these matters without your concurrence, although the decisions will have to be made. . . . If you could designate someone to act authoritatively for you, or come yourself to sit in on these meetings, it would be the proper solution to the problem."

As Herbert Hoover had done in 1932–1933, and as future presidents were to do as they approached the end of their term, Truman was attempting to prevent the entire machinery of government from running down, along with his presidency, by associating the incoming president with decisions taken by the departing administration. Like Roosevelt twenty years before, however, Eisenhower shied away from assuming responsibility without commensurate authority, and he hastened to make this clear in his response to the president's letter: "In your letter you use the word 'authoritative' by which I take it you mean that my representative [Henry Cabot Lodge] be able accurately to reflect my views. This he will be able to do, but quite naturally this will likewise be the limit of his

7. Truman, *Years of Trial and Hope*, 576.

authority since I myself can have none under current conditions."
All suggestion of having a copresidency in foreign affairs until January 20 disappeared.

Truman later recalled that at his meeting alone with Eisenhower he assured his successor that he had not thought of laying any trap or avoiding any responsibility, that he would exercise all power until Inauguration Day, and that he understood Eisenhower's reluctance to enter into policy questions before assuming office. He went on to state nonetheless that some evidence of continuity would reassure other countries and that on some foreign policy issues success might depend on such reassurance. The result, Truman concluded, was that he and his subordinates would provide information to the newcomers and in return would welcome, but not require, public endorsement or support of his administration's actions. In his words: "We will tell you about these issues and would welcome concurrence if you want to give it. . . . But we will not press for it. This is a matter on which you will have to make up your own mind on the basis of what is best for America." Truman repeated this message when he and Eisenhower joined their principal advisers in the Cabinet Room.

At this larger meeting, Acheson, fresh from New York and scheduled to return there immediately, recounted the outline of the UN debate, calling it "a most serious situation," and produced the draft of a statement he hoped would be issued by the president-elect in support of the current American stand. In addition, the draft of the joint statement to be put out by Truman and Eisenhower after the meeting contained the sentence "We both agree that it is of the utmost importance to preserve the principle that prisoners of war shall not be forcibly repatriated." Eisenhower would agree to neither suggestion. To the idea that he should issue a statement on the prisoners, he promised only that he would study the matter and would confer on it with Eden when he met the foreign secretary two days hence. He deleted the reference to the issue in the joint statement, reportedly to leave his hands entirely free.[8]

From the viewpoint of Truman and his aides, this could not have

8. Robert J. Donovan, *Eisenhower: The Inside Story* (New York, 1956), 16–17; Henry Cabot Lodge, *As It Was: An Inside View of Politics and Power in the '50s and '60s* (New York, 1976), 38–39.

been a satisfactory outcome of the meeting. In the joint statement the two men issued, there was no reference even to the modest hopes for concurrence Truman had expressed in private. The statement spoke of "a framework for liaison and exchange of information" between the two groups, but it laid almost equal emphasis on what had *not* been done: "Under our Constitution the President must exercise his functions until he leaves office, and his successor cannot be asked to share or assume the responsibilities of the Presidency until he takes office. . . . We have made no arrangements which are inconsistent with the full spirit of our Constitution. General Eisenhower has not been asked to assume any of the responsibilities of the Presidency until he takes the oath of office." By the time of Truman's final State of the Union Message on January 7, 1953, the reference to liaison had dropped away as well, and Truman's transition arrangements had been reduced to briefing mechanisms—"means whereby the incoming President can obtain the full and detailed information he will need to assume the responsibility the moment he takes the oath of office."

As he would later demonstrate by his own statements and actions once he had taken office, however, Eisenhower did in fact subscribe to the substance of the outgoing administration's stance. On November 19, the day after the White House meeting, he endorsed Truman's stand, though on his own ground and only indirectly. In New York he saw the incoming chairman of the Senate Foreign Relations Committee, who emerged from the meeting to tell reporters that the president-elect had "emphasized his agreement with the principle of no forcible repatriation of prisoners." [9] This signal, muted though it was, was good enough for Truman, who grabbed it with both hands. At his news conference on November 20, he announced that he was "very happy" to see the statement, pointedly drew the connection to his meeting with Eisenhower on the eighteenth, and declined to answer all further questions on the subject. [10] Acheson continued the fight in New York, even to the point of threatening a major break with the British, and, aided by the revelation of Eisenhower's atti-

9. Henry, *Presidential Transitions,* 485.

10. *Public Papers of the Presidents of the United States: Harry S. Truman, 1952–53* (1966), 1057–1058.

tude and by a blundering Soviet attack on the Indian proposal, saw the resolution through the General Assembly on December 3 in a form that satisfied American requirements.

Thus, with a measure of assistance from its successor and some luck, the outgoing administration was able to avoid the exhaustion of its power before the expiration of its term. It had been weakened, and therefore it was subjected to challenges that probably would not have faced a president not about to leave office. But it had not been completely immobilized, and therefore it ultimately prevailed. "Prevailing" under these circumstances, of course, meant little more than staving off defeat. It did not guarantee that the new administration would be able to have its preferred solution accepted in the armistice. Indeed, the terms of that agreement, signed on July 27, 1953, represented a softening in the American position in two respects. First, the armistice included the Indian proposal's idea of a repatriation commission, made up of neutral states, which was to take custody of all prisoners not wishing to be repatriated immediately to their home country. However, the commission was to retain custody of the POWs for no more than 120 days, after which they were to be free to go to the neutral state of their choice. This deadline removed the prospect of indefinite detention as the only alternative to repatriation, which had caused Washington's dissatisfaction with the original, unamended Indian draft. Second, the American stance underwent a subtle shift from "voluntary" to "nonforcible" repatriation, a shift that had begun in the last weeks of Truman's presidency, despite Acheson's disapproval of its presence in the Indian proposal. In the final settlement, prisoners were repatriated unless they declared, in individual interviews, that they would forcibly resist.

Moreover, success on the UN resolution endorsing America's terms for ending the Korean War, including those for prisoner repatriation, did not translate into victory on the larger question of the Korean armistice negotiations in toto; these, as Acheson later granted, "languished while 'the great external realm' waited to see what manner of men would follow us." [11] Nevertheless, on this

11. Acheson, *Present at the Creation*, 632–33. See also Carl Brauer, "The Pursuit or Alteration of Inherited Foreign Policy: Three Cases," in Federick C.

single issue Truman, Eisenhower, and the others were able to achieve a successful transition. Given a degree of (sometimes covert) cooperation between the newcomers and the outgoers, the United States government maintained its effectiveness on a matter of great moment and high contentiousness, despite the uncertainties associated with the passing of the baton.

## The Anglo-Iranian Dispute and the Change of Government in Iran

As an outgoing administration feels power slipping from its grasp, it must worry that in its declining days it will be taken advantage of by foreign powers. This was the situation that the Truman administration faced as it confronted another pressing problem for American foreign policy in the winter of 1952–1953, the dispute between Iran and Great Britain over the holdings of the Anglo-Iranian Oil Company, which the government of Prime Minister Mohammed Mosadeq had nationalized in 1951.[12] As in the case of the Korean POWs, circumstances conspired to divide the United States from its closest ally, but in this case the roles were reversed: this time it was London that was unwilling to compromise a principled stand and Washington that sought to act as mediator. For the Americans, more was at stake than the oil, important as that was. What lay in the balance was the entire position of Iran as a united, independent country standing as a bulwark against Soviet expansionist designs on the Middle East and the regions beyond. Acheson and others feared that if the stalemate continued the Mosadeq government would be overthrown and replaced by something worse—a regime dominated by the communist Tudeh party and totally subservient to the Soviet Union.

As the fall of 1952 approached, the parties were at the end of a year of acrimonious deadlock. Iran demanded that any compensa-

---

Mosher (ed.), *Papers on Presidential Transitions and Foreign Policy: Some Views from the Campus* (Lanham, Md.: forthcoming); William H. Vatcher, Jr., *Panmunjom: The Story of the Korean Military Armistice Negotiations* (New York, 1958).

12. The most complete account of the American perspective concerning this tangled dispute may be found in Acheson, *Present at the Creation*, 499–511, 679–85.

tion to the stockholders of Anglo-Iranian had to await British acceptance of Iran's right to nationalize the company; Britain, fearing the effect of such a step on its investments in other countries, refused, though it was willing to renegotiate the terms of its 1933 oil concession. The Iranians had successfully fended off a challenge to their nationalization in the International Court of Justice; the British had withdrawn all their tankers from the Iranian port of Abadan and had sent a naval force to ensure that no other tankers took their place. The flow of oil from Iran had ceased in mid-1951.

From the beginning, the United States had sought to find a compromise solution to the dispute, a stance that had caused each side to suspect Washington of favoring the other. As the months of deadlock had passed, they had witnessed recurrent friction between the United States and Britain over the extent to which Tehran's demands should be met. London was convinced that Washington did not understand what was happening within Iran or how to deal with Iranians; American officials held similar doubts about the British grasp of the situation. Even so, the two allies were feeling their way toward a highly problematic agreement on a common approach when, in October, 1951, the British government went through a transition of its own. The new Conservative government adopted a harder line than its Labour predecessor, and the series of secret negotiations ended. At the same time, those Americans who were involved in the talks were repeatedly frustrated by their inability to obtain from the Iranian government a clear, consistent statement of its terms. After a number of unproductive meetings with Mosadeq in Washington, Acheson labeled the Iranian premier "a great actor and a great gambler," who could never be trusted to stand by his commitments. Faced with this seemingly insurmountable impasse and the failure of an American initiative to break the deadlock in August, 1952, the secretary of state gave up most hope of resolving the conflict and told the British that he was prepared to pass the problem along to the next administration.

However, Truman gave new life to American efforts in October by expressing the desire that a settlement be achieved before his term ended three months hence. With this impetus, Acheson prepared one last effort, putting together with his aides a package deal involving Iranian agreement to arbitration on the question of compensation to the Anglo-Iranian company, large and immediate payments by the United States to Iran against the future delivery of oil (Truman had given written approval for the use of up to a hundred million dollars for this purpose), further assistance to Iran from American government agencies, and the delivery of the oil to Anglo-Iranian and a consortium of American companies for transport. As an added stick against the British—who, in the opinion of the Americans, were the more obstinate of the two parties—news was leaked that, should London refuse the bargain, the American companies would proceed on their own. Frantic negotiations with the two parties at issue followed.

This American effort faced a number of difficulties, including the near impossibility of obtaining a comprehensible position from the Iranian government (Acheson said that Mosadeq was "whirling like a dervish") and the hostility with which the Justice Department's Anti-Trust Division regarded the proposed cooperation among American oil companies. Other problems were more closely related to the presidential transition then taking place. Each side, for its own reasons, believed it might not be to its advantage to settle with the Truman administration.

In Iran, Mosadeq—mistakenly, as it turned out—felt himself under no pressure to come to an early agreement. When the talks in the fall of 1951 had broken down and the prime minister was preparing to leave the United States for Iran, an American official, hoping for a last-minute breakthrough, pleaded with him that his returning without an agreement would disappoint the high hopes that had been raised in Iran. "Don't you realize," Mosadeq responded, "that, returning to Iran empty-handed, I return in a much stronger position than if I returned with an agreement which I would have to sell to my fanatics?" [13] This willingness to allow the talks to drag on may have been strengthened by a trip to Tehran in October, 1952, by the president of the Cities Service Oil Company to discuss with Mosadeq the role Cities Service might play in the foreign distribution and sale of the nationalized oil formerly owned by Anglo-Iranian. What gave the visit unusual significance was the executive's known friendship with Eisenhower. There is no evidence that Eisenhower, who in any

13. Barry Rubin, *Paved with Good Intentions: The American Experience and Iran* (New York, 1981), 68.

event had not yet been elected, approved or even knew of these discussions. But the mere fact of this association with the candidate may have been enough to give Mosadeq hope that an Eisenhower administration might be more favorably inclined toward Iran's case, that Anglo-Iranian could easily be replaced by other distributors, and thus that the incentives for settlement on the Iranian side were not so great as they had appeared. In any event Iran soon thereafter broke diplomatic relations with Britain, thereby confirming each side's suspicion of the other, though the Iranians continued to rely on the United States as their interlocutor with the British.[14]

Meanwhile, London was beginning to have its own doubts about the efficacy of further negotiations through the agency of the Truman administration. Suspicions had always run high within Anglo-Iranian and in Whitehall that Washington's eagerness to settle the crisis and to press the British into accepting some of the Iranians' key demands was prompted by a desire to see American companies replace British ones as the conduit for the export of Iranian oil. These fears were only increased by the explicit inclusion of this threat in the American proposals of October, 1952. However, the British government—which, throughout this period, had better information than did its Iranian counterpart on opinions within the American government and business community—knew this to be an empty threat. In the foreseeable future, the United States oil companies would stand by Anglo-Iranian because they feared the effect on their own concessions in Iran of their acceptance of the principle of nationalization and because they distrusted the Mosadeq government. When Acheson dispatched the director of the State Department's Policy Planning Staff, Paul Nitze, in early November to tell Foreign Secretary Eden that the United States was prepared to wait no longer and would proceed to end the boycott of Iranian oil on its own, Eden was unmoved.

Eden could afford to be unfrightened for another reason: by the time he saw Nitze, he had hopes that progress on a second front might obtain British objectives with much less need to compromise on Anglo-Iranian's position. The British government had already be-

---

14. Acheson, at least, was convinced that, though no culpability attached to Eisenhower, this mission "did enhance Mosadeq's obduracy." Acheson, *Present at the Creation*, 681.

gun planning a covert operation to bring down Mosadeq and replace him with a more sympathetic figure. Shortly before the 1952 election—that is, around the time of Nitze's visit—another American arrived in London. This was Kermit Roosevelt of the Central Intelligence Agency, whom the British government had invited to hear its proposal that the two countries collaborate in the coup attempt, under the code name Operation Ajax. According to Roosevelt, both the CIA's director, Walter Bedell Smith, and its deputy director, Allen Dulles, knew of his meeting. Smith avoided any involvement in Anglo-American contacts on the subject. Dulles, who knew that Acheson opposed such an effort at overthrowing Mosadeq, made the decision to postpone further steps until Eisenhower, who by this time had been elected, took office. Apparently, neither Smith nor Dulles informed the incumbent president or secretary of state.[15] Neither Truman nor Acheson knew, therefore, that the British could have been strengthened in any resolve they might have to outwait the departing administration for its successor.

In the meantime the president and the secretary of state wanted to settle the dispute if they could and, if they could not, prepare their successors to cope with it. Truman included "the Iran problem" in his November telegram to Eisenhower calling for concurrence between the two administrations on a number of foreign policy issues. Acheson laid out the state of the negotiations at some length in his presentation to Eisenhower when the president-elect visited the White House November 18. Iranian oil was second only to the UN debate over Korea in his discussion of those substantive problems "where action was called for daily and which would have important influence in the weeks and months following the taking over of the government by the new administration." The secretary "suggested that the new administration should be closely in touch with this situation because considerable difficulties were likely to arise from

---

15. Kermit Roosevelt, *Countercoup: The Struggle for the Control of Iran* (New York, 1979); Rubin, *Paved with Good Intentions,* 77. Eisenhower was apparently much more strongly convinced of the value of covert CIA operations in general than was Truman. See Richard H. Immerman, *The CIA in Guatemala: The Foreign Policy of Intervention* (Austin, 1982), esp. 101–32.

it"; indeed, it "might be approaching a crisis as the new administration took over." [16]

Having taken these precautions, the outgoing administration continued its efforts to resolve the problem on its own time. Judicious hints were passed to the press regarding American willingness to act unilaterally if London proved recalcitrant. On November 26 the president gave Acheson written authority to meet with representatives of the American oil companies to discuss their role, and reassured by this shield against Justice Department action, they did so on December 4 and 9. Fortified by their agreement to help if Anglo-Iranian agreed, the administration pushed the British into grudgingly consenting to consider a new negotiating offer, which was presented by an American representative to Mosadeq on Christmas Day. The talks that day went well, but further discussions on December 31 less so. Still, it was felt worthwhile to reduce the proposals to writing and submit them on January 15. But it was too late. Time had run out on the Truman presidency, and Truman and his subordinates left office on January 20 with no agreement in hand.

Both the Iranians and the British refused to make the remaining concessions necessary to obtain a settlement in mid-January; both had already turned their attention to Truman's successor. Not only did Mosadeq apparently change his mind on the American plan between December 25 and 31; he also decided to open contacts with the new administration, at the highest levels. In early January, Eisenhower received an extended cable from the Iranian premier, amounting to a plea for a more favorable stand by the American government after January 20.

> I dislike taking up with you the problems of my country even before you assume office. I do so partly because of their urgency and partly because I have reason to believe that they have already been presented to you by those who may not share my concern for the future of Iran and its people [perhaps referring to Eisenhower's meeting with Truman on November 18 or that with Eden on November 20].
>
> It is my hope that the new administration which you will head will

16. Truman, *Years of Trial and Hope,* 582, 585; Acheson, *Present at the Creation,* 706.

obtain at the outset true understanding of the significance of the vital struggle in which the Iranian people have been engaging and assist in removing the obstacles which are preventing them from realizing their aspirations for the attainment of . . . life as a politically and economically independent nation.[17]

Eisenhower replied (apparently while still president-elect) that he remained completely impartial, that no one had attempted to prejudice his judgment, and that he would be glad to receive Mosadeq's further views. Even this innocuous-sounding message may have persuaded the Iranian prime minister to wait for more advantageous terms, and the Truman initiative withered.

The British, too, were in contact with the incoming administration and with rather more results. Prime Minister Winston Churchill found it convenient to stop by for a chat with the president-elect on January 6 and 7. The two ranged over the whole gamut of foreign policy problems, including Iran, that they would be facing together after Eisenhower assumed office. (When he saw Truman on the eighth, Churchill said that he hoped his conference with the head of the incoming administration had not been inappropriate; the president replied that not only did he not mind, but it was important that Churchill and Eisenhower stay in close touch.)[18]

At a more mundane level, representatives of British intelligence continued to plan for a joint Anglo-American effort to support a coup against Mosadeq. At his first meeting with them in London in November, 1952, Kermit Roosevelt had put them off by saying that he believed that Truman and Acheson would never approve the scheme but that the response from the Republicans might be quite different. The British continued their preparations nonetheless, confident in the knowledge that, as they told Roosevelt, both Churchill and Eden supported the plan. Nor were Roosevelt and Allen Dulles the only American advocates of covert action. Despite his abstention from personal involvement in discussions with the British, Bedell Smith called Roosevelt into his CIA office in early 1953 to

17. Dwight D. Eisenhower, *Mandate for Change, 1953–1956* (Garden City, N.Y., 1963), 160. Vol. I of Eisenhower, *The White House Years,* 2 vols.

18. Robert H. Ferrell (ed.), *The Eisenhower Diaries* (New York, 1981), 221–24; Acheson, *Present at the Creation,* 715.

demand, in barracks language, when the operation was going to get under way. Roosevelt assured him that a British delegation would arrive in Washington as soon as possible after Inauguration Day.

Thus, on February 3 Roosevelt's British contacts came to the capital for talks that no longer had to be shrouded from the view of top American policy makers. A meeting that included John Foster Dulles (the new secretary of state), Bedell Smith (who had moved over to become under secretary of state), and Allen Dulles (now CIA director) approved the joint venture in replacing Mosadeq and selected Roosevelt to direct it in the field. Preparations for the coup began in Tehran. The Iranian prime minister knew nothing of these activities; he continued to hope that the new American administration would support him and on May 28 sent a new message to Eisenhower painting himself as the only figure able to prevent a communist takeover of Iran and asking for a large increase in American assistance. The president waited a month before refusing the request on June 29. During the week before the reply went out, the decision was taken in Washington to proceed with the coup, and on August 16, after three days of confusion in Tehran that saw the Shah's temporary flight to Iraq and Italy and the near failure of Roosevelt's efforts, Mosadeq was removed from office by a coalition of military officers, royalists, and others disenchanted by the increasing disarray of the Mosadeq government. The new Iranian government, now under the Shah's control, negotiated a compromise agreement with Anglo-Iranian and began a strategic partnership with the United States that would last until the overthrow of the Shah in 1979.

Throughout this complicated and at times dramatic episode runs the influence of the change in American leadership. No one reading of clandestine projects being formulated by British and American officials who hoped and expected that, though they were opposed by the incumbent administration, they would be approved by the regime in waiting, can doubt that presidential transitions can affect the conduct of foreign countries toward the United States. The Iranian side, too, sought to gain an advantage from the transfer of power to what it hoped would be a friendlier administration.

Of course, one cannot read too much into the history of what did not happen. To the end, Mosadeq remained under the mistaken belief that his domestic position was growing stronger, not weaker, and therefore that he had nothing to gain from settling his disagreement with Anglo-Iranian early. Even if there had been no American transition, he might well have chosen to hold out indefinitely for better terms. Likewise, it is by no means certain that, deprived of the prospect of a potentially more amenable administration's accession to office in the near future, the British would have been induced to agree to the concessions Acheson was urging on them. London might have conducted a coup attempt on its own or, in frustration, employed open military force against the Mosadeq government. Had these unilateral steps failed, the position of the West in Iran might have been much worse than it turned out to be.

This was a case in which a good deal of foreign involvement in an American transition brought mixed results. Mosadeq failed in his effort to bypass the incumbent administration and commit the president-elect to tilt American policy further toward Tehran. On the other hand, the British were able to cooperate with American officials in circumventing the Democratic administration and preparing a scheme that could be set before its successor immediately upon its taking office. They used the transition skillfully and, from their standpoint, with success.

With a bit of timely assistance from its successor, the Truman administraion was able to stave off defeat in the UN and preserve the United States' bargaining position in the Korean armistice negotiations. Because both the Iranians and the British suspected that the new administration would not follow Truman's policy in Iran, his administration was bypassed, and it failed in its hope of resolving a festering and dangerous problem before it left office. Effective though informal cooperation between the newcomers and the outgoers ensured that the United States had only "one president at a time" in the Korean talks; when other parties thought they saw daylight between the two groups on Iran, they circumvented a lame-duck administration. In the one case the two administrations succeeded, and in the other they failed, to walk the fine line between useful cooperation and unwitting usurpation of the prerogatives of the incumbent by the successor.

# CHAPTER 8

# From Eisenhower
# to Kennedy

◆◆

We pass our problems on to each other. During the Berlin Crisis of 1961–62, a reporter asked me what my hopes were with
regard to the Berlin Crisis. I said, "I hope to be able to pass it
along to my successor."

—Dean Rusk

The transfer of the presidency that occurred in 1960–1961 was in
many ways quite different from the one that had taken place eight
years previously.[1] No divisive and debilitating issue like Korea cast a
pall over every other question of foreign policy. Bipartisanship in
foreign affairs had been solidified and, indeed, had been necessi-
tated by six years of split party control of the White House and Congress. The outgoing president, unlike his predecessor, remained
popular; a constitutional amendment, not public disapproval, prohibited Eisenhower from seeking another term. Hysteria over alleged domestic subversion and bitter partisan attacks on campaign
opponents were both passé in the calmer climate of 1960.

Nevertheless, one could also find points of similarity. Lessons
that had been learned in 1952–1953—concerning institutions, attitudes, valuable opportunities, and necessary precautions—had not
been forgotten by representatives of either party, and their application to this new transition marked a noticeable improvement over
prior successions to power. On the other hand, a number of problems and difficulties remained constants as well, putting the old and
new administrations under the same handicaps that others in their
positions had faced throughout the country's history. The transition

1. A number of documents relating to the 1960–1961 transition are in Robert L.
Branyan and Lawrence H. Larsen (eds.), *The Eisenhower Administration, 1953–
1961: A Documentary History* (New York, 1971), 1198–1377.

of 1960–1961 suffered some of the same vicissitudes, even as it carried forward the advances, of its predecessor.

Throughout the country, a basic consensus on foreign policy reigned. Both parties were in favor of containing the Soviet Union while simultaneously pursuing such opportunities for cooperation as might present themselves, such as arms control. Both advocated firmness in confronting the areas of greatest East-West tension, particularly Berlin. Neither called for dismantling the country's system of alliances or for in any way returning to a policy of isolationism. In short, both parties proclaimed the same basic national policy for the United States; when the candidates were reduced to quarreling over Quemoy and Matsu, it was clear that no fundamental differences separated them.

There was more controversy over the record of the incumbent administration in putting into practice the containment consensus. The Democrats charged that lassitude, drift, and timidity had marked the Eisenhower years and had undermined the nation's position in the world. Their party platform decried the administration's reluctance to increase spending on defense: "As a result, our military position today is measured in terms of gaps—missile gap, space gap, limited war gap."[2] The platform also implied that the administration might be wavering over Berlin and Cuba and promised more strenuous efforts toward arms control, accusing the Republicans of indifference and inaction. In all facets of foreign and defense policy, the Democrats demanded "a new urgency, persistence, and determination."

By contrast, the Republican platform pointed to the Eisenhower administration's "demonstrated firmness" and its resolve "to maintain an armed power exceeded by no other," coupled with its initiatives for East-West accommodation. The result of such a balanced policy was that "Dwight David Eisenhower stands today throughout the world as the greatest champion of peace and justice and good." Another result of two terms in power was that the Republican party brought to the days ahead "trained, experienced, mature and coura-

2. This and other quotations in this chapter from the platforms of the two major parties are taken from Schlesinger and Israel (eds.), *History of American Presidential Elections*, IV, 3471–81, 3510–16.

geous leadership"—an oblique reference to the Democratic nominee's lack of executive experience.

As the campaign was argued out over these differences, the president suffered some of the typical decline in a lame duck's influence
that Truman had experienced eight years earlier. After the Paris
summit of May, 1960, was aborted because of the U-2 incident,
the Soviet premier, Nikita Khrushchev, pointedly began to treat
Eisenhower as a caretaker, announcing that he would wait till after
January, 1961, to discuss the ongoing dispute over Berlin with the
new American president. Eisenhower later recalled that in a meeting
during this period, CIA Director Allen Dulles "quoted Tass . . . as
saying that the Soviets planned to 'scare the daylights' out of all
United States allies until I left office, apparently on the theory that
our election period would neutralize the administration into inaction." [3] This impression that the administration was simply mark-
ing time grew so prevalent that in August of 1960 Secretary of State
Christian Herter felt it necessary to issue a denial: "An illusion is
current in some quarters abroad that in foreign policy the United
States becomes paralyzed or semiparalyzed during a presidential
election period. It is well that our friends and our opponents should
fully realize that nothing could be further from the truth. The United
States—the President—can act just as quickly and forcefully during
this election period as at any other time." [4] By its actions concerning
the gold outflow question and the Bay of Pigs invasion, the United
States would demonstrate in the interregnum that it could still act
decisively, though its initiatives might not survive the transfer from
one administration to the next.

Power and office would in the end be transferred to John F.
Kennedy, the Democratic candidate. After a hard-fought campaign
against the Republican candidate, Vice-President Richard M. Nixon,
Kennedy emerged the victor by the narrowest margin of any presidential election of the twentieth century. The slenderness of his majority would incline him toward caution in both foreign and domestic affairs, at least during his first months in office. There were

3. Eisenhower, *Waging Peace,* 570.
4. Department of State *Bulletin,* XLIII (August 29, 1960), 309.

substantial changes in tone and style but no drastic policy alterations upon the changeover of administrations.

However, continuity in the substance of policy did not preclude
several innovations in the ongoing institutionalization of transitions.
One was the creation of a number of task forces set up to advise
a presidential candidate on questions of public policy. These small
groups of experts were first employed by the Kennedy campaign.
Their reports, delivered to Kennedy six days after his election,
spawned further, more specific task forces on foreign affairs; there
were some twenty-nine different task forces at work during the interregnum, and several more were set up after his inauguration. All
relied on the model of the comprehensive report prepared under the
direction of Adlai Stevenson on issues of foreign policy that would
face the new administration both before and after Inauguration Day.[5]

The incumbent administration did its part to prepare its successor. FBI clearances for the mass of appointees converging on
Washington were expedited, so that the new administration could
complete its personnel selection and the designated officials could
set about learning their jobs as quickly as possible. Eisenhower representatives also agreed with their counterparts from the Kennedy
camp on an unprecedented arrangement to allow the newcomers
government office space and secretarial help even before the new regime took over. Beginning January 3, 1961, two people named by
the incoming secretary in each department, except those of State
and Defense, would be placed on the payroll of that department; the
secretaries-designate of state and defense could select eight such
representatives.

Referring to such instances of cooperation, many of the participants in the transition recalled that it was smooth and cordial.
Eisenhower and Kennedy both made public statements at the time
describing themselves as pleased by the extent of cooperation, and
their two meetings during the interregnum were warmer and probably more productive than the stiff encounter between Truman and

5. For a discussion of the Kennedy task forces, see M. B. Schnapper (ed.), *New
Frontiers of the Kennedy Administration: The Texts of the Task Force Reports Pre-
pared for the President* (Washington, D.C., 1961); and "Pre-Inaugural Task Forces
Unprecedented in History," *Congressional Quarterly,* April 7, 1961, pp. 620–23.

Eisenhower in 1952. The Democrats had been out of office for only eight years, not twenty, and had a seasoned crop of former officials in the fields of foreign and national security policy who could apply the skills they had mastered under Truman to problems that would confront Kennedy.

On the other hand, the newcomers displayed at least the normal amount of overconfidence that causes those assuming office to believe that they know the solutions to all the country's problems and need no advice from their predecessors. Members of the outgoing administration guarded their authority to the end and followed strict ground rules on the number of Kennedy appointees who could be given briefings before January 20. Such attitudes on both sides may have contributed to the outcome of one of the most embarrassing episodes of American foreign policy, the CIA-sponsored invasion of Cuba by anti-Castro rebels in April, 1961. The operation is a textbook example of the dangers that transitions can pose for American foreign policy; it necessarily colors any assessment of this turnover of power. With the exception of the steps that led to the Bay of Pigs disaster, then, the transition of 1960–1961 bettered the record of 1952–1953 but left considerable room for improvement.

## The Gold Outflow Problem

As the Eisenhower-Kennedy transition occurred, a longstanding problem in American international financial policy came to a head. This was the depletion of the country's gold reserves and the danger this drain posed to the future of the dollar as the stable underpinning of the international currency regime established at Bretton Woods. The problem was "solved" twice—once by the Eisenhower administration as it left office and again, in a different way, by the Kennedy administration soon after it took over. The change in policy illustrates the importance of preparing the new president and his officers to "hit the ground running" as far as that is possible.

Deficits in the American balance of payments—considered necessary and even desirable as long as the West Europeans and other countries remained short of dollars after World War II—became worrying when they persisted even after the dollar gap disappeared in 1958 and resulted in a run on the dollar in the London gold market during 1960. The election of a Democratic president in November only increased fears in the financial community at home and abroad that an expansionary fiscal policy would increase the deficits in both the budget and the balance of payments and thereby further drive down the value of the dollar.[6] Immediate action seemed required.

Eisenhower, who had always feared that too ambitious a role for the United States government would overheat the economy, was particularly concerned by the strains on the dollar. He met with his senior financial and defense advisors the day after the election to discuss new corrective measures. On November 15, 1960, he issued a directive that included a package of measures designed to reduce American expenditures and increase American receipts abroad. These steps would (1) cut by more than half the number of dependents of military and other governmental personnel abroad by reducing dependents by 3 percent a month to a maximum of 200,000; (2) make minor reductions in American troop strength overseas; (3) end foreign procurement of supplies for American post exchanges and commissaries; (4) tie a greater portion of foreign-assistance loans to the purchase of American products; (5) promote exports; and (6) attempt to persuade allied countries to increase their own foreign aid programs. The order also termed a balanced budget essential.

The Eisenhower program labored under the double disadvantage of being unpopular without being assured of success. If it was to have any chance at all of effectiveness, it had to be seen as more than the temporary expedient of a departing administration—that is, bankers and foreign governments would have to be convinced that the restrictions would not be removed after January 20, 1961, and that the outflow of gold would not be allowed to resume. Cooperation would not be easy to achieve, however, because of the suspicions of both sides in the transition. Some Republicans wanted to avoid any painful actions during the interregnum, fearing their exploitation by the succeeding administration. Secretary of Defense Thomas Gates, arguing against the restrictions on American military dependents, warned, "It'll be like the bank holiday of 1933; the

6. An overview of the balance-of-payments problem is presented in David P. Calleo, *The Imperious Economy* (Cambridge, Mass., 1982), 1–24.

Democrats will be riding this white horse for the next twenty years, alleging that they had to unsnarl the mistakes of the Republicans." The Kennedy staff, meanwhile, was also recalling the Hoover-Roosevelt transition, but they remembered it as an effort by the incumbent president to "trap" his successor into commitments that would have continued Republican policies and prevented the New Deal from ever coming into being.[7]

Under these circumstances, it was not surprising that Eisenhower's first effort at a united front failed. At the November 15 session at which he issued the economic directive, the president also ordered his transition liaison officer to inform Kennedy's liaison with the administration that Eisenhower "thought it highly important" that the president-elect see Treasury Secretary Robert B. Anderson "as soon as possible on this urgent question." When the meeting took place, it proved to have as its purpose more than informing the president-elect about the facts of the case. Anderson told Kennedy that he and Under Secretary of State Douglas Dillon would soon be traveling to West Germany to discuss the gold outflow problem and to press the Bonn government to share the burden of assisting less-developed nations by creating its own foreign aid program. Would Kennedy name a representative to accompany them, thus increasing the strength of the American case? Kennedy's answer was no. His staff regarded the idea as an attempt by the Eisenhower administration to "inveigle Kennedy into underwriting its policies," and the president-elect would offer only to have Paul Nitze (who would soon be named to a post in the Kennedy Defense Department) receive Anderson's report on his return.[8]

One of the grounds for the suspicion with which the Kennedy team received Anderson's proposal, ironically, lay precisely in what had been one of the success stories of the unprecedented effort at a genuinely collaborative transition in 1952–1953—the president's budget. In his public statements on the transition, Eisenhower had stressed familiarity with the Bureau of the Budget and with the

7. Eisenhower, *Waging Peace,* 606; Arthur M. Schlesinger, Jr., *A Thousand Days: John F. Kennedy in the White House* (Boston, 1965), 126.

8. See Eisenhower, *Waging Peace,* 606–607; Schlesinger, *A Thousand Days,* 126; Paul T. David (ed.), *The Presidential Election and Transition, 1960–1961* (Washington, D.C., 1961), 228–30.

Fiscal Year 1962 budget (then in preparation) as the best single means for his successor to ready himself for the presidency. He apparently acted on this conviction, since no Kennedy aide indicated that he had been given any ground for complaint regarding the extent of budget information open to him.

But the issue for the new administration was not completeness of information, but accuracy of assumptions. The Republicans in the campaign had charged that Kennedy was a reckless spendthrift who would bankrupt the government, and the fear among some in the Kennedy camp was that the budget and the economic forecast to be presented in the Republican administration's final days were being designed to prove this allegation true. Kennedy's aide, Theodore Sorensen, was unhappy: "As I reviewed with Eisenhower's Budget officers the document with which he would take his leave of the Congress in January, it was clear that its precarious balance relied upon legislative actions, expenditure reductions and revenue expectations which they knew full well would never be realized. But it was equally clear that they had no intention of revising their estimates in the light of changed conditions, preferring to let Kennedy take the blame for the deficit."

One ought to add that (1) a deficit would have appeared anyway, since Kennedy would propose increases in both defense and domestic spending; (2) holding down expenditures had always been a concern of Eisenhower's, and this concern had only been increased by the election of a heavily Democratic Congress in 1958; (3) the president had in 1959 and 1960 waged a crusade against spending, even to the point of refusing to put money into the economy in 1960, regardless of the effect on his vice-president's campaign; and (4) he might well have presented such a seemingly quixotic budget even if he had not been leaving office. Still, the issue had arisen that was to plague more transitions than this one—the charge that the departing administration was manipulating for partisan advantage the budget it would leave behind.[9] The problem could make a collaborative ap-

9. *Public Papers of the Presidents of the United States: Dwight D. Eisenhower, 1960–61* (1961), 561; New York *Times,* November 11, 1960, Sec. 1, p. 20; Theodore Sorensen, *Kennedy* (New York, 1965), 232, 414; William B. Ewald, Jr., *Eisenhower the President: Crucial Days, 1951–1960* (Englewood Cliffs, N.J., 1981), 291–94. For comparisons of the Eisenhower and Kennedy budgets and eco-

proach to the balance-of-payments deficit more difficult, but it also spurred Kennedy's subordinates to master economic questions early, so that they would not have to rely during their early months in office on the analyses and prescriptions left behind by Eisenhower's Treasury Department.

Gold and the balance of payments next figured prominently in the transition after the Anderson mission, when Eisenhower and Kennedy met on December 6. The president spoke to the president-elect for twenty minutes on the matter, emphasizing "the way that confidence is affected by the balance or imbalance of budgets," and Anderson followed with a forty-five-minute briefing on the same subject. Eisenhower noted in his diary, "I pray that he understands it." His diary also revealed that he intended to warn the other members of NATO that, unless they increased their own military contributions to the alliance and unless other means were found to stanch the outflow of United States gold reserves, he would redeploy some American troops from Europe. Perhaps because of the example of the Anderson trip, there was no effort to have Kennedy associate himself with this step. "I told him that I informed him of this so he would not be surprised," Eisenhower later wrote, "and the decision was made and the announcement would be made in such a way as to leave him a free hand in reversing this policy if he so chooses." Such an arrangement apparently suited the president-elect; when asked after the meeting whether his advice on the balance-of-payments problem had been sought, he replied, "No, the responsibility rests with the present Administration until Jan. 20, and under the Constitution there cannot be any sharing of that responsibility, nor was it suggested that there should be." [10]

But if it did not wish to be associated with its predecessor on responses to the balance-of-payments deficit, neither could the new administration ignore the problem; indeed, the necessity of maintaining confidence in the dollar was to result in a link between the

---

nomic forecasts, see *Congressional Quarterly,* March 21, 1961, pp. 512–13, and Carl L. Figliola, "Considerations of National Security in the Transfer of Presidential Power: An Analysis of Decision-Making, 1960–1968" (Ph.D. dissertation, New York University, 1971), 123–24.

10. Ferrell (ed.), *The Eisenhower Diaries,* 382; New York *Times,* December 7, 1960, Sec. 1, p. 46.

two administrations of a completely unprecedented kind. Kennedy's difficulty lay in the selection of a secretary of the treasury. His election had been followed by further losses in the nation's gold reserves and jitters within the financial community, and, despite the anguish this caused the more liberal members of his staff, it seemed that the only nominees who might help to restore confidence were those close to the banking world, preferably Republicans. Robert Lovett, who was serving as an influential advisor on appointments, and others who were consulted all named Dillon—the incumbent under secretary of state for the Eisenhower administration. Convinced by the argument that such an appointment would send a message of bipartisanship and fiscal responsibility, Kennedy offered the post to Dillon, who, despite the strenuous efforts of Eisenhower to persuade him (as well as other Republicans) to decline a post in the new regime, finally accepted. His appointment was announced December 16, well in time for him to attend the January 19 meeting of Eisenhower and Kennedy with their senior diplomatic, military, and economic cabinet officers, at which time the outflow of American gold reserves was again discussed.[11]

Dillon's appointment and that of his deputy (also a holdover from the Eisenhower administration, who had served in the Defense Department) did not ensure continuity of policy, however. Kennedy issued revisions in the budget and economic report left by his predecessor. More immediately important to the balance-of-payments problem, the new president sent to Congress his own special message on gold and the balance-of-payments deficit on February 6, in which he announced that he was rescinding the most dramatic and controversial of Eisenhower's measures, the limitation on American military dependents abroad.[12]

Economic policy in general, including international monetary

11. Schlesinger, *A Thousand Days,* 133–36; Sorensen, *Kennedy,* 405–10; Eisenhower, *Waging Peace,* 603; Richard M. Nixon, *Six Crises* (Garden City, N.Y., 1962), 404–405; Figliola, "Considerations of National Security in the Transfer of Presidential Power," 305; Douglas Dillon, "Presidents I Have Known: Presidents as Leaders," in Kenneth W. Thompson (ed.), *The Virginia Papers on the Presidency,* Vol. XII (Lanham, Md., 1983) 1–16.

12. Kennedy's message on the balance of payments may be found in *Public Papers of the Presidents of the United States: John F. Kennedy, 1961* (1962), 57–66.

policy, constituted one of the sharper breaks between the old administration and the new, primarily because the two began with different assumptions. Eisenhower, proceeding from a great sensitivity to the danger of inflation and a distaste for governmental activism, believed that America's cloak had to be cut to fit the cloth. For him, the major task was one of trimming government expenditures abroad to a level that could be supported by the country's surplus in its balance of trade. This view led him to his order reducing the number of military dependents overseas and his threat to cut American troop strength in Europe. Kennedy, on the other hand, came into office promising to get the country moving again, at home and abroad. He and his advisors believed that the Eisenhower administration's fiscal conservatism was condemning millions of Americans to poverty and allowing the Soviet Union to forge ahead of the United States around the world. Thus, the task as the new administration saw it was to weave more cloth—to expand the economy and thereby provide the resources that would allow the government to increase its domestic, military, and foreign affairs expenditures without endangering its balance-of-payments position.

Kennedy's emphasis on expansion could be seen in his February 6 message to Congress, in which he pledged that the price of gold would be maintained at thirty-five dollars an ounce and that there would be no exchange controls or moves toward protectionism. Nor would there be cuts in American military and foreign assistance spending; indeed, these expenditures would grow. The aim would instead be to expand exports and encourage foreign investment in the United States, so as to provide a balance-of-payments surplus large enough to cover government spending abroad.

In the pursuit of these ends, Kennedy announced, he would seek to encourage exports: American commercial representatives and facilities abroad were to increase; the president of the Export-Import Bank was to submit plans for enlarging the bank's credit facilities for exports; the Agriculture Department would seek ways to step up agricultural exports; and in GATT negotiations, the United States would press for reductions in foreign tariffs and liberalization of foreign import quotas. The president also wished to draw foreign capital into the United States in other ways: he sought to make it more attractive for foreign governments and investors to make deposits and buy securities in this country; he directed the Commerce Department to increase its efforts to promote foreign travel in the United States; and he pledged to press the West Europeans to eliminate their remaining restrictions on investment in the United States.

Kennedy ordered a Treasury Department study on ways to increase international monetary reserves in addition to gold production and the growth in holdings of dollars and pounds, and he announced his willingness to use American drawing rights under the IMF for the first time to meet the balance-of-payments deficits. He would continue Eisenhower's efforts to press other countries to increase their foreign assistance programs, and he would retain the requirement that American foreign assistance be tied to purchases in the American market. But he replaced the limitation on military dependents with a less rigorous cap on foreign spending by military personnel for tourism and the purchase of durable goods. Finally, whereas Eisenhower had proposed to complement his foreign measures with cutbacks in domestic spending, leading to a balanced budget, Kennedy wished to increase spending at home and to deal with any resultant inflationary pressures through jawboning and voluntary restraint on wages and prices. Both plans were intended to bring the United States' payments into balance with receipts, but Kennedy would do so at a noticeably higher level of government expenditures.

The important point is not to be found in the details of the Kennedy program or the relative merits of the Eisenhower and Kennedy approaches. It is the fact that within three weeks of taking office the new administration was ready to unveil its proposals for coping with a serious and highly complex problem. As Kennedy himself noted in his message to Congress, the outflow of the nation's gold, while a development that required concern, was not an immediate crisis or a cause for panic. Responses to it could have been delayed past the newcomers' settling-in period, but instead Kennedy was able to present an integrated proposal almost immediately.

For this readiness to confront the demands of office early on, there were several reasons. One was certainly the political benefit of quickly overturning the unpopular Eisenhower restriction on military dependents. Others, however, could be found in the determination of the arriving administration to prepare itself to act from its first day in the White House. Both Dillon and Walter Heller, the chairman of the Council of Economic Advisers, were appointed early in the interregnum and thus had time to inform themselves on the issues they would face (and also to establish their relationship and the power each would exercise, at least in the initial period). Dillon's experience under Eisenhower meant that he was already familiar with the balance-of-payments problem. Although Kennedy refused to be associated publicly with the Dillon-Anderson mission to West Germany in December, his willingness to receive, through Nitze, Anderson's report on it allowed him to understand, before becoming president, the connections between this financial issue and the broader concerns of the alliance. Eisenhower did his part in making sure that the shrinkage of American reserves was discussed at both meetings he held with the president-elect. All these steps increased the knowledge of the incoming administration, enabled it to come to office prepared to address this question, and ensured that, though the United States' policy changed, there was no hiatus in concern or competence.

## The Bay of Pigs

By almost every criterion, the botched American attempt to overthrow the government of Cuba through clandestine support of disaffected elements of the Cuban population in the spring of 1961 presents an example of failure in all aspects of a transition. Nothing, it seems in hindsight, had been thought through carefully enough or went according to plan, but the change of administrations exacerbated every one of these already existing flaws. Ironically, American officials derived confidence from the success of the overturning of the Mosadeq government soon after the transition of 1952–1953 (and the similar operation in Guatemala the following year).[13] Cuba was not Iran, however, and the 1960–1961 transition was marred by this effort to replicate the events of eight years before.

Despite overtures by the Eisenhower administration toward Fidel Castro after his proclamation of victory over the Batista regime on

13. Richard H. Immerman, *The CIA in Guatemala: The Foreign Policy of Intervention* (Austin, 1982).

New Year's Day, 1959, Cuban-American relations steadily deterio-
rated through 1959 and 1960. Washington was concerned about several things: the increasing repressiveness of the Castro government,
particularly its summary execution of supporters of the former regime; the expropriation of American properties in Cuba without
proper compensation; the ever shriller anti-American language used
by Castro and his associates; and, above all, the rapid filling of government posts with Communists and Havana's signing of economic
agreements with the Soviet Union and China. The governments of
Venezuela, Guatemala, El Salvador, and Nicaragua were all reported to be the targets of subversion sponsored by Cuba. Havana
denied that it had become a Russian pawn, declared that its legal
system and economic policies were its own affair and not the concern of the United States, and accused Washington of conniving at
bombing raids launched by Cubans opposed to the Castro regime,
apparently from Florida. As the downward spiral of mutual recriminations continued, Eisenhower, on March 17, 1960, approved
a CIA recommendation long supported by Nixon and others within
the administration that the agency secretly train a force of Cuban
exiles for possible use against the Castro government.

While the exiles were training (primarily in Guatemala), public
and private events were pushing the Cuban and American governments further toward rupture. In July of 1960 the administration
suspended the balance of Cuba's 1960 sugar quota and was attacked
by Democratic campaigners for not doing more. United States policy toward Castro became a major and frequently heated issue in the
campaign. Kennedy appeared to accuse the administration of not
recognizing the danger of Castro's communist beliefs early enough
and, as in so many other regions, letting American policy drift
while the Soviet Union advanced. This latter line of attack culmi-
nated in an October 20 statement by Kennedy that termed the recently instituted American embargo on all exports to Cuba other
than nonsubsidized food, medicine, and medical supplies "too little
and too late," and offered a pledge: "We must attempt to strengthen
the non-Batista democratic anti-Castro forces in exile, and in Cuba
itself, who offer eventual hope of overthrowing Castro. Thus far,
these fighters for freedom have had virtually no support from our
government." Kennedy aides were later to term this passage "a rhe-

torical flourish" and "a vague generalization" thrown in to pad the speech, but to the White House, such a proposal sounded dangerously close to the secret program of training Cuban exiles for an anti-Castro invasion that the CIA had been planning for months.

Nixon knew that Kennedy had been given intelligence briefings on Cuba and claimed to have been informed by the White House that the briefings included information on Cuban invasion plans; he believed that Kennedy, through this statement, had breached the confidentiality of a matter of national security and endangered the operation's success in order to gain partisan political advantage by appearing as the tougher of the two candidates on Castro. Kennedy afterward denied prior knowledge of any invasion plans, saying that the episode was only an unfortunate coincidence, and contended that the assistance he advocated was only moral support and propaganda, not arms. The issue faded from the headlines, but, perhaps sensitive to the charge of softness on Cuba, Eisenhower issued a statement in October pledging that the United States would never permit a unilateral Cuban takeover of the American naval base at Guantanamo Bay; he also directed that the fortifications of the base be reinforced with minefields and a contingent of marines.[14]

Kennedy's election and the certain prospect of an interparty transition complicated matters but did not stop the movement of events. When he became president-elect, Kennedy had apparently not yet settled on a policy toward Cuba. Six days after the election, he asked one of the leaders of his primary task force on foreign policy to lay the groundwork for a new approach; he requested estimates both of the effectiveness of the trade embargo against Cuba and of the possibilities of a reconciliation with it. Kennedy first learned of the training of the exiles on November 18 and was given a more detailed briefing on the operation by CIA Director Allen Dulles on November 29. The project was now much more ambitious than that approved by Eisenhower some eight months previously, having evolved from the provision of a guerrilla insurgency to the

14. Accounts—on several points mutually contradictory—of this episode may be found in Nixon, *Six Crises*, 351–57; Schlesinger, *A Thousand Days*, 215–97; Sorensen, *Kennedy*, 205–206, 294–309; and Eisenhower, *Waging Peace*, 598, 613–14. See also John F. Kennedy, *The Strategy of Peace*, ed. Allan Nevins (New York, 1960), 132–34, and Neustadt, *Presidential Power*, 220–25.

preparation of an amphibious landing. But it is not clear how far the president-elect knew the plan had departed from its original conception when he asked for the continuation of preparations on the twenty-ninth. Cuba was discussed at the December 9 and January 19 meetings of Kennedy and Eisenhower, but apparently at no great length because of the limitations of time.

During the interregnum, as one participant in discussions on Cuba put it, "government floated as in a void," in which "neither the outgoing nor the incoming administrations wanted to make fundamental decisions, and most matters continued to move along existing tracks."[15] In the case of American relations with Cuba, unfortunately, those tracks led to deepening hostility and terminated, surprisingly, in a dramatic action of the sort few expected from an administration with less than three weeks to run.

The episode was touched off on January 2, when Castro— charging that, of an American embassy staff he said numbered three hundred, 80 percent were spies—ordered the contingent reduced to eleven within forty-eight hours. For Eisenhower, this action "was the last straw," not only because of the falsity of the allegations (the United States insisted that the embassy staff consisted of only eighty-seven persons, none of whom were engaged in espionage), but also because of the peremptory manner in which Castro's demand was made. The president directed that diplomatic relations with Havana be severed January 3.

At the NSC meeting on the morning of the third, at which the decision to break relations was taken, there arose the question of whether the president-elect should be informed before the announcement was made. When Eisenhower directed that Secretary of State Herter advise Kennedy through Secretary of State–designate Dean Rusk, Allen Dulles revealed that "Mr. Rusk had not been fully briefed and in detail on the Planning with respect to Cuba."[16] The

15. Schlesinger, *A Thousand Days,* 258. Schlesinger also tried to turn the transition and its necessary discontinuities to the new administration's benefit. When told that "we" could not condemn Batista publicly because "we" had supported him, Schlesinger "pointed out that the 'we' in question had changed on January 20 and that it surely was not necessary for Kennedy to identify himself with all the errors of his predecessor" (p. 246).

16. Gordon Gray Memorandum of Meeting with the President (January 9,

president ordered that Rusk be briefed immediately, but the first week of January was a late hour for the officer who was to head the State Department to learn the full story of an American policy intended to overthrow another government.

This delay by the outgoing administration was countered by a certain distance maintained by the incoming. Early in the afternoon of January 3, Herter informed Rusk of the decision to sever relations later that day and asked whether Kennedy might come to the White House for a second meeting with Eisenhower to discuss Cuba and perhaps associate himself with this move. Rusk replied that he doubted that the incoming administration would have a public reaction to the breakoff and added that it was his impression that "Senator Kennedy might feel some embarrassment in going to see the President, only because of press speculation as to what might be discussed between them, particularly in the light of the situation in Laos and in Cuba." [17] Rusk promised to check with the president-elect, but no meeting took place until the eve of the inauguration.

This, then, was the situation that confronted the newly installed administration as it attempted to gain its footing in the weeks following January 20. Although its confidentiality had been compromised by articles in the New York *Times* and elsewhere, the training of the exile forces was advancing in Guatemala. All plans for a purely guerrilla operation had been abandoned in favor of a sea and air invasion. A number of former Cuban political figures had been gathered in Florida, ready to be installed as the new government upon the collapse of the Castro regime. Allen Dulles and General Lyman Lemnitzer, the chairman of the Joint Chiefs of Staff, presented the project to Dean Rusk, Robert McNamara, Robert Kennedy, and other important new officials on January 22, and on January 28

---

1961), 4, in White House Office, Office of the Special Assistant for National Security Affairs: Records, 1952–61, Special Assistants Series, Presidential Subseries, Box 5, Folder titled "1960—Meetings with President—Volume 2(2) ," Dwight D. Eisenhower Presidential Library, Abilene, Kansas.

17. Herter Memorandum of Conversation with Dean Rusk (January 3, 1961), in Christian Herter Papers [Chronological File] July, 1960(1), Box 9, Folder titled "[Chronological File] Jan–Feb, 1961(3)," Eisenhower Library; Schlesinger, *A Thousand Days*, 127; David (ed.), *The Presidential Election and Transition*, 230–32; Eisenhower, *Waging Peace*, 613–14.

President Kennedy held his first White House meeting on the subject.

Beginning at that initial meeting and continuing with increasing force at every discussion thereafter, those immediately concerned with the planning and execution of the project pressed on Kennedy and his advisors the argument that what Kennedy as president-elect had believed a mere contingency plan on which the decision to proceed could be made in the future at greater leisure was in reality an ongoing program whose termination would entail considerable costs. Furthermore, the decision could not be long delayed, for several reasons: (1) the Guatemalan government was becoming embarrassed by the publicity about the Cubans' presence on its soil and had requested their departure by the end of April; (2) the rainy season in Central America would soon make further training impossible; (3) more advanced fighter aircraft from the Soviet Union and Cuban pilots trained in Czechoslovakia were about to arrive in Cuba, after which time the exiles would no longer be able to mount a successful invasion without the help of American ground and air forces; and (4) members of the exile contingent were themselves becoming restless for action and would be demoralized by delay. Things could not be maintained as they were for long, and the only alternative way of ending the status quo—canceling the invasion—now seemed out of the question. Since it was unlikely that other Latin American countries would receive this trained and armed force of anti-Castro Cubans, it seemed obvious that, if they were not to return to Cuba, they would have to come to the United States. But their presence in this country would make revelation of the entire scheme inevitable, with the attendant risk that Kennedy, after criticizing Eisenhower in the campaign for not taking firmer action, would appear irresolute for not employing the tool his predecessor had left him.

In deciding how to respond to these pressures, the president labored under three handicaps, all products of the transition—one a matter of knowledge, one a matter of confidence, and one a matter of institutions. The first, lack of knowledge, was the natural result of his inexperience and that of some of his advisers who had never before occupied high government positions. It was one of these aides who later attributed Kennedy's decisions on Cuba to the fact that he had been in office only seventy-seven days when he set the plan in motion.[18] Thus, the president did not know, for example, that the CIA's prediction of an uprising against Castro once the landing had taken place did not come from the agency's evaluators of intelligence, but only from its operational side. Nor could he know that the exiles believed they had been promised direct intervention by American forces if they needed it.

The president's second disadvantage lay in what has been called the "heady quality" engendered in the minds of all new presidents by their exhilaration in winning the nation's highest office. A sympathetic observer believed that Kennedy was no exception to the general rule of overconfidence in freshly minted presidents: "Everything had broken right for him since 1956. He had won the nomination and the election against all the odds in the book. . . . Intelligence was at last being applied to public affairs. Euphoria reigned; we thought for a moment that the world was plastic and the future unlimited. . . . Everyone around him thought he had the Midas touch and could not lose. Despite himself, even this dispassionate and skeptical man may have been affected by the soaring euphoria of the new day." [19]

Finally, a third burden the president had to bear was that of organization—or, more accurately, the lack of organization—that dogged the new administration as it tried to rid itself of what it saw as the overly bureaucratized White House national security structure created by its predecessor. This disdain for Eisenhower's procedures was especially marked in the case of the Operations Coordinating Board (OCB), the body designed to oversee the execution of decisions taken in the NSC and to ensure the periodic reevaluation of major policies. Because of Eisenhower's military-staff background, "during the 1960 election campaign, the OCB got tagged . . . as an invention of Eisenhower [and an example of] the allegedly unnecessary and excessive staff structure that the 'aging general' had imposed upon the government, thereby 'stifling creativity and

18. Schlesinger, *A Thousand Days*, 258. Other officials of the Kennedy administration, such as Rusk, have concurred in this opinion. See also the account in Neustadt, *Presidential Power.*

19. Authors' interview with Frank Pace, April 27, 1983; Schlesinger, *A Thousand Days*, 259, 214.

ideas.' . . . Thus it was pretty well doomed from the outset," Ike's OCB vice-chairman regretfully recalled. Kennedy's aides were not convinced of the need for such elaborate institutional devices and promptly disbanded most of them after taking over. Although preparations for the Cuban operations had never been overseen by the OCB, which was devoted primarily to more routine policies, an official who served in high posts in both administrations lamented that the disruption of the lines of communication and advice provided by the NSC system deprived Kennedy of information and assessments he needed both while the operation was being planned and once it was under way.[20]

The style of the first months of the administration may have been a handicap. As compared with its predecessors, the Kennedy team was in general younger, it contained more intellectuals, and it was more comfortable with informal, interpersonal seminars than with passing paper through official channels. This impatience with structure contributed a freshness of outlook, but it could also leave gaps in the knowledge of participants, particularly when, as in the early days, they did not know one another well. Rusk has pointed to the resulting "tendency for each one of us to sit upon our own specific responsibility and not look at problems in the whole context" as one reason that he and his colleagues did not ask searching questions about aspects of the operation that were the responsibility of others. The contrast with the orderly and disciplined way in which the same people dealt with the Cuban missile crisis one and a half years later is stark and sobering.

These unfavorable circumstances, then, faced the president at the moment of decision on Cuba: The unavoidable inexperience of many members of the administration meant that they brought too little knowledge to a difficult problem. Their overconfidence meant that they failed to recognize the limits of their knowledge and felt there was little they could learn from other parties, such as their predecessors. An unsettled organizational support structure compli-

20. Karl G. Harr, Jr., "Eisenhower's Approach to National Security Decision-making," in Kenneth W. Thompson (ed.), *The Eisenhower Presidency: Eleven Intimate Perspectives of Dwight Eisenhower* (Lanham, Md., 1984), 89–111. Vol. II of Thompson (ed.), *Portraits of American Presidents;* Schlesinger, *A Thousand Days,* 210; Dillon, "Presidents I Have Known."

cated their struggle to make the best use of the knowledge they possessed. Nevertheless, apparently, a decision had to be made. Having heard the internal debates on the issue and drawn from his subordinates what he thought were adequate assurances of the plan's success, Kennedy committed himself in early April to support a landing at the Bay of Pigs. On April 15, the invasion began.

It was, of course, a failure, plagued in every facet by setbacks that might have been foreseen but somehow were not. The pre-invasion air strikes that had been planned were inadequate. Castro's air force, even without the addition of the new Soviet fighters, was much more powerful than had been anticipated, and the exiles had too few pilots to make their air cover effective. Cuban ground forces also performed well and greatly outnumbered the exiles. One ship had somehow been permitted to carry both the reserve ammunition and the communications equipment for the invaders, making its sinking by one of Castro's planes a doubly crippling blow. Contact with the internal opposition to Castro had been poor, and in any event most of the regime's opponents were arrested within twenty-four hours of the landing. The escape route for the exiles, on which all had relied if the worst should happen, turned out to be too far away and separated from the beach by an impenetrable swamp. In almost no aspect of the plan did events proceed as those in Washington had assumed they would.

This disaster was a major shock to the administration and brought down upon it severe criticism from political leaders and the press around the world (though, interestingly enough, not from the American public, among whom approval of Kennedy actually rose). Embarrassment also gave rise to mutual resentment between the old administration and the new over responsibility for the mistakes that were revealed at the Bay of Pigs. Despite public professions of bipartisanship on both sides, Kennedy told his secretary, Evelyn Lincoln, that "it was a failure of Eisenhower to provide sufficient information earlier" that had left the new president too little time to form a task force on Cuba of his own advisers, have them examine the CIA plan thoroughly, and receive from them suggestions for its modification or even scrapping. Kennedy's already low opinion of Eisenhower's abilities was further reduced by his belief that his predecessor had allowed the upper ranks of his military and intelligence advisers, in particular the Joint Chiefs of Staff, to be filled with persons whose competence Kennedy questioned. He expressed his resentment more than once, remarking: "My God, the bunch of advisers we inherited. . . . Can you imagine being President and leaving behind someone like all those people there?" [21]

These sentiments were fully reciprocated by the former president. Although when he met with reporters at the conclusion of a Camp David meeting with Kennedy soon after the invasion attempt, Eisenhower said that all Americans should stand behind the president in matters of foreign policy, in private his comments were less favorable. That same day, before leaving for Camp David, he told friends with a chuckle—and perhaps with agreement—of a telegram he had just received from a woman in Iowa, saying: "You go down there and tell that little boy to be careful. In fact, you'd better go and take over yourself." By June, Eisenhower, noting in his diary that rumors were circulating of a crucial air strike at the Bay of Pigs canceled at the last moment by Kennedy, was saying that if the story was true, it constituted "a very dreary account of mismanagement, indecision, and timidity at the wrong time." He predicted that if the episode was fully revealed, it would lead to "a virtual repudiation of the present administration" and should be titled a "Profile in Timidity and Indecision." [22]

In fact, there was enough responsibility to go around. The Eisenhower administration failed to bring the plan to the attention of Kennedy and his top appointees early enough for them to master its details and probe its weaknesses. It is not clear that the incoming president was ever apprised of the variations the scheme had undergone since its inception in early 1960; if he had known them, he might have questioned the effectiveness of the form it ultimately took. Kennedy later complained that he should have been given the opportunity to meet more often with Eisenhower during the interregnum.

21. Figliola, "Considerations of National Security in the Transfer of Presidential Power," 146; Schlesinger, *A Thousand Days,* 295.

22. Ewald, *Eisenhower the President,* 316; Ferrell (ed.), *The Eisenhower Diaries,* 386–90. Kennedy intimates denied the air-strike rumors. See Sorensen, *Kennedy,* 299–301, and Schlesinger, *A Thousand Days,* 293–94.

However, Kennedy, through Rusk, rebuffed Herter's invitation to the White House after the severing of diplomatic relations with Cuba. Because knowledge of the operation was kept so secret under both administrations, segments of the bureaucracy that could have provided valuable information and evaluations, such as several offices in the Defense Department and the intelligence section of the CIA itself, were told of the plan only late and in general terms, if at all (see Chapter 4). General Andrew Goodpaster, a national security aide in the Eisenhower White House, stayed on for a period after the Kennedy inauguration to help smooth the transition. Unfortunately, his responsibilities had never included the Cuban operation, and he therefore could not supply the information and continuous involvement that would have been helpful to the newcomers. On the other hand, Dillon had been involved in discussions on Cuba under Eisenhower, but he was not part of Kennedy's planning group and was never asked about the evolution of policy since 1959; in fact, he was abroad when the invasion took place, and it came as a surprise to him.

The result of all these lapses was that Kennedy and his subordinates lacked the information they needed to make informed policy choices on the Bay of Pigs operation. Conceived in the closing months of an administration that would never bear its consequences, the plan matured in the period of drift and confusion that accompanied the interregnum, and the operation was launched by a new administration not yet ready to judge its practicality. On all counts, the episode was a failure, and the reputation of the 1960–1961 transition suffers for it.

Information, then, was the key to both our cases from this transition. In the instance of the gold outflow and balance-of-payments problems, the old administration provided full briefings to the new— indeed, Eisenhower and his subordinates seemed to push the facts on their successors—and Kennedy's advisers prepared themselves to work together in putting their knowledge to use in a coherent program of action almost as soon as they assumed authority. In the case of the Bay of Pigs, by contrast, perhaps because of the extreme sensitivity of the subject, the outgoing administration appears to have been more reticent and the incoming less inquiring. Once Kennedy took office, compartmentalism among members of his new team prevented them from sharing the information they had and using it to the fullest extent, with lamentable results. Both episodes demonstrate that communication between administrations, within administrations, and between political and career staffs is vital.

# CHAPTER 9

# From Johnson to Nixon

The decisions made between [Election Day] and the time of the inauguration will probably be the most important decisions that the new President will make insofar as determining the success of his administration over the next four years.

—President-elect
Richard M. Nixon

The transition from Lyndon Johnson to Richard Nixon in 1968–1969 was, by most accounts, the least disruptive interparty transition the country had seen. The changeover occurred with remarkably little rancor, the incumbent proved exceptionally forthcoming with information and access, the incoming team approached its outgoing counterpart with respect and cautious deference, and the new Nixon administration promised more continuity than change in the appointments it made and in the foreign policy it set forth.

The relative success of this turnover of authority was partly attributable to the operation of the transition-easing mechanisms that had developed since World War II. This was the first transition to be governed by the Presidential Transition Act of 1963, legislation designed to authorize government funds for transition activities and to increase cooperation between president and president-elect. President Johnson referred to the act in early September when he announced the appointment of Charles Murphy, a veteran public servant who had assisted Truman in the 1952–1953 transition, as his transition chief and invited presidential candidates Hubert Humphrey, Richard Nixon, and George Wallace to appoint their own transition representatives, which they did. Johnson also adhered to the spirit of the act by providing each candidate with periodic intelligence briefings by high administration officials, sometimes including himself. At Johnson's urging and under Murphy's direction, all the departments and agencies of the government prepared briefing books that would be used to acquaint incoming officials with their new responsibilities. Both Humphrey and Nixon, following the precedent set by Kennedy, authorized the establishment of a number of task forces to provide a mixture of campaign advisory and post-election planning functions. As if all this preparation were not enough, the Brookings Institution commissioned a series of papers on the national problems that would confront the new president, later published as *Agenda for the Nation*. Brookings made the galley proofs of this book available to the candidates prior to the election, following a precedent set in 1960.[1]

After the election, the administration allocated a twenty-room office suite in the Executive Office Building and additional office space elsewhere to President-elect Nixon. Nixon himself chose to establish transition headquarters at the Hotel Pierre in New York City, which offered a central location and yet distance from Washington. Additional task forces were authorized, a talent hunt operation was established, and the process of interviewing candidates was begun, using $450,000 provided by the Presidential Transition Act. Since the Nixon transition spent about $1.5 million, government funding had to be supplemented by private contributions. At President Johnson's request, Nixon appointed former Under Secretary of State Robert Murphy as his special foreign policy liaison. Murphy was given an office next door to Secretary of State Rusk's and took part in many of Rusk's meetings. Nixon's transition chief, Franklin Lincoln, Jr., worked closely with Charles Murphy to designate transition representatives in various departments and agencies, to identify the positions to be filled, and to assure access to information and assistance.

These measures, while impressive, could not in themselves assure a smooth transition, as the subsequent transitions of 1976–1977 and 1980–1981 suggest. More important were two other factors: first,

1. Laurin Henry, "Presidential Transitions: The 1968–69 Experience in Perspective," *Public Administration Review,* XXIX (September–October, 1969), 471–73; Henry Graff, "Transition at the White House," *New Leader,* LI (December 30, 1968), 3–7; Franklin B. Lincoln, Jr., "Presidential Transition, 1968–1969," *American Bar Association Journal,* LV (June, 1969), 529–33; Figliola, "Considerations of National Security in the Transfer of Presidential Power," 226–34, 249–52.

the incumbent had not been a candidate in the presidential contest, and second, Nixon and Johnson seemed to be in basic agreement in their views on American objectives. In both respects this transition resembled the two that preceded it; yet it took place in a new context. The new administration would have to come to terms with the relative decline in American power and the breakup among the public and various leadership groups of the cold war consensus on foreign policy, brought on in no small measure by the continuing conflict in Vietnam, which was far and away the dominant issue of the campaign.

President Johnson shocked a national television audience on March 31, 1968, with the announcement that he would not seek another term. That marked the moment the transition of 1968–1969 may be said to have begun. The announcement came as part of a speech on American foreign policy in Vietnam that laid the basis for peace talks with North Vietnam and linked the effort to make peace with the decision not to stand for reelection. The search for peace was so important, declared Johnson, that "I do not believe that I should devote an hour or day of my time to any personal partisan causes."[2] By taking himself out of partisan politics, Johnson hoped he could continue to address the nation's foreign policy problems unencumbered by the constraints of campaigning for office. He intended to pursue his peace initiative with the North Vietnamese; he wanted to complete the nonproliferation treaty and engage the Soviet Union in arms-limitation negotiations before his term expired. Unfinished business remained with North Korea, which had captured and imprisoned the crew of the intelligence ship *Pueblo* in January, 1968. The administration also believed that initiatives in the Middle East and with Communist China might be broached before it left office.

At the same time, Johnson recognized that, while taking himself out of the campaign would give him more time to work on these problems and might minimize charges of partisan opportunism, the declaration of his noncandidacy meant the slow but sure ebbing of his political power. The central challenge and problem of his re-

2. Lyndon B. Johnson, *The Vantage Point: Perspectives of the Presidency, 1963–1969* (New York, 1971), 435.

maining months in office would be to preserve the authority without which diplomacy would be ineffective. He believed that if he provided the candidates with information about foreign policy during the campaign and transition, they would understand and concur with his actions. This support would in turn help preserve his own authority. Johnson took the extraordinary step of conducting intelligence briefings himself for candidates even prior to the conventions. He met with Robert Kennedy on April 3, Nelson Rockefeller on June 10, Eugene McCarthy on June 11, and George Wallace and Richard Nixon on July 26, saying later that he wanted no hasty remark made on the campaign trail that might derail negotiations.[3]

Once the general election campaign began, Johnson intensified his efforts to keep the candidates informed. Humphrey, of course, received information by virtue of being vice-president. Immediately after the Republican convention Johnson invited Nixon and Agnew to the LBJ Ranch, where he, Secretary of State Dean Rusk, former Deputy Defense Secretary Cyrus Vance (who was currently engaged in negotiations with the North Vietnamese in Paris), and CIA Director Richard Helms gave the Republican candidates a full-scale intelligence briefing. In addition to the periodic briefings that the candidates subsequently received, Johnson also initiated conference calls with Nixon, Humphrey, and Wallace in mid- and late October to inform them of the latest developments in the negotiations with the North Vietnamese. All told, Johnson logged at least seven conversations with Nixon between the end of the conventions and Election Day.[4] These efforts did help to keep the campaign from undercutting diplomatic efforts, though not completely.

Johnson's effort to retain maximum political power continued after the election was over. He clearly believed and hoped that cooperation and assistance on his part would be met with support and deference from Nixon. Nevertheless, the inherent ambiguity of their relationship was demonstrated by a dispute that erupted after their first postelection meeting on November 12. Perhaps overwhelmed by

3. Johnson, *The Vantage Point*, 554.

4. Richard Nixon, *RN: The Memoirs of Richard Nixon* (New York, 1978), 322–30, mentions four of these; Johnson, *The Vantage Point*, 554–55.

Johnson's presence and hospitality, Nixon emerged from the meeting to say:

> If progress is to be made on matters like Vietnam, the current possible crisis in the Mideast, the relations between the United States and the Soviet Union with regard to certain outstanding matters . . . it can be made only if the parties on the other side realize that the current administration is setting forth policies that will be carried forward by the next administration. . . . I gave assurance in each instance to the Secretary of State and, of course, to the President, that they could speak not just for this administration but for the nation, and that meant for the next administration as well.[5]

Later in the week Nixon pulled back from this sweeping statement of support when he responded to reporters' questions by saying that his statement was based on an understanding that he would be consulted on any major decisions. Not surprisingly, the suggestion that the president had given the president-elect veto power was not well received at the White House, already acutely aware of the president's diminishing power. Johnson quickly called a press conference to dispel the impression that Nixon had become a kind of co-president, announcing, "The decisions that will be made between now and January 20 will be made by this President and by this Secretary of State and by this Secretary of Defense." No more was said publicly, and the two went on to constructive collaboration.[6]

Nixon, of course, was no novice to government and brought to the presidency extensive acquaintance with foreign policy problems and some firm convictions about how the office should be organized. Relatively little time was spent on personnel. The foreign policy appointments Nixon and his associates did make promised continuity more than change. Like his predecessors, Nixon retained the heads of the CIA and the FBI. Democrats Sargent Shriver and Charles Yost became ambassador to France and permanent representative to the United Nations, respectively. And in Henry Kissinger, the new assistant for national security affairs, Nixon had appointed

5. Johnson, *The Vantage Point*, 556.

6. *Ibid.*, 556–57; Henry, "Presidential Transitions," 476–77; New York *Times*, November 11, 1968, p. 34.

an academic who was known for his attachment to Nixon's political rival Nelson Rockefeller and who had also carried out special assignments for the Kennedy and Johnson administrations. Secretary of State–designate William P. Rogers had substantial government experience as attorney general during the Eisenhower administration. Although Rogers' foreign policy experience was limited, Nixon admired his negotiating skill and administrative abilities. Secretary of Defense–designate Melvin Laird came to his office after sixteen years in Congress, where he had served on the Defense Subcommittee of the House Appropriations Committee. Rogers and Laird, like Kissinger, were given broad discretion in selecting their staffs, and each retained a significant number of Johnson administration personnel.

Nixon and his foreign policy team spent more time during the interregnum redesigning the foreign policy machinery then designing a new foreign policy. An Institute for Defense Analysis study of the national security process made available to Nixon after the election and critical of the informal approach of the Kennedy and Johnson administrations helped confirm Nixon's preference for the more structured approach of the Eisenhower administration. Henry Kissinger, aided by Morton Halperin, who had served in Johnson's National Security Council staff, and General Andrew Goodpaster, who had served President Eisenhower as staff secretary, devoted himself to the task of re-creating a more orderly process designed to give the president "real options" (rather than presenting him with a bureaucratic consensus) and to integrate specific issues in an overall strategy. This tended over time to centralize in the White House control over important foreign policy problems. The immediate result was National Security Decision Memorandum 2 (NSDM2), signed by Nixon on January 19, one day before the inauguration. As the White House explained, the National Security Council (which under President Johnson had fallen into disuse) would "be reestablished as the principal forum for Presidential consideration of foreign policy issues." The NSC would meet regularly, usually once a week, with a formal agenda. Its work was to be buttressed by a structure of subcommittees called interdepartmental groups or IGs, consisting of representatives of all the relevant agencies, who would draft policy analyses presenting the facts, problems, and options on a given issue. The subcommittees' reports would be screened before presentation to the full NSC by an interagency review group of senior officials and chaired by Kissinger as national security adviser "to insure that the issues, options, and views [were] presented fully and fairly."[7] In discussions of the proposal during the transition, some officials recognized that this arrangement would enhance the role of Kissinger and his staff at the expense of the State Department particularly. But sooner or later they realized that, whatever their objections, the arrangement was what the president wanted.

President-elect Nixon's unusually serious focus on this vital area reduced—without eliminating—the relational ambiguities within the foreign affairs bureaucracy that would plague other administrations. It also allowed him to take hold of the government more quickly. Nixon and Kissinger made few public statements about the substance of foreign policy during the transition, though privately they initiated contact with the North Vietnamese, spoke with a Soviet representative about a possible transition summit, and sent former Pennsylvania Governor William Scranton as a personal envoy to the Middle East. On Vietnam and on Soviet-American relations, the president-elect said little, apparently willing to consider shifts in policy but prepared to proceed only after a review of the information and options available. In sum, the incoming team did as little as possible to undercut publicly the authority of the incumbents.[8]

Despite this, Johnson's hopes for what he could accomplish in his final year as president were wholly fulfilled only in the case of the *Pueblo*. Postelection negotiations won the release and return of eighty-two crewmen just before Christmas, removing one foreign policy problem from the plate of the new administration. Virtually nothing was done on the Middle East and Communist China initiatives, as all concerned chose to wait for the new administration to take office. As for Johnson's highest priorities, peace talks with North Vietnam and arms limitation talks with the Soviet Union, Johnson would leave office knowing that some progress had been made but also painfully aware of how the electoral campaign and

7. "President's Report to the Congress on United States Foreign Policy," *Public Papers of the Presidents of the United States: Richard M. Nixon, 1969* (1970), 123–24.
8. Kissinger, *White House Years*, 38–53; Nixon, *RN*, 337–51.

external events had intruded on the diplomatic process in both cases.

## Vietnam

President Johnson announced a partial bombing halt of North Vietnam on the same evening that he announced his noncandidacy for the presidency. This meant that the United States would continue to bomb only the part of North Vietnam south of the twentieth parallel. This unilateral action, he hoped, would lead to serious peace negotiations. The effort to conduct peace talks, however, was necessarily affected by the nomination and election campaigns and by the coming transfer of leadership. Johnson in his memoirs commented, "I am certain the fact that 1968 was an election year influenced Hanoi and affected the attitude of numerous Americans concerning our dealings with the North Vietnamese and our search for peace." [9] He believed that domestic criticism of the war increased North Vietnamese obstinacy and that the North Vietnamese often played for the American audience rather than negotiating seriously.

Vietnam, of course, had become a deeply divisive issue domestically. In late January, 1968, the North Vietnamese had launched a massive assault on many key South Vietnamese cities during the holiday season of Tet. Although the offensive failed, many Americans were shocked by the communists' show of strength. As the war continued, seemingly without end, President Johnson's political support on both right and left eroded, and even before Tet a significant challenge to his policies had already been mounted within the Democratic party. Senator Eugene McCarthy's astonishing showing in the New Hampshire primary on an antiwar platform and Senator Robert Kennedy's entry into the race as an antiwar candidate revealed a party profoundly at odds with itself. The party's eventual nominee, Vice-President Hubert Humphrey, was selected at the Democratic convention in July amid bloody clashes between police and antiwar demonstrators, and bitter disagreements among convention delegates over the Vietnam plank of the platform. Humphrey confronted

9. Johnson, *The Vantage Point*, 513.

the same dilemma his opponent Richard Nixon had faced in 1960: how far to defend the administration of which he was a part, and how far to distance himself from it.

Basically, Humphrey did not agree with Johnson's policy on Vietnam, but he found it difficult to overcome his steadfast loyalty to the president. He and his staff had drafted a compromise platform on the war, proposing a complete bombing halt and an increased role for the South Vietnamese army, but when President Johnson objected that this undercut the administration's policy, Humphrey capitulated and adopted the Johnson plank.[10]

With Johnson's announcement that he would not seek reelection and the subsequent opening of peace talks between the Americans and the North Vietnamese, Republican candidate Nixon told reporters he would "observe a personal moratorium" on comments about the Vietnam War in order not to jeopardize the negotiations. This strategy of silence allowed Nixon to refrain from specific commitments about Vietnam—and thereby avoid alienating potential supporters—and focused attention on the divisions within the Democratic party. Thus Nixon conveyed the sense of agreeing with American policy in the broadest sense but disagreeing on tactics. The new Nixon administration would not be hemmed in by promises made on the campaign trail months earlier.

It took over a month after Johnson's speech for the North Vietnamese and the Americans to agree on a site for the peace talks and once begun, the Paris talks seemed little more than sterile propaganda exercises, as spokesmen for both sides repeated the same arguments. The United States insisted that North Vietnamese forces be withdrawn from South Vietnam; the North Vietnamese insisted that *all* American bombing of the North cease before any substantive issues would be discussed. During the summer the American negotiators, led by Cyrus Vance and Averell Harriman, maintained the position that a complete bombing halt would come only when the North had accepted three conditions: 1) entry into prompt and serious negotiations that included the South Vietnamese; 2) no North Vietnamese violation of the demilitarized zone separating

10. Stanley Karnow, *Vietnam: A History* (New York, 1983), 80.

North and South Vietnam; and 3) no large-scale North Vietnamese artillery attacks against South Vietnamese cities.[11] In mid-October the North Vietnamese negotiators suddenly softened their position and agreed to engage in serious talks with the United States and with South Vietnam. After two more weeks of further negotiation and clarification, Johnson, on October 31, announced a breakthrough at the talks, with the American election less than a week away. The North Vietnamese had agreed to allow South Vietnamese participation in prompt and serious negotiations, and the United States had agreed to cease bombing North Vietnam.

All of this diplomatic activity so close to the election set off alarm bells in the Nixon campaign and in Saigon. In the last analysis, neither the candidates, the president, nor the countries involved in the war could keep the American presidential campaign and diplomacy apart. The timing of the breakthrough suggested first that the North Vietnamese had the American election campaign very much in mind as they negotiated, though other factors could have contributed to their more conciliatory attitude. The Tet offensive, widely misreported at the time as an American defeat, had dealt a severe blow to the North Vietnamese; continuing American and South Vietnamese ground attacks and air strikes probably also weakened the North Vietnamese. They may also have been under pressure to be more forthcoming from their Soviet and Chinese allies. Nevertheless, the desire to influence the American election should not be discounted. Vice-President Humphrey, who had trailed badly in the polls as September drew to a close, on September 30 "cut the umbilical cord" that had bound him to the president by making a nationally televised speech in Salt Lake City in which he promised to cease all bombing of North Vietnam without conditions if he was elected. Widely interpreted as a repudiation of the administration's policy in Vietnam, the speech may have led the North Vietnamese to prefer Humphrey over Nixon as president. A preelection "breakthrough" by the administration of which Humphrey was part might contribute to a Humphrey victory.

Speculations about North Vietnamese motivations were seldom more than that, but the effects of the campaign and the negotiations

11. *Ibid.*, 513–14; Nixon, *RN*, 324–25.

on the South Vietnamese are easier to document. The South Vietnamese had resigned themselves to taking up a greater share of the
military burden once Washington signaled in early 1968 that there
would be no further escalation of American forces in Southeast
Asia. This increased their fear that the Paris talks might result in a
secret agreement between Washington and Hanoi for an early and
rapid withdrawal of American troops from an increasingly unpopular war. Both Nixon and Johnson have noted in their memoirs
that one consequence of Humphrey's September 30 speech was to
increase South Vietnamese anxieties on this point. Thus, when the
United States and North Vietnam announced a breakthrough in the
Paris talks on October 31, the South Vietnamese government balked
and on November 2 declined to join the talks. The effect of this decision was to puncture a good-sized hole in the peace balloon inflated
by Johnson's announcement two days earlier. It also may have cost
Humphrey the election, which was extremely close. Nixon speech
writer William Safire later noted, "When people later wondered
why Nixon thought so highly of President Thieu, they did not recall
that Nixon probably would not be President were it not for Thieu." [12]

Nixon and his supporters were also naturally suspicious of the
timing of the breakthrough announcement. Nixon was convinced
that, while Johnson did sincerely want to set peace talks in motion,
the president was not above using the war for partisan purposes.
From a secret source in Johnson's innermost circle, Nixon learned
that the political liaison between the White House and Humphrey
was very close, suggesting a connection between the campaign and
the breakthrough announcement. This confirmed Nixon's conviction
that whatever Johnson did "was weighed a second time on a strictly
political scale." [13] The announcement on October 31 had not come as
a total surprise, however, because the Nixon campaign had developed sources of information on Vietnam independent of the administration. Henry Kissinger, who had worked with both the Kennedy
and Johnson administrations and had served in 1967 as a secret

12. William Safire, *Before the Fall* (New York, 1975), 88; Nixon, *RN,* 328;
Johnson, *The Vantage Point,* 513–18, 548; John P. Roche, "Lecture," in Morton
Kaplan *et al., Vietnam Settlement: Why 1973, not 1969?* (Washington, D.C.,
1973), 151.
13. Nixon, *RN,* 327.

emissary from Johnson to the North Vietnamese through French intermediaries, contacted the Nixon team during the campaign and, according to Nixon's memoirs, provided three substantial messages about the Vietnam negotiations then in progress.[14] Another informant was Anna Chennault, a committed Republican with close ties to the China lobby who was on good terms with Ambassador Bui Diem, the South Vietnamese representative to the Paris talks.

President Johnson in turn had reason to believe that Nixon had the capacity to use the peace talks to his electoral advantage. In the midsummer of 1968 the CIA told Johnson of the efforts of Anna Chennault to establish a line of communication between the Nixon campaign and the Saigon government. Nixon turned down Chennault's suggestion, and there is no evidence that Nixon himself used such channels to urge the South Vietnamese to hold out because he would give them a better deal. Nevertheless, Chennault remained active and in contact with the Nixon campaign. On November 1 the FBI's tap on the South Vietnamese embassy picked up a phone call from Madame Chennault to Saigon urging South Vietnamese officials to hold firm because they would get more favorable terms with Nixon. As Johnson noted later, the effort by people "who claimed to speak for the Nixon camp" encouraging Saigon to stay away from Paris paid off.[15]

The best summary of the entire episode is that offered by Safire: "Should Democrats be proud of the manipulation of foreign policy for political ends against a political deadline and should Republicans be proud of letting supporters, once removed from the campaign itself, seek to frustrate those manipulations? No. It was not one of American politics' finest hours."[16] Nixon himself seemed to quash the hopes of the South Vietnamese for a harder line toward North Vietnam when he stated after his meeting with President Johnson on November 11 that on Vietnam (as on the Middle East

14. *Ibid.*, 323; Karnow, *Vietnam,* 585. Kissinger does not mention any of this in his memoirs, though he discusses his previous Vietnam involvement under President Johnson in *White House Years,* 230–35.

15. Thomas Powers, *The Man Who Kept Secrets: Richard Helms and the CIA* (New York, 1979), 197–200; Safire, *Before the Fall,* 88–91; Johnson, *The Vantage Point,* 548.

16. Safire, *Before the Fall,* 91.

and the Soviet Union) the Johnson administration could speak for the incoming administration as well.

On November 26 the South Vietnamese agreed to join the Americans in Paris, perhaps because of Nixon's statement, which suggested that they had little to gain by holding out further. The talks quickly bogged down over the shape of the negotiating table, reflecting a dispute on the standing and designation of the parties who were to sit around it. The North Vietnamese proposed a four-sided conference table, one side apiece for the North Vietnamese, the United States, the South Vietnamese, and the Viet Cong. Saigon argued that this granted de facto recognition to the Viet Cong and in effect meant that the parties to the talks accepted Hanoi's interpretation of the war as a civil war. The South Vietnamese preferred instead an arrangement of the conference table that made clear that the war was a two-sided war.

In mid-January, the Soviet Union agreed to a compromise on behalf of North Vietnam. The agreement that emerged was for a circular table without nameplates, flags, or markings—an arrangement that would allow the communists to speak of four sides and the Americans and South Vietnamese to speak of two. The parties also agreed to rotate the speaking order of the four delegations for each meeting. Urged on by the administration, Nixon privately signaled and then publicly stated his support for this compromise proposal, which broke the procedural deadlock four days before the inauguration. This enabled the Paris negotiations to get started and allowed outgoing Johnson administration officials to celebrate a success as they left office. Another indication of Nixon's interest was his appointment of Henry Cabot Lodge to replace Averell Harriman as ambassador to the Paris talks the day after the inauguration. At Nixon's request Vance remained on the delegation for another month. Later Kissinger would come to regard Nixon's agreement to the proposal for a circular table as a tactical error because it allowed the North Vietnamese to make the war seem like Nixon's war sooner.[17]

During the interregnum Nixon and Kissinger also began to develop their own approach to Vietnam. They reviewed the options

17. Kissinger, *White House Years*, 52–53; Henry, "Presidential Transitions," 476; Johnson, *The Vantage Point*, 552; New York *Times*, January 17, 1969, p. 1.

available to them; without informing Johnson, Harriman, or Vance, they initiated contact with the North Vietnamese to indicate their negotiating position (which was similar to that of the Johnson administration); and they articulated a theory of linkage that made progress in other areas of Soviet-American relations contingent on progress in Vietnam. The difference this transition made manifested itself quite early in the new administration: by March, 1969, Nixon had ordered the secret bombing of North Vietnamese sanctuaries in Cambodia, had informed the Soviets that progress in areas of interest to them would depend on progress in Vietnam, and had begun sending hints of his desire to make contact with the government of Communist China.[18] Despite these tactical shifts, the war dragged on, and the Paris talks produced no formulas acceptable to the parties involved. It was only in 1972, another presidential election year, that serious negotiations began. Nixon's large lead over George McGovern in that campaign meant that neither North nor South Vietnam had the leverage to affect the election results.

## Arms Limitation Talks

The Kennedy administration had come into office in 1961 loudly proclaiming the existence of a missile gap, but it soon discovered that the United States remained far ahead of the Soviet Union in nuclear weaponry. By the mid-1960s Moscow had moved rapidly toward invulnerable second-strike forces along the American model: missile silos were being hardened and a buildup of offensive missiles was under way. More disturbing to American military planners was the evidence that the Soviets were installing an antiballistic missile (ABM) system around Moscow. Consequently President Johnson in 1967 and 1968 found himself under increasing pressure from Congress and the Defense Department to authorize development and deployment of an American ABM system (to protect American mis-

18. Karnow, *Vietnam,* 591–93; Kissinger, *White House Years,* 125–30, 165–71, 237–67 *passim;* Nixon, *RN,* 343–50, 380–82; Carl Brauer, "The Pursuit or Alteration of Inherited Policy: Three Cases," in Frederick C. Mosher (ed.), *Papers on Presidential Transitions and Foreign Policy: Some Views from the Campus* (Lanham, Md., forthcoming). Some of the options forwarded to Kissinger by outgoing Johnson officials were disclosed in the New York *Times,* January 12, 1969, p. 1.

siles and/or cities) and of multiple independently targetable reentry vehicle (MIRV) technology (to overwhelm Soviet defenses with greater numbers of missiles). Both Secretary of Defense McNamara and Secretary of State Rusk thought the time had arrived when both the Soviet Union and the United States might agree to limit offensive and defensive nuclear defensive systems and thereby forestall spending a great deal of money on systems that they doubted would materially enhance the security of either side.[19]

The negotiations to limit the spread of nuclear weapons, begun in 1964 and concluded in the summer of 1968, suggested that an agreement to limit nuclear arms might be possible. Indeed the smaller non-nuclear nations made it a condition of their signing the nonproliferation treaty that the superpowers would engage in discussions on the problem of offensive and defensive nuclear weaponry. Although the Soviets had rebuffed Johnson when he had entreated Soviet Premier Alexei Kosygin to consider strategic arms limitation at their meeting in Glassboro, New Jersey, in 1967, they signaled their willingness to engage in such negotiations in May and June of 1968, once they knew the nonproliferation treaty would be signed. The reason for the shift in Soviet policy may never be known for sure. But with the United States on the verge of developing sophisticated new weapons systems—the ABM and the MIRV—the Soviets may have wanted to freeze the Americans where they were. The Soviets may also have calculated that by engaging in negotiations with a willing Johnson administration, they could exact commitments that would bind the next administration.[20]

In any case, when the United States and the Soviet Union signed the nuclear nonproliferation treaty in the summer of 1968, they also agreed privately to discuss holding a summit conference later in the year to begin talks on limiting strategic nuclear weapons. On July 1 both sides announced their agreement in principle to hold such a conference. On August 21 they were to announce that a summit conference of Johnson and Kosygin would be held in Leningrad on September 30.

19. John Newhouse, *Cold Dawn: The Story of SALT* (New York, 1973), 67–102; Johnson, *The Vantage Point*, 479–80; Thomas Wolfe, *The SALT Experience* (Cambridge, Mass., 1979), 1–5.
20. Newhouse, *Cold Dawn*, 107–108.

This gave the administration only a short time to work out a negotiating position. Led by officials in the Defense Department, it agreed on a preliminary set of proposals by late August. The proposals essentially called for a limitation of ABM systems together with a freeze on ICBM (intercontinental ballistic missile) and SLBM (submarine launched ballistic missile) deployments and no freedom to mix these latter two categories of weapons.

These preparations would later strike the incoming Nixon administration as hurried and somewhat illogical, since there seemed to be little direct presidential involvement. The apparently haphazard quality of the process would be one reason why the Nixon administration would approach SALT so cautiously. When its review of the Johnson administration's SALT proposals was complete, however, the Nixon program was said to be not very different from Johnson's.[21]

The day before the summit was to be announced, the Soviets invaded Czechoslovakia to put down a government drifting too far from socialist orthodoxy. The United States felt it had no choice but to cancel the joint announcement, and when President Johnson telephoned the candidates to inform them of his decision, each candidate assured Johnson of his support.

In spite of the invasion, Johnson and the Soviets continued to hope that the summit and the launching of negotiations could take place before Johnson left office. Each tacitly understood that talks would have to wait until the shock of the Czech invasion had begun to subside and until the results of the presidential election campaign were known. On November 14, a week after the election, Soviet Ambassador Anatoly Dobrynin told Presidential National Security Assistant Walt Rostow that his government felt it important to create a positive atmosphere for Senate ratification of the nonproliferation treaty and wished not to lose momentum in the missile talks. President Johnson could set Soviet-American relations on a stable course for the next administration if the talks were opened before he left office. When Johnson realized that Moscow really did want to go

21. *Ibid.*, 113–32, describes the Johnson SALT preparations in depth. See also Alton Frye, "U.S. Decision Making for SALT," in Mason Willrich and John B. Rhinelander, (eds.), *SALT: The Moscow Agreements and Beyond* (New York, 1974), 70–83, and Chalmers Roberts, *The Nuclear Years* (New York, 1970), 99.

ahead with the summit and the talks, he first sought support from Senator J. W. Fulbright, chairman of the Foreign Relations Committee. Fulbright commented that Johnson's plan was "not an orthodox action for a man leaving office," but wished Johnson success in his effort.[22]

Johnson then turned to the more difficult task of persuading President-elect Nixon to support the proposed summit. Emissaries from the White House and from the Soviet Embassy as well contacted Nixon's transition foreign policy group, which was being managed by Kissinger, to solicit support for the idea.

To make the idea more attractive—and in acknowledgement of the transition—Johnson suggested that Nixon himself accompany him to Leningrad to attend the summit; or if not Nixon, anyone he chose to select as an observer would also be welcome. Johnson explained that the Americans and the Soviets had devised a three-part scenario for the talks. First, there would be an exchange of technical papers setting forth each side's general positions; second, Johnson and the Soviet leaders would meet at the summit, now planned for late December, to try to reach agreement on the broad principles to guide the negotiators; and third, based on the agreed-upon broad principles, there would be a continuation of the technical negotiations, which would be under the full control of the new president.

Nixon and Kissinger resisted Johnson's overtures. Although sympathetic with the president's eagerness to make a breakthrough for peace, Nixon and Kissinger nevertheless had no desire to be bound by commitments Johnson might make. They thought the proposed summit came too soon after the Czech invasion, they saw little evidence that the Soviets were prepared to negotiate seriously, and they wanted the opportunity to take stock and pursue their own policies once in office. A Soviet emissary was told in late November that Nixon did not want a preinauguration summit and that if one were held, Nixon "would have to state publicly that [he] would not be bound by it."

On hearing this, the Soviets quickly lost interest in the summit, even though Johnson administration officials continued to urge that arms limitation talks should begin as soon as possible. As late as

22. Newhouse, *Cold Dawn*, 136; Kissinger, *White House Years*, 49.

December 15, Defense Secretary Clark Clifford, on the weekly television news program "Face the Nation," was strongly urging an early American-Soviet meeting to launch strategic arms negotiations. The Nixon team evidently did not inform the Johnson administration about what they had told the Soviets, though Johnson could easily guess what had happened.[23]

Another casualty of the Czech invasion and the transition was early Senate ratification of the nonproliferation treaty. Despite the invasion, Johnson was anxious to proceed with ratification and even considered calling a special session to act on the treaty, but many of the senators with whom Johnson spoke considered the move ill advised. Nixon let it be known that he would prefer the Senate to wait. It did. Nixon submitted the treaty to the Senate in early February, and the Senate finally approved it in March, 1969, allowing the new administration to share credit for its enactment.[24] In effect, the president-elect had vetoed Johnson's plans, demonstrating the comparative impotence of the lame-duck president.

More successful was the effort on the part of the incoming administration to equip itself for dealing with the Soviets. As noted earlier, the new administration retained the services of many who had considerable government and foreign policy experience. Kissinger drew heavily on personnel from the State Department, the Defense Department, and the CIA in building the national security adviser's staff. Since these individuals had served in the Johnson administration, they provided a substantial amount of continuity as well as expertise. Morton Halperin, for example, had spearheaded the internal policy process for SALT for the Johnson administration in the summer of 1968. Both Secretary of State Rogers and Secretary of Defense Laird retained a rather remarkable number of Johnson officials, and when the American SALT delegation was announced in the fall of 1969, its principal members—Gerard Smith (the delegation head), Paul Nitze, Royal Allison, Harold Brown, and Raymond Garthoff—each had served at high levels of the Johnson administra-

23. Johnson, *The Vantage Point,* 489–90; Nixon, *RN,* 346; Kissinger, *White House Years,* 49–50.
24. Johnson, *The Vantage Point,* 490.

tion and, with the exception of Smith, had been involved in the Johnson SALT policy process.[25]

Second, the new foreign policy machinery constructed during the transition allowed the new administration to use the foreign affairs bureaucracy to take stock of the American position in the world and explore various options available to the country in light of that position. This review had already begun during the interregnum when Nixon and Kissinger worked out the concept of linking progress on SALT with progress in various other problem areas, especially Vietnam and the Middle East. They knew that the Soviets were eager for arms talks to begin and wanted some movement on the questions of Berlin and the German border. To get these sets of negotiations going, the Soviets would have to help the United States in those areas of special concern to Americans. Nixon, who during the campaign suggested that he would "restore our objective of clear-cut military superiority in the aggregate," indicated at his first presidential press conference that the aim of his administration would be for "sufficiency" rather than "superiority." He also said that he was willing to proceed with strategic arms limitation but "in a way and at a time that will promote, if possible, progress on outstanding political problems at the same time."[26]

The Soviets' desire to get SALT under way as soon as possible was shared by many leading Democratic politicians, editorial writers, and officials in the State Department and the Arms Control and Disarmament Agency. Nixon and Kissinger, however, were in no hurry to get on with SALT. They mistrusted Soviet motives, discounted the urgings of State Department officials as reflective of a bias toward negotiation, and questioned the thoroughness of the Johnson SALT proposal preparations. First, they felt, much more needed to be known, and they used the new White House–centered national security policy system to send out a blizzard of questions to get the bureaucracy's attention and to provide better answers and more options.

25. Newhouse, *Cold Dawn*, 110–19; Gerard Smith, *Doubletalk: The Story of the First Strategic Arms Limitation Talks* (Garden City, N.Y., 1980), 37–72.

26. Kissinger, *White House Years*, 129–38; Nixon, *RN*, 346–47, 415.

Within ten days of taking office the Nixon team had issued a dozen National Security Study Memoranda (NSSM), and by April 30 the number was up to fifty-five. Several concerned SALT. The administration's study and review of various arms limitation options was not complete until mid-June, 1969, though as various observers noted, the Nixon negotiating position for SALT was not very different from the Johnson position. Thus, it could be argued, as Johnson had contended in pressing for a summit, that a year had gone by with no arms control negotiations nor anything else to show for the time lost. Indeed, what did occur during that year was the American deployment of MIRVed ICBMs, which would bedevil later arms control talks.[27]

In essence, MIRVs would make verification much more difficult, since no satellite camera could detect how many warheads a particular missile carried. This problem confronted American defense planners much sooner than they expected, because they significantly underestimated the speed with which the Soviets would develop and deploy their own MIRVed missiles. If any agreement not to deploy such missiles could have been negotiated, it would have had to come before significant testing had occurred. The first American test took place in August, 1968, making 1968–1969 the best time to negotiate a MIRV ban. According to journalist Chalmers Roberts, "Had the superpowers met in the fall of 1968, at the time MIRV tests for Poseidon and Minuteman III missiles were about to get under way, they might have been able to agree on a mutual freeze and thus have prevented escalation of the nuclear arms race."[28] The transition itself, of course, was one reason why the summit did not take place, though it is impossible to say what might have happened had 1968 not been an election year. Perhaps if the election had come out differently, President Humphrey would not have felt it necessary to undertake the review that President Nixon undertook. Certainly the Czech invasion and possible Soviet hesitations to limit MIRV development might have played important parts in preventing agreement.

27. Newhouse, *Cold Dawn*, 140–43; Frye, "U.S. Decision Making for SALT," 77–83; Kissinger, *White House Years*, 147–49.

28. Roberts, *The Nuclear Years*, 106–107; Wolfe, *The SALT Experience*, 8; Smith, *Doubletalk*, 15–19.

The transition did cost time, but it gave the incoming administration the chance to equip itself with the information and the organization necessary to the conduct of serious negotiations. The goal of an incoming administration often is to "hit the ground running," but there is danger in acting without sufficient preparation or information. By moving deliberately, the new administration gained arms control proposals in which it had confidence in exchange for the time that had been lost.

The Johnson-Nixon transition, then, displayed some of the typical features of transition, revealing the ambiguous relationship of president and president-elect. It also provided some instructive departures from the norm in the efforts of the incumbent to hold on to his authority, in his efforts to pursue negotiations, and in the overall smoothness of the transfer.

# CHAPTER 10

# From Ford to Carter

Every new Administration feels it has a mandate for new foreign policy. . . . To be sure, the new men soon discover that the problems they face are more intractable and lasting than they had expected—and the virtues of continuity come to be appreciated more than the merits of innovation. Proud claims of originality quietly give way to statesmanlike appeals for bipartisanship on behalf of the enduring national interest.

—Zbigniew Brzezinski

The transition of 1976–1977, the fourth such interparty transfer of power of the postwar period, exhibited points of both continuity and contrast with the transitions that had preceded it. It differed from the earlier turnovers of authority in at least three ways: First, it took place after the breakdown of the containment consensus that had undergirded earlier transitions. Second, foreign policy issues played a smaller role in the 1976 general election campaign than in any other contest since the Second World War. As in 1948, when Truman defeated Wallace for the Democratic nomination, and 1952, when Eisenhower defeated Taft for the Republican nomination, the key debates and decisions about foreign policy were made during the nomination process within each party. Third, unlike the three previous occasions, in this transition the incumbent president was a candidate in the election and lost. On the other hand, the measures of institutionalization that had accumulated in prior years were, in the main, preserved, and some new measures were added.

Between 1968 and 1976 the war in Vietnam shattered the anticommunist consensus of the Cold War. Unlike Hubert Humphrey in 1968, George McGovern had run in 1972 calling for a fundamental reordering of the country's diplomatic objectives and a shift in the emphasis given to foreign versus domestic goals. Jimmy Carter's success four years later was partly due to his ability to bridge (and blur) the differences between the Humphrey and McGovern camps within the Democratic party, but his election did not mean that consensus had been reestablished. It had in fact been further fractured by the recriminations arising from the collapse of South Vietnam in 1975, by the souring of détente (which began as early as 1973), and by the rising concern over human-rights abuses during the mid-1970s. New issues, such as the demonstrated power of OPEC, divided Americans in new ways. Without the supporting structure that had been provided for over twenty years by the containment consensus, the foreign policy debate in the campaign was often unfocused, and the possibility arose of sharp changes in direction with the arrival of a new administration.

During the campaign Carter talked of introducing moral principles into the country's diplomacy and made a strong plea for a more urgent push by Washington for the control and eventual abolition of nuclear weapons. His pledges on both questions were ambitious though ambiguous, as was his discussion of them in his inaugural address. Carter's willingness to advocate fresh approaches sometimes brought him criticism, as it did when he refused to follow the example of every postwar president in pledging to assist Yugoslavia if that country were invaded by the Soviet Union.

Carter's opponent, President Gerald Ford, when he spoke of foreign policy, argued that the experience he had gained in the White House and as minority leader of the House of Representatives made him far better qualified than Carter to direct the nation's foreign affairs. Ford defended American policy toward the Soviet Union, though he dropped the use of the word *détente,* and he claimed that the United States had a good record in doing all that reasonably could be done to promote the worldwide observance of human rights. At the same time, he attacked as naïve Carter's proposal to reduce defense spending. Ford's greatest handicap in the campaign was the suspicion that he was not equal to the demands of the presidency, an impression that was strengthened when, in one of the two campaign debates that year, he denied that Poland, or the rest of Eastern Europe, was dominated by Moscow. The ensuing controversy over the president's understanding of the Soviet Union's control over the region was also practically the only occasion in the entire campaign in which attention centered on foreign policy.

Although the race tightened considerably in its final days, Ford became the first incumbent president defeated for election since 1932 and only the third of the twentieth century. In 1952–1953, 1960–1961, and 1968–1969 the outgoing president had not been a candidate for reelection. Truman, Eisenhower, and Johnson all sought to aid their parties' standard-bearers and were no doubt disappointed when the election was won by the other party. Still, none had to feel that the outcome had been a personal repudiation of him and his administration. Each might have believed (Eisenhower with more reason) that if only he had headed the ticket, victory might have been achieved. The successor of each, meanwhile, could view him as something of an elder statesman, not a recent electoral opponent. The psychological climate between the two sides in these transitions was therefore reasonably friendly.

Ford's partisans, on the other hand, felt all the frustrations attendant upon a campaign effort that was almost, but not quite, successful. Carter's supporters were tempted by the usual disdain for the advice of a defeated opponent and by overconfidence in their own prescriptions. Both smarted from the partisan attacks of the campaign. These resentments hampered the development of trust between the two camps and impeded communications in some, though certainly not all, areas. Cooperation in matters such as the budget, which had marked some earlier transitions, was not present to the same degree now; Carter staffers claimed they were frozen out of OMB. Secretary of State Cyrus Vance, however, would later praise his outgoing counterpart, Henry Kissinger, for the cooperative spirit that governed the transition in the State Department. Kissinger provided Vance office space, ready access to information, regular discussions on a variety of foreign policy problems, and the opportunity to have some policy decisions postponed for the new administration to consider. In at least two instances—policy toward Rhodesia and a review of the Subic Bay agreement with the Philippines—Vance requested and received such a postponement.

It was fortunate that no crisis demanding an immediate decision arose during the interregnum. There was no counterpart to the Korean POW dispute of 1952, the breakoff of relations with Cuba in 1961, or the opening of the Vietnamese peace negotiations in 1968–1969. This year the world was more quiescent as it waited for the arrival of the new president. The outgoing administration continued its talks on the terms of an IMF loan to Great Britain designed to tide that country over its balance-of-payments problems, and an agreement was finally achieved before Inauguration Day. Ford did take one initiative with foreign policy implications by proposing statehood for Puerto Rico. But the time at which the step was announced was so late—December 31, 1976—and the setting so incongruous—the bottom of a Vail, Colorado, ski slope that Ford had just successfully negotiated—that Congress did not take it seriously, and the proposal was allowed to lapse. In general, attention remained fixed on the intentions of the incoming administration.

To help it transform its plans into reality, the Carter staff assembled the largest transition organization ever seen to that time. It began with Carter's directive to commence preparations, issued once he was sure he would win the nomination after his victory in the Pennsylvania primary in the late spring. This planning was formalized after the convention with the establishment of the Carter-Mondale Policy Group, under the direction of Jack Watson. Although organizationally and physically separated from the campaign organization, the Watson staff operated on $150,000 diverted from the federal funds allocated to the Carter campaign. After the election, using money supplied under the Transition Act, it grew to over three hundred employees (divided into task forces corresponding to federal departments and agencies) and spent $1.7 million.

There was one other significant new measure of institutionalization. In January of 1977, the Civil Service Commission issued a directive allowing the new administration that year, and each new administration thereafter, temporarily to double the number of positions politically exempted from the regular civil service. This innovation, which the commission stated was intended to encourage orderly transitions, gave fresh administrations more freedom to reassign personnel in accordance with their ideas on reorganization and policy change.[1]

With these tools, the 1976–1977 transition might have been expected to be a relatively smooth transfer of power. To be sure, there

1. Bruce Adams and Kathryn Kavanaugh-Baran, *Promise and Performance: Carter Builds a New Administration* (Toronto, 1979), chs. 2 and 3; John Osborne, *White House Watch: The Ford Years* (Washington, D.C., 1977), 440–50.

were many instances of bipartisan cooperation, and both administrations avoided some pitfalls that had trapped participants in earlier transitions. Inevitably, however, several problems emerged.

The election rivalry between Ford and Carter, of course, hurt chances for collaboration during and after the campaign. In addition, the structure of the Carter preelection transition organization—a separate group operating parallel to the campaign staff—reduced communications between the two and encouraged later hostility between them. Once the election had been won, the campaign team, headed by Hamilton Jordan, became suspicious of the Watson transition group and fearful that campaign staffers would be excluded from appointments in the new administration. A struggle between Jordan and Watson for the ear of the president-elect ensued, and with Jordan's victory much of the Watson organization's transition planning was discarded.

The new administration's difficulties extended beyond its own ranks to Capitol Hill. Although Carter came into office with large Democratic majorities in both houses, many of his fellow partisans were far less convinced of the need for fiscal restraint than he. He also faced a Congress that contained most of the men he had defeated for the Democratic presidential nomination the year before, many of them in positions of prominence. Therefore, the new Congress gave the new president only the briefest honeymoon. When the young administration took actions that offended congressional sensibilities—confronting the legislators with an overly ambitious list of requests, for example, and canceling cherished though uneconomical water projects—there was little inclination among members to overlook mistakes and give Carter the benefit of the doubt. In foreign policy the new administration unintentionally left an impression of well-meaning overeagerness and inexperience in at least two important areas—arms control and human rights.

## Arms Control

The Ford administration could take credit for having made some progress in arms control, but its goal of signing a SALT II treaty proved elusive. In November, 1974, President Ford and Soviet General Secretary Leonid Brezhnev reached an agreement in the Soviet city of Vladivostok to limit each side to 2,400 strategic launchers (ICBMs, SLBMs, and bombers), of which no more than 1,320 could be equipped with MIRVs. Within this framework the SALT II negotiations were launched, and both sides expressed optimism that a formal treaty could be signed within a year.

Two different but related sets of issues soon emerged to test those hopes and prolong the negotiations. First, both sides had developed new kinds of weapons, and each wanted the other's to be included in and limited by the new treaty. Defense planners in the Pentagon argued that the new Soviet Backfire bomber had sufficient range to reach the United States and so should be counted as a strategic launcher within the overall ceiling. The Soviets rejected this view and countered with the demand that the new American cruise missiles should be banned if they had a range of over 350 miles. Because the two kinds of weapons were not comparable, negotiators found it very difficult to find acceptable compromises.

Second, the Ford administration found its policy of détente under increasing attack from domestic critics. The erosion of executive authority due to Vietnam and Watergate dovetailed with increased congressional activity that limited the president's freedom of action in foreign affairs. Abroad, Soviet complicity in the intervention of twelve thousand Cuban troops in Angola fueled a new debate about American-Soviet relations, the value of détente, and the reliability of the Soviet Union as a negotiating partner.

In January, 1976, fourteen months after the Vladivostok accords, Secretary of State Kissinger made what turned out to be a last-ditch effort to conclude a treaty when he traveled to Moscow at Brezhnev's invitation to consider some new approaches. While an agreement in principle was not reached, Kissinger returned hopeful that a compromise was within sight in which the United States would limit the range and number of some of its cruise missiles, provided that the Soviet Union would reciprocate with the Backfire bomber in a similar manner.[2]

The political campaign, however, had already begun to intrude

2. Henry Kissinger, "The Strategic Arms Limitation Treaty," in Kissinger, *For the Record* (Boston, 1981), 207–208; Cyrus Vance, *Hard Choices: Critical Years in America's Foreign Policy* (New York, 1983), 47; New York *Times*, January 25, 1976, Sec. 4, p. 4, January 26, 1976, Sec. 1, p. 15.

on the negotiations. Kissinger's salvage mission came too late, as SALT, détente, and Kissinger himself were already under attack from candidates in both parties. Faced with a stiff challenge from Governor Ronald Reagan for the Republican nomination and with opposition within his own administration, President Ford chose not to accept the proposed compromises. Instead the White House suggested to the Soviets in mid-February that the controversial issues be put aside and a treaty be signed containing only those points that had been agreed upon. The Soviets rejected this alternative, since they wanted cruise missiles dealt with; neither side produced new proposals, though the SALT delegations in Geneva continued to meet. Thus, the requirements of electoral politics effectively put the SALT negotiations on hold until after the election or, in the event of a Ford loss, after Inauguration Day. Ford himself later second-guessed his decision to defer SALT, by recalling Nixon's landslide victory in 1972, to which the SALT I agreement probably contributed. A SALT II agreement with the Soviets consummated in the summer of 1976 might easily have tipped the scales for Ford in November. Arms control might have helped against Carter, but, unfortunately for Ford, he had to face Reagan first.[3]

Carter criticized the Ford administration several times during the election campaign for not pursuing SALT negotiations vigorously enough, making it clear that arms control was high on his own agenda. During the campaign Carter received CIA briefings, convened a set of meetings with Democratic foreign policy experts (including Dean Rusk, Paul Warnke, Paul Nitze, Cyrus Vance, Harold Brown, and Zbigniew Brzezinski), and solicited general foreign policy memoranda from Vance, Brzezinski, and George Ball. These familiarized the candidate with the basic issues at stake in the negotiations. As a signal of his intentions Carter authorized Averell Harriman, who traveled to Moscow in September, to inform Brezhnev that if Carter were elected, he would move quickly to sign a SALT II agreement based on the Vladivostok accord and incorporating a compromise on the Backfire and cruise-missile issues that Kissinger had been unable to resolve.[4]

3. Ford, *A Time to Heal*, 357–58, 437.
4. Strobe Talbott, *Endgame: The Inside Story of SALT II* (New York, 1979), 39–40; Vance, *Hard Choices*, 30; New York *Times*, July 27, 1976, Sec. 1, p. 17.

Carter's statements and personnel decisions after the election seemed consistent with that message. At an early postelection news conference the president-elect said that he hoped the departing administration was continuing to push for a SALT agreement (though he almost certainly knew it would not and probably could not) and that he was committed to freezing the number of missiles, warheads, and overall throw weights at current levels and then lowering those levels step by step. In subsequent press conferences he emphasized his intention to engage the Soviets in a two-step process in arms control negotiations: first, "fairly rapid" ratification of a SALT II agreement and, then, moving to a substantial reduction in nuclear weapons on both sides.

Quick completion of a SALT II treaty was also implied in the decision to retain the services of several of Ford's top officers. They included William Hyland, deputy director of the National Security Council staff, Roger Molander, another Ford administration expert on SALT, and David Aaron, a former official of both the Kissinger NSC staff and the Arms Control and Disarmament Agency. Two members of the Ford administration's SALT II delegation in Geneva, Ralph Earle and Edward Rowny, remained as members of the Carter administration's delegation, and Harold Brown and James Schlesinger, who had been participants in the SALT negotiations during the Nixon and Ford years, were named to the cabinet. Continuity in personnel usually suggests continuity in policy, and each of these men presumably had a stake in concluding the SALT II negotiations.

While these and other personnel decisions were being made, the Carter postelection transition teams in the various departments were preparing their reports on the tasks and outstanding issues in each department, all designed to get the new administration quickly "up to speed." SALT naturally figured heavily in the Pentagon, NSC, and State Department studies. The Ford administration, meanwhile, arranged with the Soviets a recess of the Geneva negotiations until after the new president had assumed office.[5]

The Soviets, for their part, undoubtedly observed the transition

5. New York *Times*, November 16, 1976, Sec. 1, pp. 32–33, November 20, 1976, Sec. 1, p. 8; Talbott, *Endgame*, 40–50; Zbigniew Brzezinski, *Power and Principle: Memoirs of the National Security Adviser, 1977–1981* (New York, 1983), 74–78.

with curiosity, interest, and concern. Brezhnev stressed the importance of completing the stalled talks, contending that the Ford administration had delayed an accord because of election-year politics. Brezhnev also reportedly conveyed a message to Carter through Secretary of the Treasury William Simon, who had been in Moscow. In it he promised no crises during the transition, so that there could be an early resumption of the talks.[6]

A current of dissatisfaction with the SALT status quo nevertheless lay beneath the surface indications of continuity. This came to play a decisive role in the arms control proposals the new administration would offer the Soviets within two months of taking office. Key figures within the Democratic party, including Jimmy Carter himself, believed that the Vladivostok accords and the Ford-Kissinger SALT II framework hardly deserved the label *arms control,* since neither involved real reductions in nuclear weapons. Vice-presidential nominee Walter Mondale said, "It looks like both sides took their weapons programs, stapled them together, and called the result a breakthrough." Zbigniew Brzezinski, in a memo to candidate Carter in February, 1976, argued that the present SALT ceilings were too high and should be lowered. Senator Henry Jackson, whose support of any arms agreement would be essential, had criticized the Kissinger proposals for leaving Soviet "heavy missiles" untouched. As a candidate and then as president-elect, Carter had emphasized his commitment to a substantial reduction in dependence upon nuclear weapons as an instrument in international relations, a point he reiterated in his inaugural address when he spoke of eliminating all nuclear weapons from the earth.[7]

Nuclear arms reductions were something both the dovish and hawkish wings of the Democratic party could agree on, though for quite different reasons. Doves wanted to see the arms race slowed on both sides; hawks wanted to see a reduction in Soviet ICBMs, which they believed were increasingly threatening American land-based ICBMs. In either case the possibility of "leapfrogging" the Vladivos-

6. New York *Times,* December 5, 1976, Sec. 1, p. 1, December 4, 1976, Sec. 1, p. 12, January 19, 1977, Sec. 1, p. 4.

7. Peter Ognibene, "SALT II and Beyond," *New Republic,* February 5, 1977, p. 17; Brzezinski, *Power and Principle,* 149–50; Talbott, *Endgame,* 48–53; Jimmy Carter, *Keeping Faith: Memoirs of a President* (New York, 1982), 212–17.

tok accords to consider negotiating actual reductions in nuclear arsenals seemed one well worth exploring. During the interregnum and
early months of the Carter presidency, then, officials developed two
sets of options for pursuing arms control.

The first set of options the new administration devised were variations of the Vladivostok accords. Under that rubric it could accept
Soviet claims that the Backfire was not a strategic weapon, it could
seek a trade-off between the Backfire and the cruise missile, or it
could suggest to the Soviets, as the Ford administration had done in
February, 1976, that the Backfire and cruise-missile issues be de-
ferred and a treaty signed based on what had already been settled.
Of the Vladivostok-based options, this latter, "deferral" option had
the most support within the administration, though the Soviets had
rejected it once already.

The second set of options entailed making specific proposals em-
bodying deep cuts in the nuclear arsenals of both sides and establishing limits on the qualitative improvement of strategic weapons. The
ceiling on strategic launchers would be lowered from 2,400 to a
level between 1,800 and 2,000; the ceiling on MIRV launchers
would be lowered from 1,320 to between 1,100 and 1,200; an entirely new subceiling would be added for MIRVed ICBMs; flight testing of existing ICBMs would be limited; and development, testing,
and deployment of mobile ICBMs or any new ICBMs would be
banned. The "comprehensive proposal," as the package came to be
called, did not count the Backfire as a strategic launcher, and it limited the cruise missile only to a range of 1,550 miles.

Those in the administration who favored a Vladivostok-based option, led by Secretary of State Vance and chief SALT negotiator
Paul Warnke, argued that it offered the best prospect for a rapid conclusion of the SALT II negotiations and would provide a more stable
foundation for Soviet-American relations. Consecrating the Vladivostok accord would establish continuity between American administrations and enhance Soviet confidence in arms control negotiations. Those who favored deep cuts, including Vice-President
Mondale and Secretary of Defense Harold Brown, stressed the importance of achieving arms reductions and not mere limitations;
having criticized the previous administration for not pursuing arms
control strenuously enough, they wanted to take a bold step that

would distinguish them from their predecessors. Part of the difference between the two was over tactics, since both agreed that at some point an effort to negotiate deep cuts would have to be made. Vance, who was scheduled to take the proposals to Moscow in late March, had doubts that the comprehensive approach could succeed without extremely difficult negotiations involving substantial compromise on both sides. This would open the administration to charges of giving in to the Soviets, which might make treaty ratification more difficult. One indication of the potential problems the comprehensive approach would encounter came in a letter Carter received from Brezhnev in late February that amounted to a negative, even "chilling," response to arms control proposals Carter had included in a letter sent to the Kremlin several weeks earlier.[8]

After substantial debate, President Carter in mid-March decided that, despite the political and negotiating risks, he wanted to go beyond Vladivostok and seek deep cuts in nuclear arsenals. Vance disagreed, but once the decision was made, he devoted himself to its success. Nevertheless, he persuaded the president to include a fallback proposal in case the Soviets rejected the entire concept of the comprehensive one. At a news conference shortly before Vance's departure, President Carter announced that the secretary of state would be seeking Soviet agreement for substantial reductions in the number of strategic missiles and bombers each side would be allowed. He also revealed that the United States had a fallback proposal based on Vladivostok if reductions could not be achieved.

The Soviets were anything but receptive and turned down both proposals immediately without offering any new counterproposals themselves. Soviet Foreign Minister Andrei Gromyko, in a news conference of his own, pointedly remarked, "One cannot talk about stability when a new leadership arrives and crosses out all that has been achieved before."[9] The bold proposal for deep cuts and the way it was handled came quickly to be seen as a diplomatic blunder for the fledgling administration.

In spite of the March blowup, neither side wanted to see strategic arms negotiations untracked, and they agreed to schedule a meeting

8. Vance, *Hard Choices,* 48–52; Talbott, *Endgame,* 46–62; Brzezinski, *Power and Principle,* 154–60; Carter, *Keeping Faith,* 218–19.
9. New York *Times,* April 7, 1977, Sec. 1, p. 11.

between Vance and Gromyko in Geneva in May. By then the administration had repackaged its arms proposals to make them appear more like the Vladivostok accords and the compromise envisioned by Kissinger in January, 1976, though they retained key ideas from the comprehensive proposal. The Soviets found this version more acceptable, and it became the basis of the negotiations. Two more years were spent refining the agreement, but by the time the SALT II treaty was submitted to the Senate in 1979, prospects for ratification were far from auspicious. By then the Carter administration had gained a reputation for being too soft on the Soviets, in part because it had appeared to retreat from the original proposal for deep cuts when faced with their coolness to it. The Soviet Union's actions in Africa, its naval buildup, and its introduction of SS-20s in Eastern Europe deepened American suspicions of Soviet intentions. Posturing for the 1980 presidential campaign guaranteed that the treaty would become a partisan issue. The Soviet invasion of Afghanistan, of course, removed any question of ratification.

Critics and analysts, in post-mortems of the Soviet rebuff of the deep-cuts proposal, pointed to several transition-related causes. Some argued that inexperience in the young administration caused it to misjudge Soviet suspicions of the very public way that the new proposals were announced. President Carter's "open diplomacy" may have appeared to the Soviets as a propaganda ploy to capture world opinion and not as a serious negotiating position. The eagerness of the new team for a new approach may also have caused the administration to underestimate the extent to which Brezhnev was personally committed to Vladivostok as a result of hard bargaining within the Politburo. Others thought that the Soviets might be testing the new president as they had tested some previous new presidents. By being less public, by returning to the Vladivostok framework, and by persisting in pushing for arms control, the administration subsequently sought to show that it had learned the right lessons from the episode, but much damage had been done.[10]

Finally, some critics pointed to what they regarded as a still unresolved contradiction between the administration's goals in arms con-

10. Talbott, *Endgame,* 66–80; Brzezinski, *Power and Principle,* 160–69; New York *Times,* March 24, 1977, Sec. 1, pp. 1, 10, March 31, 1977, Sec. 1, p. 10; Vance, *Hard Choices,* 52–57.

trol and its human rights policy. How, they asked, could the administration expect the Soviets to be receptive to new arms control proposals while at the same time pointing to abuses of human rights in the Soviet Union? Secretary of State Vance disagreed with these critics' premises. He later wrote: "I do not believe our human rights policy was the cause of the failure of the Moscow negotiation, although it did affect the general atmosphere in which the talks took place. Our position on human rights matters had undoubtedly irritated the Soviets, but it did not cause them to reject our proposals. The Soviets were much too pragmatic to let their deeper security interests be jeopardized by matters that were only an irritant." [11]

## Human Rights

The setback in Moscow would nevertheless affect the ongoing debate within the government and the country over another issue close to the president's heart. The Carter administration entered office with a view of ethics in foreign policy that differed sharply from its predecessor's. In place of Kissinger's realpolitik, Carter proposed to listen more closely to public opinion at home and to rely more heavily on America's moral influence abroad. The new president believed that by giving renewed emphasis in all his words and actions to traditional American concepts of right and wrong, especially by applying these standards to the country's foreign policy, he could recapture the popular support squandered in the Vietnam and Watergate years. Public backing could then undergird official action, making the country stronger abroad. Moreover, an ethically sensitive foreign policy would gain respect and trust from the governments and peoples of other countries.

With these presuppositions, it was almost inevitable that Carter would make the protection of human rights abroad a major point of emphasis. Using the United States' diplomatic resources to persuade other governments to behave justly toward their citizens—or at least ceasing to support those governments that continued to act unjustly—was a perfect illustration of the resharpened moral awareness that he hoped would characterize all American actions. Nothing

11. Vance, *Hard Choices*, 54–55.

seemed more likely to command public support everywhere than a forthright stand in favor of those basic rights to which everyone was entitled simply by virtue of his or her status as a human being.

In the 1976 campaign, Carter sought to appeal to these sentiments by attacking the Ford administration for indifference toward human rights and by promising to infuse American diplomacy with a concern for individuals. He summed up his stance in an address to the Foreign Policy Association in New York in June: "We and our allies, in a creative partnership, can take the lead in establishing and promoting basic global standards of human rights. We respect the independence of all nations, but by our example, by our utterances, and by the various forms of economic and political persuasion available to us, we can quite surely lessen the injustice in the world. We must certainly try." [12]

Carter could expect to profit politically from this position. One campaign foreign policy adviser later said: "Human rights was an issue with which you could bracket Kissinger and Ford on both sides. It appealed to Henry Jackson and others on the right in the sense that it applied to the Soviet Union and its treatment of Jews, and it appealed to the liberals in terms of Korea and Chile. So it was a beautiful campaign issue, an issue on which there was a real degree of public opinion hostile to the Administration." Patrick Caddell, the campaign's pollster, found it "a very strong issue across the board."

Still, the sincerity with which Carter embraced the cause should not be underestimated. Human rights was an issue to which, because of his firsthand experience of the effects of the civil rights movement in the South and his deep religious convictions, he could be expected to warm. A campaign aide recalled, "I don't think the people who were putting the issue of human rights before Carter realized how receptive he would be for personal reasons." [13]

12. Jimmy Carter, *A Government as Good as Its People* (New York, 1977), 115–22. This compilation of Carter's speeches and other statements was intended, in his words, to give "as broad a picture as possible of the campaign" by providing elucidation of his "most deeply held beliefs" (pp. 8, 9). See also Jimmy Carter, *Why Not the Best? Why One Man Is Optimistic About America's Future* (Nashville, 1975).

13. Quotations in this and the preceding paragraph are from Elizabeth Drew, "A Reporter at Large: Human Rights," *New Yorker,* July 18, 1977, pp. 36–62. This

With all of these forces at work, the noteworthy fact is not that the new Carter administration was determined to act forcefully on behalf of human rights in its first months but that it had evidently come to so few conclusions about how this might be done. The transition of 1976–1977 deposited President Carter and his subordinates in office willing to promote respect for human rights around the world. Unfortunately, it left them with no very clear ideas on the means by which this might be accomplished or the relationship this goal bore to other objectives. The administration assumed power without knowing what its human-rights policy was.

Certainly, the incoming team did not ignore human rights during the interregnum. In a postelection press conference on November 16, Carter stated, "I think the allocation of foreign aid and the normal friendship of our country would be determined or affected certainly by the attitude of those countries toward human rights." [14] Many of those appointed in the State Department, particularly to second-echelon posts, had been associated in some way with the human rights movement. Vance, as secretary of state–designate, met in New York with Soviet dissident writer Andrei Amalrik, and, according to a Vance aide, "there was talk then that our foreign policy had to draw strength from the moral feeling of the people, its innate sense of decency." [15]

These public statements and actions were on a fairly high level of generality. Private discussions were only somewhat more specific. Vance had advised Carter on a number of foreign affairs issues during the campaign and on October 24, at Carter's request, had sent the candidate a memorandum suggesting goals for a possible Carter administration. [16] The document argued that human rights should be

---

article, based on numerous interviews, gives an extremely thorough and valuable account of the new administration's actions on human rights in its first six months.

14. U.S. Congress, House of Representatives, *International Development Institutions Authorizations—1977: Hearings Before the Subcommittee on International Development Institutions and Finance of the Committee on Banking, Finance and Urban Affairs on H.R. 5262*, 95th Cong., 1st Sess., 86.

15. Mark L. Schneider, "A New Administration's New Policy: The Rise to Power of Human Rights," in Peter G. Brown and Douglas Maclean (eds.), *Human Rights and U.S. Foreign Policy: Principles and Applications* (Lexington, Mass. 1979), 3–13; Drew, "Human Rights," 38.

16. The memorandum is reprinted as an appendix in Vance, *Hard Choices*, 441–62.

one of the primary elements of Carter's diplomacy, but did not go beyond broad-brush statements concerning implementation. An informal preinaugural meeting of the Carter NSC on January 5 commissioned more than a dozen studies on a broad range of topics but gave no assignments on human rights.[17]

In the transition papers drawn up for the incoming administration, the State Department included one on human rights, probably the first transition paper ever prepared on the subject. Faced with widespread uncertainty on how Carter's campaign statements on human rights would be translated into policy and with large perceived differences on this issue between the Kissinger and Vance State Department teams, the paper consisted less of an attempt to direct the new appointees than a plea for guidance from them. In general, it "stressed a need for greater definition of human rights objectives, additional analyses of responsibilities under new laws, institutional resources to direct the policy, and answers to a set of complex questions. Those questions included how high a priority was to be given human rights, how the human rights objectives would interrelate with other interests, how effective this policy would be and how it would affect other interests and objectives."[18]

Jody Powell, the president's press secretary, later recalled that he and his colleagues firmly believed that human rights would be of great importance in the Carter administration, but he added, "What nobody could predict was that an opportunity would present itself to make the point so dramatically so early."[19] A series of events almost immediately began to force the administration to apply its general attitude in specific and contentious circumstances. The first occurred less than a week after its accession to office, when on January 26 the State Department issued a statement condemning the reported harassment and detention by the Czech government of the signers of Charter 77, a petition calling for the respect for human rights in Czechoslovakia. A day later, it followed this unprecedented action—the first occasion on which it had ever publicly charged a signatory of the Helsinki Accords with a violation of those agree-

17. Brzezinski, *Power and Principle,* 8.

18. Schneider, "A New Administration's New Policy," 9. Schneider was one of the human-rights activists named to posts in the Carter administration; he was appointed deputy assistant secretary of state for human rights.

19. Drew, "Human Rights," 38.

ments—with an equally stern warning to the Soviet government against trying to silence one of its most prominent dissidents, Andrei Sakharov. The department made headlines for the third successive day on the twenty-eighth by releasing upon its receipt a letter to Carter from Sakharov requesting the president's help in protecting Sakharov's and others' human rights in the Soviet Union.[20]

When Soviet Ambassador Anatoly Dobrynin telephoned Vance on January 27 to protest the press release on Sakharov as an interference in the internal affairs of the USSR, he caught the secretary unaware, since Vance had not even seen the release. Vance rebuked his subordinates for this lapse, but at a news conference on the thirty-first he stood by the substance of the release. Carter admitted on January 30 that he had not known of the statement in advance either, asserting that it "should have been said by myself" or Vance but adding that its message "was my attitude." When the president and the secretary met with Dobrynin, and Carter vowed not to retreat from his emphasis on human rights, however, the White House press release on the meeting did not mention human rights at all, and reporters discovered only by accident that the subject had come up. The episode came to a furious close in mid-February when, in Moscow, Sakharov received and released to the press Carter's reply to his letter. Once again the Soviets protested Carter's actions.

This uproar over the Sakharov corresponence was followed closely by another over military assistance. The Carter administration had to decide quickly on any changes it desired in the Ford budget for Fiscal Year 1978, since amendments had to be submitted to Congress by late February. Debate over the extent to which the human-rights record of potential recipients should determine their allocation made a conclusion especially hard to reach, and the process of review was a difficult one, filled with contentiousness.[21]

20. Department of State *Bulletin,* LXXVI (February 21, 1977), 137–46, 154; *Public Papers of the Presidents of the United States: Jimmy Carter, 1977* (1977), Vol. I, 100; New York *Times,* January 27, 1977, Sec. 1, p. 1, January 28, 1977, Sec. 1, p. 1, January 29, 1977, Sec. 1, pp. 1, 2, January 31, 1977, Sec. 1, p. 1, February 18, 1977, Sec. 1, p. 2, February 19, 1977, Sec. 1, pp. 1, 6; *Economist,* February 5, 1977, p. 49.
21. Drew, "Human Rights," 41–42; Patrick Breslin, "Human Rights: Rhetoric or Action?" Washington *Post,* February 27, 1977, pp. 1, 3.

On February 24 Vance announced the result of the administration's review almost offhandedly. In the course of his testimony before a Senate appropriations subcommittee he was asked by the chairman, Senator Daniel K. Inouye, whether Carter was so committed to human rights that he was prepared to reduce or eliminate aid to "some of our friends who have not maintained similar commitments to human rights." "Yes," Vance answered. "We have made some cuts out of human-rights concern." He listed Argentina, Ethiopia, and Uruguay as the "three that come to mind." Military assistance to Ethiopia and Uruguay would be eliminated, and arms sales credits to Argentina would be reduced to one-third of the level proposed the previous year. Assistance to other countries that had been considered for cuts—Zaire, South Korea, the Philippines, Brazil, and others— would be spared because of overriding political or security concerns. "Have they [the three countries targeted] been informed?" inquired Inouye. Vance answered, "If they haven't, they will be notified." Referring to the television cameras and the journalists in the hearing room, the chairman responded drily, "They are notified now."

Hard on the heels of the announcement of the security-assistance decisions came the appearance of the annual reports on the human-rights practices of all countries receiving American economic or military assistance. They were sent to Congress by the State Department in early March and released to the public on March 18. These annual assessments had been mandated by Congress over the opposition of the Ford administration. The first set of reports, submitted in November, 1975, had, at Kissinger's direction, been couched in general terms, containing specifics concerning neither nations nor rights violations, and legislators had attacked it as a violation of congressional intent.[22]

This second set of reports was therefore the first to single out particular countries for criticism. It had in reality been prepared by December, 1976, in the closing months of the Ford presidency, and the new administration had had only a few weeks in late January and

22. U.S. Congress, Senate, *Human Rights Reports Prepared by the Department of State in Accordance with Section 502(B) of the Foreign Assistance Act, as Amended, Submitted to the Subcommittee on Foreign Assistance of the Committee on Foreign Relations, United States Senate,* 95th Cong., 1st Sess.

February to conduct a hurried review and introduce several slight changes in the format and text. Nevertheless, because the reports were made available in the midst of the new administration's many other human-rights initiatives, they were received at home and abroad as part of its campaign and taken as representative of its thinking. Any criticism engendered by the reports consequently fell on Carter and his top foreign policy advisers.

Criticism was not long in coming. Stung by the abrupt cut-off or reduction of aid requests and by the publication of the country reports, El Salvador, Guatemala, Argentina, Uruguay, and Brazil angrily rejected all United States military assistance (though in several of these cases both sides later quietly agreed to restart the flow of aid), and Brazil renounced its mutual defense pact with the United States. George F. Kennan argued, "We have enough on our platter, dealing with the traditional items of foreign policy," and complained of "zealots" who wanted to make the State Department "a human rights factory." [23]

On the other hand, a series of human-rights activists testifying before a Senate subcommittee described some aspects of the administration's outspoken public stand as "impressive" and "forthright" but said the cuts in military assistance thus far proposed on human-rights grounds were not very significant. Vance's refusal to recommend cuts in aid to such countries as South Korea because of security interests at stake there was termed "disturbing," and one rights activist warned that unless the administration asked for further reductions, "questions will arise about the depth of its commitment to human rights." Finally, they demanded an announced overall strategy; in the words of one human-rights advocate, "Ad hoc action is not policy." [24] These divisions were reproduced within the State De-

23. A. Glenn Mower, Jr., *The United States, the United Nations, and Human Rights: The Eleanor Roosevelt and Jimmy Carter Eras* (Westport, Conn., 1979), 167. See also the cautionary remarks of British Foreign Secretary David Owen in New York *Times*, March 4, 1977, Sec. 1, p. 9.

24. U.S. Congress, Senate, *Human Rights: Hearings Before the Subcommittee on Foreign Assistance of the Committee on Foreign Relations, United States Senate, on Human Rights Issues and Their Relationship to Foreign Assistance Programs*, 95th Cong., 1st Sess., 3–41 *passim.* See also Drew, "Human Rights," 42; David Weissbrodt, "Human Rights Legislation and U.S. Foreign Policy," *Georgia*

partment, where relations between the human-rights staff and some other bureaus were described by a Congressional Research Service study as "little better than chaotic." [25]

The final shock came with the failure of Vance's arms control mission to Moscow. Throughout its first two months in office the administration had asserted that its public protests on Soviet human-rights practices would have no effect on superpower arms talks. At least in public, these views were not shared in Moscow. A warning in *Pravda* on March 13 that American outspokenness on human rights could poison the atmosphere of the SALT negotiations was followed a day later by a statement from Paul Warnke, just before he was sworn in as head of the Arms Control and Disarmament Agency and chief SALT negotiator, that discussions of human rights should not affect efforts at arms control. On March 21 Brezhnev, in his first public comment on the subject, strongly complained of Carter's stress on human rights. The next morning at a breakfast meeting with congressional leaders, Carter professed to be unworried: "Some people are concerned every time Brezhnev sneezes." [26] Vance's frigid reception in Moscow at the end of March chilled such optimism.

After the breakdown of the Moscow talks, the administration quickly developed a greater concern with the relationship between advocacy of human rights and other American policies. Less than two weeks after Vance returned from Moscow, he and Brzezinski reportedly met with the president on April 12 and submitted a memorandum saying that human-rights policy since January 20 had been

---

*Journal of International and Comparative Law,* VII (Summer, 1977), 231–87; Thomas A. Balmer, "The Use of Conditions in Foreign Relations Legislation," *Denver Journal of International Law and Policy,* VII (Spring, 1978), 197–238; Washington *Post,* February 27, 1977, Sec. C, pp. 1, 4.

25. U.S. Congress, Senate, *Human Rights and U.S. Foreign Assistance: Experience and Issues in Policy Implementation (1977–78): A Report Prepared for the Senate Committee on Foreign Relations by the Foreign Affairs and National Defense Division, Congressional Research Service, Library of Congress,* 96th Cong., 1st Sess., 80. See also Mower, *The United States, the United Nations and Human Rights,* 171; David Southerland, "State Department Rights Proponents Flex Muscles: But More Traditional Bureaucrats Resisting," *Christian Science Monitor,* June 27, 1977, p. 7.

26. New York *Times,* March 14, 1977, Sec. 1, p. 1, March 15, 1977, Sec. 1, p. 1, March 23, 1977, Sec. 1, p. 1.

"loose" and "generally counter-productive." The "strained relations" with several countries resulting from the blunders of the past several weeks had thus far elicited no serious retaliation against American interests or citizens abroad, but Carter's public comments on human rights stood "in danger of misinterpretation as intervention in internal affairs." [27]

The secretary of state apparently obtained the presidential backing he desired for a change in course, since on April 30 he convened a meeting of senior State Department officers to order that any future public censure of individual countries for human-rights violations be limited to a short list of states such as South Africa and the smaller Latin American and African countries that were not "important to the national security." Furthermore, any criticisms that *were* made had to be approved personally by Vance or by Under Secretary Warren Christopher. Vance told the others that he was acting on the express authority of the president, who had been convinced by the April 12 briefing to "tighten down the hatches."

Vance himself attempted to lay down the definitive interpretation of the administration's human-rights policy in a speech at the University of Georgia Law School on April 30, Law Day. [28] He announced that the United States would adopt a broad definition of human rights—including "rights of the person," civil and political rights, and economic and social rights—and would work to promote all three. In an effort to achieve consistency in American policy toward different countries, the secretary outlined a series of questions on the scope, trend, and responsibility of violations that he and others intended to ask "as we determine whether and how to act." He warned, however, that, no matter what the standard, "in the end, a decision . . . is a matter for informed and careful judgment. No mechanistic formula produces an automatic answer."

The tests outlined in Vance's address were to be applied in specific instances by the Interagency Group on Human Rights and Foreign Assistance, established by an NSC directive on April 1. The Interagency Group was to pass on all proposals for economic aid, examining the human-rights record of each suggested recipient, before

27. Roger Morris, "Blithering Diplomats," *Politics Today,* V (September–October, 1978), 36. See also *Human Rights and U.S. Foreign Assistance,* 69, 91.
28. Department of State *Bulletin,* LXXVI (May 23, 1977), 505–508.

they were incorporated into the president's budget request. What this body did for economic assistance, the Arms Export Control Board was to do for military assistance, foreign military sales, and other defense-related forms of aid. For other areas of policy, Brzezinski, acting on Carter's January 12 request, submitted to the president on April 30 a memorandum setting out specific goals in human rights for each of the four years of his administration.[29]

A successful transition would have ensured that the administration would take these steps in December and January, before the inauguration, not in April. With earlier planning, at least some of the difficulties it encountered in its first three months in office could have been avoided. The human-rights policy, like the efforts at arms control, could have gotten off to a smoother start.

Of course, many factors, not all of them under the control of Carter and his officials, played a part in the problems of the first quarter of 1977. The reports on individual countries were a legacy of the Ford administration. No matter how softly they were worded, they would have aroused the displeasure of the states whose conduct was criticized. On the other hand, it is improbable that any reports and any budget cuts likely to be approved, no matter how emphatic, would have left human-rights activists satisfied. Far-reaching and innovative, the SALT proposals might well have been rejected by the Soviets even if human rights had never become an issue.

Still, the impression remains that the administration handicapped itself in meeting these challenges by failing to define and articulate its human-rights policy early on. By late spring, executive officials were saying as much themselves. One contended that events during the transition that were beyond the administration's control mandated action: "We had to define where we stood. We were confronted with it right away." Lack of preparation, however, meant that this early stand would not be well coordinated within the administration or with other areas of policy. Another of the president's foreign policy advisers said in midsummer, "The whole thing sort of acquired a dynamic of its own."[30]

29. *Human Rights and U.S. Foreign Assistance,* 36–42; Brzezinski, *Power and Principle,* 48–56.

30. Donald P. Kommers and Gilbert D. Loescher (eds.), *Human Rights and American Foreign Policy* (Notre Dame, 1979), 226; *Human Rights: Hearings . . .*

Until this lack of coordination diminished, beginning in April, the administration's human-rights advocacy lacked answers to three questions that could make it into coherent policy: First, what did Washington mean by "human rights"? Second, what were likely to be the most effective tactics in advancing the chosen conception of human rights? Third, what other American objectives could be subordinated to a human-rights campaign, and to which would it have to yield? The Carter administration left its search for the answers until the final stage of the transition—the period once it was in office. Despite a transition effort of unprecedented size and expense, it did not succeed, at least in this area of policy, in preparing itself adequately for the responsibilities of power.

On arms control, by contrast, early preparation was greater, but hopes for immediate success were even higher, and the inclination to introduce dramatic changes in policy was just as strong. Was it the mark of a newcomer to begin by proposing such a far-reaching change in the American stance—or to announce beforehand that the United States had a fallback position ready if the deep cuts were rejected? When it launched the initiatives on both arms control and human rights, the Carter administration, like any new administration, was still finding its feet. The desire to move quickly and to differentiate itself from its predecessor may have betrayed it into mistakes that proved costly later.

---

*on Human Rights Issues and Their Relationship to Foreign Assistance Programs,* 72–73; Brzezinski, *Power and Principle,* 125; Drew, "Human Rights," 41; *Christian Science Monitor,* June 27, 1977, p. 7.

# CHAPTER 11

# From Carter to Reagan

Being the friend of the United States is like living on the banks of a great river: the soil is wonderfully fertile and there are many other benefits, but every four years or eight years, the river, flooded by storms that are too far away to be seen, changes its course, and you are left in a desert, all alone.

—President Mohammad Zia
ul-Haq of Pakistan,
as paraphrased by
Alexander Haig

Of all the postwar transitions, the transfer of authority that took place in 1980–1981 most resembled the one that had immediately preceded it. Like the Ford-Carter transition and unlike the three others of the postwar period, the transition from Jimmy Carter to Ronald Reagan was between two men who ran against each other in the presidential election, and was, as a result, freighted with all the suspicion and disdain that opposing campaign staffs tend to hold toward each other. Dragged down by a divisive challenge within his own party from Senator Edward Kennedy (as Ford had been hurt by his struggle with Reagan in 1976), a soaring inflation rate resulting partly from huge increases in oil prices, and the national frustration that welled up in reaction to Iran's detention of its American hostages for over a year, Carter suffered a decisive defeat at the hands of the Republican challenger. The Republicans also captured the Senate, making this the first transition since 1952–1953 to witness a turnover in party control of at least one house of Congress simultaneously with that in the White House.

The Reagan campaign staff imitated the 1976 Carter campaign by beginning to plan for a transition even before the Republican party's convention officially made the governor its standard bearer. The transition planning group reported to Edwin Meese, who figured prominently in the president's campaign staff; there would be no repeat of the Jordan-Watson struggle that reduced the impact of Carter transition planning.

As Jimmy Carter had in 1976, Ronald Reagan ran as an "outsider" and attributed the nation's problems to "those bureaucrats in Washington." Reagan also attacked the incumbent administration's entire approach to foreign policy, as Carter had done against Ford in 1976. But foreign policy played a much more central role in the 1980 campaign than it had four years earlier. Reagan charged that Carter had no coherent strategy for confronting Soviet advances, such as Moscow's steadily increasing military spending and its invasion of Afghanistan, and no clear sense of what the administration's policies, such as its stand on human rights, were doing to the American alliance system. The prolonged public debate over Carter's embargoes—of grain shipments to the Soviet Union and of American participation in the 1980 summer Olympics in Moscow—that were intended as responses to events in Afghanistan, and the ignominious failure of the attempted hostage rescue mission in Iran, only served to lend credence to Republican charges of ineptitude. So anxious was the Reagan campaign staff to separate itself from the incumbent administration that at first it refused intelligence briefings, saying that the candidate wanted to be free to criticize President Carter without worrying about betraying sensitive information. Only when war broke out between Iran and Iraq in late September did Reagan and his vice-presidential nominee, George Bush, consent to a briefing on the war by CIA director Stansfield Turner.

With this contentious beginning, it was almost inevitable that, despite unprecedented effort and expense, the transition would be rough. Reagan's victory, like Carter's before him, meant yet another reexamination of basic American foreign policy, with substantially different emphases and approaches to conform with the Reagan world view. Charges that a "window of vulnerability" had been opened and assertions that the SALT II treaty negotiated by the Carter administration was "deeply flawed" meant yet another new approach to arms control. Reagan had been a vocal critic of the Panama Canal treaties, negotiated under both Republican and Democratic presidents. Campaign statements about restoring "official" relations between Taiwan and the United States made it plausible to think that, as president, Reagan might repudiate the normalization of relations with Communist China, first undertaken by Nixon and continued by Carter. The Peking government predictably reacted with outrage, Bush found it necessary to contradict his senior running mate, and the press played up the story, with all its negative implications about Reagan's foreign policy competence. At this point Reagan backed down, but the episode revealed how different was the Republican candidate's approach to foreign policy from that of his immediate predecessors. Once in office, the new administration's policies did not necessarily follow the course suggested by this campaign oratory: it accepted the Panama Canal treaties, it chose to abide by the "flawed" SALT II treaty as long as the Soviets did, and it would in time seek to promote sophisticated technology transfers to Peking.

The outgoing administration, on orders from the president, made an effort to be helpful, but it was inhibited from doing anything before Election Day that indicated it might lose. After the election it was distracted by the hostage crisis, and its members sometimes found themselves frustrated and puzzled by the approach and attitudes of their incoming counterparts. When Carter met with Reagan on November 20 for the traditional postelection meeting between president and president-elect, Carter had a list of fifteen or twenty subjects he wanted to bring to Reagan's attention. The president-elect, in Carter's recollection, said very little during the meeting and did not even bother to take notes of what was apparently a rather detailed briefing, though at the end he did request a copy of Carter's notes. The president, like his predecessors in the same situation, left the meeting unsure "how much we accomplished" and with a sense that the president-elect did not fully appreciate the magnitude of the tasks in the office he would soon be assuming.[1]

The Reagan transition effort was the largest yet. Using three million dollars in private and public transition funds, it established an organization of over one thousand paid staff and volunteers and sent approximately a hundred transition teams into federal departments and agencies. In the foreign and defense policy areas alone four

1. Carter, *Keeping Faith,* 578; Washington *Post,* November 6, 1980, p. A30, November 7, 1980, p. A10; New York *Times,* September 27, 1980, p. A8. *Cf.* Truman's account in his memoirs of his interregnum meeting with Eisenhower.

teams of experts dealt with management, budget, policy, and personnel issues in the State Department, the Defense Department, the Central Intelligence Agency, and other agencies involved in international matters. The work of these teams was loosely overseen by Meese, the director of the transition organization, by his assistant, William Timmons, by Richard Allen, President-elect Reagan's senior advisor on foreign policy, and by David Abshire, who was designated the overall coordinator for the foreign policy transition.

Much of the work that these transition teams did was not used, and some of it was probably harmful. The challenging attitude of some transition-team members toward the agencies they were investigating angered many employees of those agencies and made them less helpful and cooperative than they might have been otherwise. State Department personnel, in particular, resented the presence on the transition team of congressional staffers who seemed interested primarily in seeking out information ordinarily denied to Congress by executive privilege. Some transition-team members who traveled abroad complicated administration diplomacy in such areas as Central America, East Asia, and South Africa by signaling significant policy shifts. The sheer size of the transition organization made it difficult to police members who claimed to speak for the incoming administration, and senior transition officials several times had to issue warnings that team members should be more circumspect in their public pronouncements. In none of the foreign and national security policy agencies did the leader of the transition team in a particular agency become its head, though some were appointed to other posts. Since most cabinet appointees prefer to oversee their own preparations, a significant amount of work was done twice.[2]

Not all that was done during the transition went for naught, to be sure, but what happened (or did not happen) virtually guaranteed that the new administration would get off to a slower start in foreign policy than in domestic policy. In general the Reagan team took

2. Laurence I. Barrett, *Gambling with History: Reagan in the White House* (Garden City, N.Y., 1983), 82–83; New York *Times,* November 12, 1980, p. A7; Haig, *Caveat,* 64–72. Haig's abrupt dismissal of the transition team made him a hero to members of the State Department. Meese's transition work came back to haunt him several years later when his management of the organization's finances came under scrutiny.

longer than its predecessors in making appointments. In foreign affairs its appointments to intermediate positions were particularly slow, usually coming months after the inauguration. Adding to the confusion was the fact that word went out from the main transition team shortly before the inauguration that no presidential appointee of the outgoing administration was to be at his desk in any executive department on the morning following the inauguration. This rule would have created serious problems in the State Department, where so many policy positions were occupied by presidential appointments. Convinced of the difficulties the rule posed, Secretary-designate Alexander Haig was able to have exceptions made for a number of State Department personnel.[3]

The grueling and extensive confirmation hearings on the nomination of General Haig as secretary of state made it harder for him, in particular, to focus on other preinaugural matters. He devoted much of the time he did have to the development of a document laying out the roles and relationships of the various officials and agencies in foreign affairs. Haig's draft presidential memo, which he presented to the White House for the president's signature on Inauguration Day, did not win the approval of key members of the White House staff, and no alternative plan was negotiated. As a result, the new administration took office with the issue of foreign policy structure unsettled, in spite of Reagan's campaign promise that "my administration will restore leadership to U.S. foreign policy by organizing it in a more coherent way. An early priority will be to make structural changes in the foreign policymaking machinery so that the Secretary of State will be the President's principal spokesman and adviser."[4]

If the incoming administration had wished, it could have overcome these obstacles and moved more rapidly, but it had decided during the interregnum to make domestic issues its primary concern in its first months in office. As Reagan's advisers began charting the

3. David D. Newsom, "Presidential Transitions and the Handling of Foreign Policy Crises: The Iranian Hostage Crisis from Carter to Reagan," in Kenneth W. Thompson (ed.), *The Virginia Papers on the Presidency,* Vol. XVIII (Washington, D.C., 1985), 103–104.

4. I. M. Destler, Leslie H. Gelb, and Anthony Lake, *Our Own Worst Enemy: The Unmaking of American Foreign Policy* (New York, 1984), 225.

course for the new administration in its first months in office, they deliberately set out not to repeat mistakes many said the new Carter administration had made.

First, the new administration would focus its early attention on a few, albeit vital, initiatives, rather than dissipating presidential energy, losing public attention, and overwhelming Congress with a host of issues. Second, key Reagan aides would seek to preserve the appearance of a strong and effective presidency by associating the president with a string of successes and avoiding a connection with any "losses."

Working on these assumptions, the Reagan team chose to focus intently on reductions in spending and tax rates and on large increases for national defense. Several forces converged to make this so. The president himself clearly intended to make his mark by sharply reducing the scale and scope of the federal government except in national defense. Influential advisers like Congressmen Jack Kemp and David Stockman forcefully pressed their view that the country faced an "economic Dunkirk" unless dramatic actions were taken. Public opinion polls showed that domestic economic issues headed the list of public concerns; they also suggested public willingness to give some of the Republican ideas a try. The new administration could underscore its break with the past by pressing for "economic recovery" legislation.

The new administration's strategy proved to be remarkably successful, as far-reaching budget cuts and significant tax rate reductions swept dramatically through a surprisingly pliant Congress. Only later, after he left the government in 1985, would David Stockman, one of the principal architects of the administration's strategy and the director of OMB, say that the new administration had acted "recklessly" in these early months. This strategy also meant that foreign affairs was put on hold to the greatest extent possible. Foreign policy initiatives, particularly if controversial, were avoided so that public attention would not be diverted from the president's economic recovery program. When, for example, Secretary of State Haig sought to make an immediate issue and example of Central America, presidential aides Meese and Baker compelled him to wait until late February, after the president had made two televised speeches on the economic recovery program. They did not want to dilute the impact of those speeches by generating "background noise" in Congress and in the press.[5]

Finally, the new administration generally subscribed to the view that, before any major foreign policy initiatives were taken, especially with respect to the Soviet Union, there would have to be a major improvement in the nation's defense posture. The Reagan campaign had made clear its commitment to oversee a significant increase in defense spending early in 1980. At that time President Carter had proposed a 3 percent real increase for the 1981 defense budget, and Reagan had countered that 5 percent would be the minimum necessary to assure the nation's security. As the year wore on, pressure from elements within the administration and within Congress pushed the defense budget far beyond the $142.7 billion the president had initially proposed. In early December, 1981, House and Senate conferees approved a defense budget of $160.1 billion, and Senator John Tower, the incoming chairman of the Armed Services Committee, indicated that he was working closely with the Defense Department transition team to prepare a supplemental request for improvements in weapons programs to present to the new Congress in January. Not to be outdone, President Carter, in his final budget message, proposed $6.3 billion extra for the Defense Department for Fiscal Year 1981 and a 5 percent real increase for Fiscal Year 1982, thus accepting the figure that candidate Reagan had used a year earlier. Since the Reagan team had committed itself to spend 2 percent more on defense than Carter had, it raised its annual increase to 7 percent and, in the first year, applied that to Carter's higher proposal. Thus, President Reagan's proposals on defense spending, revealed in early March, 1981, sought an increase by over 14 percent in Fiscal Year 1982 and by about 7 percent a year thereafter, for an average of more than 8 percent, as compared with Carter's proposed average increase of about 5 percent, for the same period (Fiscal Years 1982–1986).

Ironically, this political gamesmanship tended to hide the substantial agreement between the two administrations on defense strategy.

5. David A. Stockman, *The Triumph of Politics: Why the Reagan Revolution Failed* (New York, 1986); Barrett, *Gambling with History,* 84–85; Haig, *Caveat,* 126–30.

According to Secretary of Defense Caspar Weinberger, "The principal shortcoming of the defense budget we inherited was not so much that it omitted critical programs entirely in order to fully fund others, but rather that it failed to provide full funding for many programs it conceded were necessary but felt unable to afford." In short, transition energy on foreign and defense policy was directed at preparing an unprecedented defense buildup rather than developing diplomatic initiatives.[6]

The transition itself took place during a period when an unusually large number of foreign policy issues required attention. Most of the fifteen to twenty subjects President Carter discussed with President-elect Reagan concerned foreign policy. In some of these cases the incumbents conducted their business with a free hand partly because the incoming team was preoccupied with other matters. In Poland the success of the Solidarity labor movement in challenging the government had made the Soviets nervous. In early December American intelligence agencies detected troop movements that suggested that the Soviets were preparing to invade Poland. Privately and publicly the Carter administration let the Soviets know that an invasion would have far-reaching consequences for East-West relations. Additionally, the administration conferred with AFL-CIO leaders about organizing a worldwide boycott of Soviet goods, secured the agreement of some allies to adopt economic sanctions, and prepared a list of weapons to be transferred to China, the Soviets' major adversary along their Asian border, in the event of a Soviet invasion of Poland. Reagan foreign policy advisers, who had been briefed on the situation, echoed the warnings emanating from the government. The feared invasion did not take place, and the American threats may have played some part in deterring it, though there is no way of

6. Samuel Huntington, "The Defense Policy of the Reagan Administration, 1981–82," in Fred I. Greenstein (ed.), *The Reagan Presidency: An Early Assessment* (Baltimore, 1983), 84–90; New York *Times,* June 27, 1980, p. A17, October 29, 1980, p. A24, November 12, 1980, p. A26, December 19, 1980, p. A1; William Greider, "The Education of David Stockman," *Atlantic* (December, 1981), 35. For a detailed account of how OMB under Stockman led the charge on Congress see Frederick C. Mosher and Max O. Stephenson, Jr., "The Office of Management and Budget in a Changing Scene," *Public Budgeting and Finance,* II (Winter, 1982), 23–41; Stockman, *The Triumph of Politics,* 106–109.

knowing for sure. On the other hand, the Carter administration decided to defer action on a request from the Polish government of $3 billion in economic assistance, a request considered too large to be weighed seriously by a lame-duck administration.[7]

In the Middle East, some momentum remained from the signing of the Camp David accords in 1978, and President Carter sought to sustain it by meeting with Israeli Prime Minister Menachem Begin ten days after the election. The president, however, found Begin generally unwilling to engage in substantive discussions. This was his first indication that "my power as a defeated President was not equal to that of one who is expected to remain in office." Reagan advisers had publicly supported the Camp David accords, but both the Israelis and the Egyptians preferred to mark time, waiting for the new administration. Critics of the Reagan administration's policies in the Middle East, including former President Carter, would later contend that the new administration's early failure to press for negotiations considerably weakened American influence in the area.[8]

Another pending issue was the sale of sophisticated AWACS aircraft to the Saudi Arabians, which the Carter administration believed necessary but which promised to mobilize the supporters of Israel in opposition. President Carter offered to take the heat and push the sale through if President-elect Reagan so desired, but the Reagan camp declined the offer. Haig, for one, did not believe that the lame-duck Carter administration had the requisite political capital to push through so controversial a sale. He thought that the measure had a much better chance of passage under a new administration experiencing its honeymoon with Congress. Indeed, the sale only barely won congressional approval even during the honeymoon. When the administration proposed it in the summer of 1981, it encountered a storm of controversy. The acrimonious and noisy

7. Brzezinski, *Power and Principle,* 463–69; Carter, *Keeping Faith,* 584; Washington *Post,* December 3, 1980, p. A1, December 8, 1980, p. A1; New York *Times,* November 22, 1980, p. A1.

8. Carter, *Keeping Faith,* 575–76. Begin did not meet with President-elect Reagan, but West German Chancellor Helmut Schmidt, a later visitor, did. Reagan also met during the transition with Mexico's President Jose Lopez-Portillo. See New York *Times,* November 10, 1980, p. A6, November 24, 1980, p. A1.

debate unnecessarily offended the Saudis and strained relations with the Israelis.[9]

One issue on which the Carter administration actively solicited and received assistance from the Reagan team during the interregnum involved pressing the government of South Korea to commute the death sentence of Kim Dae Jung, a political dissident. At Carter's request, Reagan officials passed the word to the South Korean government that relations between the United States and South Korea would be harmed if Kim Dae Jung were executed and that the election of a new president did not mean that the United States would cease to oppose such an act.

Two other issues are especially illustrative of the unique problems of this transition: Central America and, of course, Iran and the hostage crisis, which dominated Carter's final year as president and probably contributed to his defeat in the election. In both cases the impending turnover of authority would figure in the calculations of leaders abroad.[10]

## Central America

Two early targets of the Carter administration's human-rights policies had been Nicaragua and El Salvador. Both were led by right-wing oligarchs, and both were infamous for domestic political repression. Consequently, soon after Carter took office, both found themselves cut off from American economic and military aid. When some aid was later resumed, it came too late to save either regime. In 1979 the Nicaraguan and Salvadoran dictatorships fell: in Nicaragua a broad coalition of opposition groups led by the Sandinistas overthrew Anastasio Somoza Debayle, and then in El Salvador reform-minded military officers overthrew dictator General Carlos Humberto Romero. In each case the Carter administration sought to support the "progressive center" against right-wing reactionaries on one hand and against Marxist revolutionaries on the other.

In El Salvador this meant providing economic and some military

9. Haig, *Caveat*, 175–80.
10. Carter, *Keeping Faith*, 577–89; Barrett, *Gambling with History*, 85–87; Haig, *Caveat*, 56–64, 174–77.

support for the junta that replaced Romero, while applying pressure on it to take control over right-wing death squads responsible for killing thousands of civilians. The five-man junta of four military officers and Christian Democrat party leader José Napoleón Duarte announced in March, 1980, a land-reform project and the nationalization of banks and coffee-exporting firms in a bid to undercut the power of the landed oligarchy, a move supported and encouraged by the United States.

In the case of Nicaragua, as domestic opposition to Somoza mounted in the summer of 1978, the administration sought to end the civil strife and help negotiate a peaceful and early transition from dictatorship to democracy. Under the auspices of the Organization of American States, a three-nation mediation team with members from Guatemala, the Dominican Republic, and the United States attempted the creation of a strong post-Somoza political center in that country. These efforts were overtaken by events, and a regime dominated by the Marxist-oriented Sandinistas took power instead. From that point on, in 1979–1980, American policy was to urge the Sandinistas to hold the elections they had promised, to uphold civil and religious liberties, and to maintain a large private business sector. As incentives, the Carter administration provided low-interest loans, a seventy-five-million-dollar aid package, and favorable rescheduling of debts in an effort to moderate the Sandinistas and prevent them from becoming too close to the Cubans or Soviets. Defending this policy, Secretary of State Vance warned: "By extending our friendship and economic assistance, we enhance the prospects for democracy in Nicaragua. We cannot guarantee that democracy will take hold there. But if we turn our back on Nicaragua, we can almost guarantee that democracy will fail." [11]

Throughout 1980, domestic critics on the left and the right assailed the administration's Central American policies. Liberals argued that, because of continuing human-rights violations in El Salvador, American military and economic support for the Salvadoran junta should be withdrawn. The assassination of Archbishop Oscar

11. Barry Rubin, "Reagan Administration Policymaking and Central America," in Robert S. Leiken (ed.), *Central America: Anatomy of Conflict* (New York, 1984), 300; New York *Times*, October 8, 1978, p. 11.

Romero, leader of the Salvadoran Catholic Church and an outspoken critic of the junta, in March, 1980, underscored their concern. The junta seemed unwilling or unable to control violent groups with ties to the country's armed forces. Such a regime, liberals said, did not deserve American support. Conservatives charged that the victory of the Sandinistas in Nicaragua demonstrated the wrongheadedness of the Carter human-rights emphasis. Jeane Kirkpatrick, in an article that would bring her to the attention of candidate Reagan, contended that the application of human-rights concerns in both Iran and Nicaragua had led to the replacement of "moderate autocrats friendly to American interests" by "less friendly autocrats of extremist persuasion." For Kirkpatrick and others of like mind, the principal enemy of human rights remained the Soviet Union, and events in Central America had to be viewed in that larger perspective. This became especially persuasive when Nicaragua's foreign policy in 1979–1980 supported the Soviet positions on Afghanistan, Kampuchea, and Poland, and when the Sandinistas signed a series of trade agreements with the Soviets.[12]

The Republicans, in challenging the administration's foreign policy, adopted Kirkpatrick's thesis in the 1980 party platform: "We deplore the Marxist Sandinist takeover of Nicaragua and the Marxist attempts to destabilize El Salvador, Guatemala, and Honduras. We do not support United States assistance to any Marxist government in this hemisphere and we oppose the Carter Administration aid program for the Government of Nicaragua." Intended for the domestic audience, this statement carried to Central America as well and may well have had some effect on subsequent events. Throughout the region conservative businessmen and army officers believed that a Reagan administration would allow them to respond more forcefully to what they perceived as a leftist offensive throughout Central America. Leftist guerrillas in El Salvador meanwhile began making plans for a general offensive against the Duarte-led junta, apparently with the support of Cuba and Nicaragua. Overall, the election and

12. Walter LaFeber, *Inevitable Revolutions: The United States in Central America* (New York, 1984), 229–56; Jeane Kirkpatrick, "Dictatorships and Double Standards," *Commentary*, LXVIII (November, 1979), 34.

transition threatened to undermine the carrying out of Carter administration policy in the region.[13]

The Reagan victory in November accelerated these trends, as all sides assumed that the new administration would take the pressure off the right to deal with the left in El Salvador and to confront the Sandinistas in Nicaragua. The American ambassador to El Salvador, Robert White, took rumors of an attempt at a right-wing coup in El Salvador seriously enough to fly to Washington to urge Reagan advisers to send some sort of message against this. Later those advisers, including Jeane Kirkpatrick, now part of the Reagan entourage, informed visiting Salvadoran businessmen that the new administration would resume military aid to El Salvador but coupled that with a warning against a rightist coup.

The coup did not materialize, but the American election seemed to set off a new round of violence in El Salvador. On November 27, security forces seized and assassinated six leaders of the political opposition in a move some asserted was "aimed at dealing a severe blow to the left before Reagan is inaugurated." Then, on December 2, four American missionary women were murdered, allegedly by a right-wing death squad. The Carter administration responded by suspending economic and military aid on December 5 and demanding through Ambassador White, that the killers be brought to justice. A bipartisan presidential mission, led by Assistant Secretary of State for Inter-American Affairs William G. Bowdler and a former under secretary of state under President Ford, William D. Rogers, was dispatched within several days to determine if the Salvadoran security forces were involved. By giving the mission a bipartisan character and by keeping Richard Allen informed "at every step," the Carter people clearly hoped to present the Salvadoran government with a unified front and shore up the administration's waning political influence.

The mission held a series of meetings with Ambassador White, the governing junta, church officials, police officials, and others.

13. New York *Times*, August 4, 1980, p. A3; Robert White, "Turnabout in U.S. Policy," in Mark Falcoff and Robert Royal (eds.), *Crisis and Opportunity: U.S. Policy in Central America and the Caribbean* (Washington, D.C., 1984), 201–15.

The emissaries won from the junta a commitment to move quickly to find those responsible for the killings and urged the junta to make the military high command more responsive to civil authorities, to implement the reform program, and to open a dialogue with democratic leaders of the opposition to seek a negotiated end to the internal conflict. Based on the mission's report, President Carter on December 17 announced a resumption of economic assistance. Military assistance was not resumed.[14]

The work of the transition teams and of those purportedly helping with the transition undermined the administration's efforts. Cleto DiGiovanni, Jr., a former CIA official visiting El Salvador in early December, claimed to speak on Reagan's behalf and reportedly carried a message that the Reagan team's stated opposition to a right-wing coup should be disregarded. The Reagan transition team disavowed DiGiovanni and other "pretend emissaries" traveling abroad, and Allen circulated a memo to the foreign policy transition team asking that members control their comments. A transition team member with better credentials, General Vernon Walters, reportedly also traveled to Central America to promise support for the conservative military regimes there. Meanwhile, back in Washington, a report by a transition team criticized Ambassador White for supporting the measures on land reform and bank nationalization announced by San Salvador in March, 1980. This leaked to the press, as did a list of ambassadors and foreign service officers targeted for replacement (which included both White and Bowdler). At this, Ambassador White publicly charged the Reagan team in mid-December with undermining his position: "That list totally undermined my authority and my effectiveness at the very time the United States needs the most leverage." Meese responded that no authorized member of the transition team had said anything to undercut the authority of any ambassador anywhere, reinforcing the impression that the transition had gotten rather out of control.[15]

14. Department of State *Bulletin,* LXXXI (February, 1981), 68–69; New York *Times,* December 7, 1980, p. A8.

15. "An Ambassador Under Fire," *Newsweek,* December 22, 1980, p. 53; New York *Times,* November 16, 1980, p. A17, November 20, 1980, p. A35, November 29, 1980, p. A1, December 7, 1980, p. A8, December 10, 1980, p. A1, December 11, 1980, pp. A11, A15.

On December 27 the top Salvadoran guerrilla commander announced that the insurgents would begin their final offensive before January 20, so that Ronald Reagan would find an "irreversible situation" by the time he reached the presidency. Although heavy fighting was reported the next day, the promised offensive began in earnest on January 10. The guerrillas struck at between forty and fifty locations throughout El Salvador and seized four radio stations in the capital city of San Salvador to broadcast an appeal for a general strike and a popular insurrection against the government. In the cities they used hit-and-run tactics to demonstrate the government's impotence; in the countryside they boarded buses and exhorted surprised passengers to take up arms. Faced on one hand with demands to punish the junta for not controlling the right-wing death squads and on the other with the strategic concern over the possibility of a Marxist-led victory, the Carter administration announced on January 14, a week before the inauguration, that five million dollars in "non-lethal" military aid would be sent to El Salvador. The decision was made easier by the discovery that the insurgents were using Soviet-made weapons supplied by Nicaragua, Cuba, and other communist countries. Several days later, on January 17, President Carter authorized an additional five million dollars in "lethal" military aid to help replenish the depleted stocks used by the government forces. In these last days of the Carter administration Ambassador White refused a Pentagon-inspired request that he sign a cable asking for seventy-five American military advisers and additional military aid for El Salvador. White believed that the request ultimately could be traced back to the Reagan transition team in the Pentagon. He strongly disagreed with the policy implicit in the request, believing it signaled a shift from seeking a negotiated settlement to pushing for a military solution.

At the same time that it resumed military assistance to the Salvadoran government, the Carter administration in its final days suspended further disbursements of its seventy-five-million-dollar package of economic aid to Nicaragua to protest Nicaragua's role in aiding the Salvadoran rebels. Documents taken from captured leftist guerrillas and other intelligence sources revealed that Nicaragua had taken a direct role in supplying arms and material to the Salvadoran leftists for their January offensive. Moreover, after Reagan's victory in November, the Sandinistas tightened their control at home. They prohibited opposition political rallies, increased censorship, and extended their control of the economy. The Catholic hierarchy, which had withheld its opposition, increasingly registered its unhappiness with the course the revolution was taking.

Nicaraguan leaders sometimes argued that these measures were undertaken in anticipation of implied threats from the incoming administration. Foreshadowings of the course the Sandinistas would take, however, were already apparent in mid-1980. By then they had begun a military buildup, created an expanded state security system, postponed promised elections until 1985, and prohibited "disinformation" about the nation's economy and security affairs. According to New York *Times* correspondent Shirley Christian: "The leaders of the Sandinista front intended to establish a Leninist system from the day they marched into Managua, whether they called it that or not. Their goal was to assure themselves the means to control nearly every aspect of Nicaraguan life, from beans and rice to religion." According to this view, the American transition affected only the pace of events in Central America, not basic political goals.[16]

In late September, 1980, the deputy assistant secretary of state for inter-American affairs was sent to Managua to make sure that the Nicaraguan government understood that American aid would continue only if Nicaragua provided no assistance to the Salvadoran rebels. The aid cutoff then, was consistent with these warnings. Whether the Carter administration would have acted differently toward El Salvador or Nicaragua had there been no election is difficult to say; certainly the election results made it harder for Carter to resist pressure to increase military assistance to El Salvador to help counter the rebel offensive, if that is what he wanted to do. Similarly, on Nicaragua, the views of the incoming administration had been made clear in the Republican platform, and the incentives within the incumbent administration for a tougher policy toward the Nicaraguan government increased. As Ambassador White saw it, "At that time Carter, Mondale, and Muskie were totally involved in the Iranian hostage crisis . . . and career officers—who are vulnerable to political revenge—whether at State, CIA, or the Pen-

16. Shirley Christian, *Nicaragua: Revolution in the Family* (New York, 1985), 170–96, 306.

tagon, started to say, looking toward the Reagan Administration, 'Well, we'd better try and burnish our image for the new fellow.'"[17] On the other hand, many career officials continued faithfully to pursue the policies of the Carter administration and found themselves reassigned or relieved of duty once the turnover had taken place.

By the time President Reagan took the oath of office, it had become clear that the guerrillas' "final offensive" in El Salvador had failed. That failure disposed Secretary of State Haig to give high priority to El Salvador. Here was an opportunity to dramatize the differences between the two administrations, to challenge leftist radicals in a vulnerable position, and to seize the initiative within the administration. "Mr. President, this is one you can win," Haig reportedly told the president. As promised, White, Bowdler, and others associated with the Carter administration's policy in Latin America were replaced; additional aid for El Salvador was requested from Congress; and wheat sales and economic aid to Nicaragua were suspended. On February 23 the State Department issued a white paper detailing charges that the Soviet bloc, Cuba, and Nicaragua had supplied arms to the Salvadoran guerrillas. Administration officials talked at times of "going to the source" of Marxist subversion in Central America—by blockading Cuba.

Nevertheless, the administration's actions fell short of the approach Haig sought, and came closer to an extension of Carter policy. On March 3 the United States announced that it was sending an additional twenty military advisers and twenty-five million dollars in military equipment to El Salvador. This was much less than Secretary Haig had been asking for. And less than a month after the publication of the white paper, a State Department spokesman accused the press of overemphasizing Central America. For the rest of 1981 Central America would be treated in a more low-key manner by the administration.[18]

17. Jeff Stein, "The Day of Reckoning Is Coming: An Interview with Robert E. White," *Progressive* (September, 1981) 23; Rubin, "Reagan Administration Policymaking and Central America," 316; Barrett, *Gambling with History,* 205; Department of State *Bulletin,* LXXXI (February, 1981), 69; White, "Turnabout in U.S. Policy," 204–205.

18. Haig, *Caveat,* 117–29; Rubin, "Reagan Administration Policymaking and Central America," 302–306; Barrett, *Gambling with History,* 207.

In the months that followed, the new administration argued that, in supplying economic and military aid to the Duarte regime, it was essentially carrying out a policy that had been laid down by the Carter administration. Reagan officials did not seek a reversal of the program for land reform and bank nationalization. There was no right-wing coup, and the United States government took steps to ensure that elections promised for 1982 would indeed take place.

As for policy toward Nicaragua, the administration moved slowly after the initial suspension of aid. In mid-February, 1981, on instructions from Washington, the American ambassador to Nicaragua met with Sandinista leaders to inform them that the United States had decided to withhold new disbursement of American assistance until it was satisfied that the Sandinistas were no longer giving supplies to the Salvadoran guerrillas. In response, the Nicaraguans told the ambassador that Managua had taken a firm decision not to permit Nicaraguan territory to be used for transferring arms to El Salvador. On April 1, 1981, the president, in light of evidence of slowed but continuing arms traffic, formally cut off disbursement of the final fifteen million dollars in assistance made available the previous year. Beyond this, however, American policy seemed to be on hold. In part this was because of the preoccupation with other matters, but the long vacancy at the desk of the assistant secretary for inter-American affairs certainly contributed. The nominee to this position was finally confirmed in mid-June. In August he traveled to Managua to discuss an American plan to reduce friction between the two countries, but the Sandinistas rejected the American conditions for the resumption of aid. In November the CIA submitted to the president a plan for channeling aid to Nicaraguan exiles seeking to overthrow the Sandinista government.

While the Reagan policies sometimes resembled those of the Carter administration, the style of American foreign policy had clearly changed. The fact that human rights played a less central role in American policy meant that there was significantly less public pressure on the Salvadoran government to curb the excesses of its security forces, though the American chargé d'affaires continued to press privately for movement in the investigation of the killing of the American missionaries, and Congress continued to insist that aid be made conditional on an improvement in the observance of human rights. The Carter human-rights policies had to a considerable degree been based on mandatory legislation, and the new administration found that its freedom to change previous policies was restricted by such laws. Another constraint was the reluctance of public opinion—and the military—to become heavily involved militarily and turn Central America into "another Vietnam."

In sum, the election and transition events prompted unintended consequences and complicated the efforts of the Carter administration to carry out the foreign policy it desired. Some of this could probably have been avoided. In particular, a smaller, more manageable transition team would have made fewer problems for all concerned. The Reagan team's transition decision to put foreign policy questions on the back burner, its lack of a settled decision-making process for foreign policy, and its desire to put as much distance as possible between itself and the preceding administration produced a policy that ran the risk of forfeiting congressional support. This quickly led to an embarrassing retreat on Central American policy, which in turn emboldened liberal and moderate critics of the administration.[19]

## Iran and the Hostages

The consequences of the transition for another foreign policy issue—the crisis over the American hostages in Iran—were much more positive. Whereas the deadline of January 20 energized the right and the left in Central America, further polarizing the region and creating foreign policy problems, the deadline served as a spur to speed the negotiations on the hostages. But even in this case the transition posed potential problems.

When militant Iranian students stormed the United States em-

19. Christopher Dickey, "Obedezco Pero No Cumplo" in Leiken (ed.) *Central America: Anatomy of Conflict,* 43; I. M. Destler, "The Elusive Consensus: Congress and Central America," in *ibid.,* 319–23; New York *Times,* December 27, 1980, p. A1, January 11, 1981, p. A3, January 14, 1981, p. A3, January 19, 1981, p. A11; Haig, *Caveat,* 127–31; Department of State *Bulletin,* LXXXI (February, 1981), 68–69. The Department of State *Bulletin,* LXXXI (April, 1981), 11, 22, reprints statements by the president and the secretary of state insisting that they are continuing Carter administration policy.

bassy and took its staff hostage in November, 1979, American officials hoped that the crisis would end quickly. Contrary to their hope, however, the resolution of the problem took about fourteen months. A series of secret negotiations developed early in 1980, but these ultimately failed, as the hostage crisis itself became hostage to the continuing confusion over who had authority in the new revolutionary government of Iran. Carter administration officials who had made their arrangements with Iran's westernized and secular leaders, President Bani-Sadr and Foreign Minister Ghotzbadeh, found that the country's religious leaders could and did exercise veto power on the government's decisions.

On April 1, the day of the Wisconsin primary, President Carter called in the press early in the morning to make a prearranged statement about Iran that was supposed to set in motion a process by which the hostages would be freed. It soon became clear that the Iranian government would not follow through with the scenario that had been planned, and that the hostages would not be freed. On April 7 the administration announced the breaking of diplomatic relations and the imposition of a total economic embargo. On April 11 the president gave the go-ahead for a rescue attempt to take place on April 24.

Throughout this period President Carter's actions and statements were given special scrutiny because the presidential primary contest was in full swing. In 1968 President Johnson, by removing himself from the presidential contest, had sought to reduce allegations of personal or partisan motivation in his negotiations with the North Vietnamese. Carter, a candidate himself, had no such protection. Thus, many came to believe that the April 1 announcement had been made with the Wisconsin primary in mind; Reagan supporters would seek to exploit that belief in the fall with their warnings of an "October Surprise."

After the failure of the rescue mission, the resignation of Secretary Vance, and the appointment of Edmund Muskie as his successor, a period of policy reassessment set in, and the hostage issue moved from the center of public attention. The administration continued to seek to make contact with the Iranians and learned that the economic measures against Iran were beginning to hurt. In Iran the internal political crisis intensified as the Iranian clerics sought to tighten their control over the government. A new parliament was inaugurated on May 28, but it immediately fell into a long period of inactivity as it examined the credentials of its members. It was not until August that a new prime minister was chosen. Thus, the Iranians, too, let the hostage crisis slip off center stage.[20]

Suddenly, on September 9, after months of inaction, Sadegh Tabatabai, an Iranian with close family ties to the Ayatollah Khomeini, indicated to the Americans through the German foreign minister and the American embassy in Bonn that Iran was ready to work to resolve the crisis. Apparently, the death of the Shah in late July and the worldwide economic and political pressure had begun to move key figures within Iran. Tabatabai's credentials were confirmed when Khomeini made a speech on September 12 repeating the earlier proposal that Tabatabai had made through the Germans. In his speech Khomeini set forth four demands or conditions to which the Americans would have to agree before the hostages would be returned: the return of the Shah's wealth, the unfreezing of Iranian assets, the withdrawal of legal action against Iran, and an American pledge of nonintervention in Iranian affairs. President Carter found the proposals "generally acceptable" and authorized Deputy Secretary of State Warren Christopher to travel to Europe to share the American counterproposals with European leaders and to meet secretly with Tabatabai.[21]

Surprisingly, the Iranian insisted that the issue be resolved before the anniversary of the hostage-taking, *i.e.*, November 4, 1980, the date of the American presidential election. One member of the monitoring team on the hostage crisis later suggested two possible reasons for this. First, a deadline would be useful in forcing agreement among feuding elements within the Iranian government. Second, the Iranians had a well-deserved reputation for being shrewd bargainers and "would probably calculate that any president, as-

20. Harold Saunders, "Beginning of the End," in Warren Christopher *et al.*, *American Hostages in Iran: The Conduct of a Crisis* (New Haven, 1985), 287–89; Carter, *Keeping Faith*, 496–521; Gary Sick, *All Fall Down: America's Tragic Encounter with Iran* (New York, 1985), 306–307.

21. Carter, *Keeping Faith*, 557–59.

sured of four years in office, would be less likely to compromise than a president fighting for his political life." [22]

By the time serious negotiations began, the fall presidential campaign was in full swing. Candidate Reagan had pledged shortly after being nominated not to bring the hostage crisis into the campaign, but he had also refused to be briefed by the administration. Reagan thus felt free to respond to Khomeini's speech of September 12 by urging that the United States should simply agree to most of the Ayatollah's conditions; the exception was the promise to return the Shah's wealth, since that was not in the hands of the American government. Although President Carter rebuked his Republican opponent the next day for having made public, point-by-point responses to the Ayatollah's conditions, Reagan's statement was "not unhelpful," according to Secretary of State Muskie. As the Washington *Post* noted, Reagan's statement freed the administration "of the anxieties it has felt that Mr. Reagan would hover on the right, threatening to undercut any Carter effort to negotiate the hostages' return." The administration could negotiate knowing that, in effect, Reagan had endorsed the main points of its position. [23]

Although the administration's contacts with the Reagan camp on the Iranian problem were minimal at most throughout the campaign, it successfully engaged in a sustained effort to inform members of Congress about the ongoing crisis. This effort served the valuable purpose of keeping Congress behind the president and forestalling political criticism from that direction.

The Reagan camp recognized and feared the possibility that Carter might arrange to bring back the hostages shortly before the election. Had the president been able to do so, it might have gained him a second term. Reagan aides often referred to the "October Surprise," trying to discredit in advance any sudden breakthrough as mere political manipulation. This allegation in itself could have had the effect of chilling negotiations. In fact, the outbreak of war be-

22. Sick, *All Fall Down,* 309–10, 319–20.

23. Gary Sick, "Military Options and Constraints," in Christopher *et al., American Hostages in Iran,* 164–70; Washington *Post,* September 15, 1980, p. A20, September 16, 1980, pp. A1·, A20–21. Candidate John Anderson joined Reagan in suggesting that the United States agree to three of the four conditions set down by Khomeini.

tween Iran and Iraq in late September did just that—first, by delaying the return to Iran of Tabatabai, with whom Christopher had been negotiating in Europe, and second, by diverting and absorbing the attention of the Iranian leadership.

The war did make the Iranians acutely aware of their diplomatic and economic isolation, increasing their incentive to resolve the crisis. When Mohammed Ali Rajai, the new Iranian prime minister, traveled to the United Nations to ask for sanctions against Iraq for invading Iran, he found himself receiving instead a steady round of reprimands from scores of countries. The prime minister refused to meet with American officials, but he did not prevent the exchanges that were taking place between officials of the two governments through the German intermediaries. Thus, in late October, with about two weeks left before election day, the hostage issue creeped back into the campaign. On one side, the President began to express cautious optimism that the hostage crisis would shortly be resolved. He felt encouraged by Iran's new willingness to discuss specific terms of an agreement and by the Iranian parliament's scheduling a major debate during the last week of October to discuss the conditions of an agreement with the United States. On the other, candidate Reagan, stung by attacks on his foreign policy credentials, declared that he did not "understand why 52 Americans have been held hostage for almost a year now." [24]

Events in Iran continued to favor the Republican challenger, even though, unlike the Nixon camp in an analogous situation in 1968, Reagan partisans had no way to control those events. The Iranian parliament repeatedly postponed debate on the Ayatollah's conditions for lack of a quorum, as hard-line members boycotted the proceedings. Then, early on Sunday, November 2, the parliament finally achieved a quorum, debated for three or four hours, and voted. Carter canceled his day's schedule of campaign appearances, notified Reagan and Anderson of the latest developments, and returned to the White House to study and prepare a response to the Iranians'

24. Saunders, "Beginning of the End," 292; Brzezinski, *Power and Principle*, 500; Abraham Ribicoff, "Lessons and Conclusions," in Christopher *et al.*, *American Hostages in Iran*, 381; Sick, "Military Options and Constraints," 164; Washington *Post*, October 21, 1980, p. A1, October 22, 1980, p. A1.

proposals. The parliament had chosen to approve the Ayatollah's four points (which the Americans considered negotiable), had assumed responsibility for the hostages, and had designated Algeria as the sole authorized channel for negotiation. But it had also included some terms that were unacceptable to the United States. An American response designed to keep negotiations going was drafted and sent. That evening Carter issued a brief public statement describing the parliament's proposals as a "significant development" that "appeared to offer a positive basis" for an acceptable settlement. The president refused to predict when the captive Americans might come home, but he promised that his actions "would not be affected by the calendar or the impending election." Some later speculated that the Iranians thought Carter would have no choice but to comply with their demands for electoral reasons.

Unfortunately for the president, the newspapers and airwaves during the next two days were full of stories commemorating the first anniversary of the taking of the hostages and speculating on the prospects for the return of the hostages in light of the recent events. Patrick Caddell, Carter's pollster, detected a precipitous decline in the popular standing of the president and a dramatic shift to the Reagan side during these two days. Few others were prepared for the Reagan landslide that took place on November 4.[25]

With the campaign over, Carter redoubled his efforts to resolve the issue that had bedeviled his final year as president. He spent part of the week after the election reviewing and approving documents that would be the basis of Deputy Secretary Christopher's negotiations in Algeria. Both Carter and the State Department, in separate statements, reminded the country that until January 20 the constitutional responsibility for pursuing the hostages' freedom remained with the Carter administration. Administration officials promised to keep the president-elect fully informed on how the administration was proceeding, a procedure that would allow him to make known any objections.

President-elect Reagan preferred that the crisis be resolved before he took office and offered support for Carter's continued efforts to

25. Carter, *Keeping Faith*, 563–67; Washington *Post*, November 3, 1980, p. A1; New York *Times*, November 5, 1980, p. A1.

negotiate during the interregnum. In late December, the Iranians finally produced a counteroffer to the one Christopher had taken to Algeria. It included a demand for twenty-four billion dollars as a guarantee against the settlement of future claims and counterclaims on the Iranians. The United States immediately rejected this as an unreasonable and even ridiculous amount. With the negotiations apparently deadlocked, officials held out virtually no hope that the hostages would regain their freedom by January 20. At this point Edwin Meese, head of Reagan's transition team, warned the Iranians on December 29 that they should not expect a better deal on the hostage crisis than what the Carter administration was offering. This amplified President-elect Reagan's comment, on hearing of the Iranian demands, that "I don't think you pay ransom for people that have been kidnapped by barbarians." [26]

In pressing for a last-ditch effort to break the deadlock, Carter officials deliberately exploited the uncertainties created by the coming turnover of authority and highlighted President-elect Reagan's blunt language about the crisis as an added incentive for the Iranians to come to terms. If no agreement was reached by January 20, a whole new team of negotiators would have to take over, a new set of criteria for a settlement might be established, and a good deal of time would pass before negotiations could resume. These arguments apparently had the desired effect. Christopher later observed that the January 20 deadline made some of the parties in the negotiations willing to do things that might have horrified them under a more leisurely timetable; it also made the Iranians more pliable at the end. [27] On January 6 the Americans received a more forthcoming response from Iran, after the Algerian intermediaries had made clear to the Tehran government the constraints under which the negotiations were taking place. General terms for the hostages' release were worked out by Friday, January 16, but snags in the complicated financial arrangements delayed the actual transfer until January 20,

26. Washington *Post,* December 29, 1980, p. A10.
27. Carter, *Keeping Faith,* 572–73; Washington *Post,* November 6, 1980, p. A1; New York *Times,* December 30, 1980, p. A10; Sick, "Military Options and Constraints," 170; Warren Christopher, introduction to Christopher *et al., American Hostages in Iran,* 6.

shortly after President Reagan took the oath of office. While on the inaugural stand Carter heard the good news that the plane carrying the hostages had left Iran. At Reagan's request, Carter flew to Frankfort, West Germany, shortly thereafter to welcome them back. Many felt that the Iranians had deliberately stalled in order to deliver one final humiliating blow to the departing president.[28]

Carter was largely unsuccessful in involving and committing the incoming administration to the agreement. A diary entry of January 2, 1981, which he included in his memoirs, notes the continuing reluctance by Secretary of State–designate Haig and National Security Adviser–designate Richard Allen to be briefed on the Iranian situation. No deputies to Haig or Caspar Weinberger, who would be the new secretary of defense, had yet been named. One member of the transition team, Fred Ikle, had been designated, but the president obviously felt that the issue was not receiving the high-level attention it deserved: "We presumed [they] . . . were avoiding the top-level briefings on some of the very sensitive issues in order to keep the full responsibility on the incumbents. If this was the reason it was fine with me. . . . However we felt that with thorough briefings there would be a much smoother and more effective transition of authority to the Republican leaders."[29]

Haig apparently received briefings shortly thereafter, but less than two weeks remained before the inauguration when he received clearance for three of his close associates to sit down with informed Carter officials to be briefed on the details of the negotiations then transpiring in Algiers. Moreover, R. T. McNamar, incoming deputy secretary of the Treasury Department, has reported that, at least in that department, officials from the secretary down were so consumed with the fast-paced developments surrounding the hostage crisis that they did not have the time to brief their successors fully, on Iran or anything else.

One consequence of this lack of involvement was that when the new administration took office, it seriously considered abrogating the entire agreement that had just been made. Some who favored

28. Carter, *Keeping Faith*, 2–14, 592–95; Brzezinski, *Power and Principle*, 507–508.
29. Carter, *Keeping Faith*, 591. See also Sick, *All Fall Down*, 334.

abrogation did so on domestic political grounds; others apparently believed that the United States had paid a ransom for the hostages' return. Both Haig and Allen strongly urged the president to abide by the agreement because national honor was at stake and because a ransom had not in fact been paid. In the end this view prevailed and was confirmed by a State Department statement issued February 18. The statement announced that a review of the agreements had taken place, and, having considered all the circumstances carefully, the new administration had decided "to approve implementation of the agreements in strict accordance with the terms of the agreements." [30] The United States would honor its obligations under international law.

In virtually all of the cases discussed in earlier chapters, elections and the transitions that accompanied them tended to delay negotiations. In the case of the hostages in Iran, however, the transfer of administrations on Inauguration Day probably acted more as a spur than as an obstacle. When combined with Carter's own determination to resolve the problem before leaving office and the Iranian need for funds and military equipment, the transition apparently helped to speed the negotiating process.

On the other hand, the end of the hostage crisis vividly revealed the potential for contradiction between international law and the outcome of a democratic political process. The new administration came surprisingly close to rejecting the hostage agreements, even though the government had committed itself. Most disturbing of all was the extent to which such a decision might have been made in ignorance. It would presumably have been based on the assumption that the American government had paid a ransom for the return of its hostages, when in fact the only money that changed hands was Iranian. Such a lack of information, while endemic to transitions, demonstrates the danger they may pose to informed diplomacy.

30. Haig, *Caveat*, 69, 78–81; Newsom, "Presidential Transitions and the Handling of Foreign Policy Crises," 105; Department of State *Bulletin*, LXXXI (March, 1981), 17.

# CONCLUSION

What we call the beginning is often the end
And to make an end is to make a beginning.
The end is where we start from.

—T. S. Eliot
"Little Gidding"

A review of the five postwar interparty transitions suggests a few generalizations. In the first place, campaign statements and commitments have consistently been a source of difficulty to new presidents, either constraining actions that later seem desirable, or embarrassing them when they find it necessary to break some of their promises. This was true of Eisenhower on liberating Eastern Europe, Kennedy on Cuba, Nixon on nuclear superiority, Carter on human rights, and Reagan on Formosa and China.

Second, despite the weakening of the American consensus in foreign affairs, it appears that in most instances the *objectives* of incumbents and incoming administrations have been basically similar. Both sides in 1952–1953 wanted a settlement in Korea; in 1960–1961, an overthrow of the Cuban government and an end to the gold crisis; in 1968–1969, peace in Vietnam and arms limitations; in 1976–1977, respect for human rights in foreign countries and arms limitation; and in 1980–1981, return of the hostages and encouragement of democratic, non-Marxian regimes in Central America. Among these cases there was a clear difference of opinion between the two sides—which did not appear until well after the interregnum—only in the case of action to be taken in Iran in 1952–1953.

But of course there were real differences, not in ultimate goals but in style, tactics, priorities, and pace. In a few unpleasant and unpopular situations, like the Vietnam War and the hostage crisis, incoming presidents preferred resolutions before they were inaugurated. But on issues carrying the promise of political benefits, the usual aim of incoming administrations had been to delay action and commitment until after the inauguration. They have sought to take charge of, and seek credit for, actions that might be taken by either side, as the incoming Nixon administration did on the nonproliferation treaty in 1968–1969. In a few instances (the AWACS sale to Saudi Arabia, for example), those coming into office have urged delay even when it might be politically costly to them to take the issue on.

On this question the newcomers have usually won. Our cases suggest that, in the area of foreign affairs, delay has been the most frequent effect of transitions. It may be seen in the British-Iranian oil problem in 1952–1953, the gold crisis (and possibly the Bay of Pigs) in 1960–1961, the Vietnam peace talks and the arms negotiations in 1968–1969, the arms limitation talks in 1976–1977, and Central American policy in 1980–1981. The only instance in which a transition may have speeded up a solution was the return of the hostages in 1981, and it may never be known whether, or to what extent, the scheduled inauguration of Reagan spurred the Iranians to reach a settlement. It should be stressed that delay does not mean simply the same action at a later time. It often has important substantive effects. Some of them are unfortunate—deaths in a war (such as in Korea and Vietnam) or failure to ban new weapons (like MIRVs in 1968–1969) in arms negotiations. Others can be favorable—a sounder bargaining position after a reappraisal of the issues at stake, or a refusal to be bound by an artificial January 20 deadline.

The case studies also show that contacts between representatives of an incoming president, both before and after his election, and officials of foreign governments are not uncommon. They cause few problems as long as they are limited to getting acquainted, conveying information, and assurances that current policy will be maintained. When the newcomers make promises of new policies or seek to negotiate with other states on their current relations with the United States, difficulties are probable. In the former case the foreign officials are led to wonder who speaks for this country. In the latter the intervention is likely to be construed as undercutting the current administration—as it often is.

It can also be observed that the career people in the foreign affairs agencies, particularly in the Foreign Service, are and long have been the central butt of the criticisms of the incoming presidential teams. They are seen as the groups least to be trusted. Over the years they have been characterized as subversives, reactionaries, taxeaters, cookie pushers, and covert supporters of the previous administration. They are convenient targets with few outside allies to defend them. This situation is ironic because the success of every incoming team depends on them.

Career officers working on problems on which an incoming administration is widely expected, or is committed, to introduce a reversal or other major change in policy are in a particularly difficult situation. If they identify and work faithfully with the outgoing administration, their future careers may be endangered, even effectively terminated. Best illustrated among our cases by those involved in policy on Central America, this condition is probably most prevalent among senior Foreign Service officers, many of whom serve as ambassadors, assistant secretaries, and their deputies.

The agency transition teams that have operated after the election, especially in the Carter and Reagan transitions, are widely considered overgrown, out of control, and insufficiently tied to persons who would later assume office in the new administration. They are relatively ineffective and often a source of embarrassment to the incoming team.

The five transitions since World War II lend wavering support to the hypothesis that transitions are likely to be less turbulent and less rancorous when the incumbent president has not been a candidate for reelection. The first three, when the winning candidates were Eisenhower, Kennedy, and Nixon, were on average smoother and more civil than the last two, when the winners were Carter and Reagan. Those first three transitions had other advantages, though none was an undiluted model of benevolent virtue. One strength was that, on underlying policies and goals, there was still a consensus in the land, though by 1968–1969 it was strained because of the virulent opposition to the Vietnam War. By 1976 the consensus had been severely challenged within the two parties as well as between them, and in 1980–1981 it was virtually invisible. Another factor was the nature and backgrounds of the successful candidates themselves.

Eisenhower and Nixon were—as modern presidents go—old hands in government, wise to the ways of Washington. Eisenhower was particularly well qualified in foreign affairs and national defense, and Nixon had been for eight years a vice-president. The contrast with Carter and Reagan could hardly be sharper. Indeed, both of the latter ran against the government itself.

The conventional wisdom among transition watchers is that of these five transitions, Nixon's in 1968–1969 was the smoothest and most effective, and Reagan's in 1980–1981, the rockiest. The Johnson-Nixon transfer had a number of strengths. In the first place, the two knew each other well and came from comparable environments. They shared a strong intention to make the transition successful. Johnson made more strenuous efforts to prepare his successor than any other outgoing president in the postwar period. Probably more than most other incoming presidents, Nixon appreciated the importance of preparation, of continuity, and of cooperation with the outgoing group. He brought into the foreign affairs side of his administration a number of officials who had gained experience in the Eisenhower days, and he retained in many important (though largely inconspicuous) posts personnel inherited from Johnson. With the help of his national security aide, Henry Kissinger, he was prepared with a firm procedure for decision making in foreign affairs by the time of inauguration. However one may feel about the nature of the plan and its effects on the distribution of power in the executive branch, it seems to have suited Nixon well. On January 20, 1969, he was ready—probably readier than the other new presidents in this thirty-year period—to move toward his ambitious foreign policy goals.

But the transition of 1968–1969 was not an unalloyed success, as none are. With his October 31 public announcement of the opening of peace negotiations on Vietnam, Johnson aroused suspicions that he was manipulating foreign policy for partisan purposes. His quest for an interregnum summit justifiably fueled fears of a last-minute bargain that would hamper the freedom of action of the new administration. The Nixon team did not then or later develop an effective formula for resolving America's greatest overseas problem—the Vietnam War. Its interregnum machinations behind the scenes before the election were certainly not helpful to the quest for successful peace negotiations in Paris. Furthermore, the White House—centered apparatus it established for decision making created deep divisions among the agencies and personnel in foreign affairs. It, and the style by which it was introduced, laid the framework for the bureaucratic infighting, back channels, suspicion, concern about secrecy, and phone taps—in short, the things that would bring the Nixon administration down five and one-half years later.

In contrast, the Carter-Reagan transition, especially in foreign affairs, was at best a difficult one. Neither the new president nor any of his immediate aides was familiar with Washington or with foreign affairs. Their views of the world, their ideology, differed radically from those of any recent administration. They therefore placed little trust in their predecessors or in those who worked for their predecessors. They were the slowest of all new administrations since 1945 to fill their presidential appointment slots.

Yet, when measured against its own standards and priorities, the early Reagan administration was surprisingly effective. It accomplished little that was new in foreign policy, but that was its intent—to keep foreign policy on the back burner until the domestic program and the budget were wrapped up, and to do nothing about arms control, at least until American arms were built up. The only positive priority in the international arena was an enormous increase in the defense budget (along with sharp reductions in domestic outlays and in tax rates). This was accomplished with astonishing success.

Thus, it is difficult to grade transitions as a whole—to term them good or bad, effective or ineffective. Like Nixon's and Reagan's, each had strong and weak points. Eisenhower's aides successfully delayed action on the British-Iranian oil dispute until they were in a position to overthrow Mosadeq. But Eisenhower's and Dulles' failure to defend public servants from charges of Communist sympathies damaged several significant sectors of the foreign affairs agencies and probably had a widely unhappy effect on the morale of their personnel. Kennedy's new team prepared itself effectively for the gold-outflow problem, partly by retaining as secretary of the treasury a Republican under secretary of state. But the preparation for, and the conduct of, the Bay of Pigs affair were at best dismal. Carter's objectives with regard to human rights were widely endorsed at the time of his election, but they were inadequately supported by programs of inducement and coordination with other goals.

With the comfortable hindsight of the 1980s, it is possible to speculate on the longer-range effects of some of these transitions. The Eisenhower delay on Iran in 1952–1953, which led to the overthrow of the Iranian government and the reinstallation of the Shah, may have had longer-range implications for the United States' willingness to intervene covertly to influence the political coloration of other governments. It apparently gave rise to popular antagonism in Iran both to the United States and to the Shah, which grew over the years to lead to his overthrow and expulsion and to the taking of the American hostages in 1979. Kennedy's Bay of Pigs had one constructive effect. It provided extraordinary preparation and training for the people who would confront the Cuban missile crisis a year and a half later. The style, tactics, and system embedded in the conduct of foreign affairs during the Nixon interregnum may well have contained the seeds not only of the opening to China, SALT I, and détente, but also of the corrosive climate and devious conduct that led to Watergate. Carter would hardly have sent Secretary of State Vance to Moscow with a proposal for substantial arms reduction had he anticipated the Soviet reaction and the consequent long delay in effective negotiations. When SALT II was finally signed, the political climate had cooled, and the treaty was never ratified. Reagan's increases in defense expenditures, coupled with tax reductions, were certainly major sources of the enormous deficits of the 1980s, to which some people attribute the American trade deficits, the precarious financial condition of Third World nations, and many other problems.

All of these examples suggest the importance to a new administration of careful study, exploration, and anticipation as far into the future as possible before undertaking major initiatives. During the months following the election and inauguration, a new presidential team is most tempted to act but is also most vulnerable.

History's confounding of expectations ought also to induce caution among outside observers who seek to assess transitions. The difficulty of declaring a particular transfer of power a success or not, in either the short or the long term, rests in part on the fact that transitions necessarily serve differing, even contradictory purposes. The interregnum is said to be both too long and too short—and both criticisms have some validity, though for contrasting reasons. Indeed, transitions are largely composed of antinomies and paradoxes.

The turnover of power, especially in the modern era, requires more than the mutual toleration of incoming and outgoing officials; it demands their active collaboration in an extended task of immense complexity and delicacy. Yet, these two groups harbor all the antipathies of recent adversaries, and in a democracy the case could hardly be otherwise. Political appointees, particularly those with no prior government experience, must also cooperate with and depend on career personnel; the wiser they are, the more rapidly they recognize this. Still, one of the things they will learn with experience is that they should not rely exclusively on any one source of information and advice, for each has some bureaucratic interest to protect. That two groups as dissimilar in background and expectations as permanent government employees and newly arrived members of the young administration will quickly accept each other seems in the abstract improbable. But their harmony is not only an ideal; in a number of cases since World War II it has been an accomplished fact.

At the heart of the differing requirements lies the reality that a transition is a Janus-like institution: it looks both forward and backward and must serve the cause of both preservation and renewal. As the *Economist* recently put it (referring to a polity other than the United States), "No democracy is complete until it has practised alternation of government, the art of proving that change can be compatible with continuity." [1] Some transitions may be more successful at meeting the goal of change, some that of continuity. If they are to serve the country effectively, they cannot ignore either. The effectiveness of transitions—not only keeping the government running smoothly but also bringing about change in policy and direction—depends heavily upon the openness and extent of communications between those coming in and those going out and upon the degree to which they respect and trust one another. This is true at all levels of administration. Attitudes of suspicion and hostility may have lasting effects upon an incoming group that combines inexperience and limited acquaintance with cockiness.

1. *Economist*, August 17, 1985, p. 12.

Transitions are more likely to be happy and productive the less the preceding political campaigns have been bitter, ideological, and personal, and the more that members of the new administration have given serious, early thought to problems they will face. The crucial element in the success of any transition is most often the spirit, the experience, and the wisdom of the newcomers. They must dispel their illusions that everything they find is bad and must be corrected; that their predecessors (and the career staff) are incompetent; that change in government can be easy and quick; and that government agencies should be run as nearly as possible like closed corporations, protected from congressional and public scrutiny. They must learn, and learn rapidly, that the federal government is different and is difficult, that they too will be leaving in a few years, and that in the meantime they are operating as trustees in the people's interest.

Eliot's words about ends and beginnings are never more relevant than at times of presidential transitions, which mark both an end and a beginning for the participants immediately involved. But for the country as a whole the change of administrations is neither a complete halt nor a wholly new start, but only an interval in an ongoing history. Individuals and the particular administrations they serve are but transient elements in this continuing national development. Their attitudes are important, for without the proper spirit no institution will work. Organizational changes are also important, for institutions help to shape attitudes. Most of the problems of transition can be handled with grace and effectiveness, given a reasonable supply of sophistication and goodwill on all sides. But sophistication has often been a rare commodity among newcomers, and goodwill has not been in abundant supply on either side. These deficiencies can surely be ameliorated, but only if it is recognized that transitions form both an opportunity and a responsibility to serve the nation.

# Recommendations of the Commission on Presidential Transitions and Foreign Policy (1987)

### CAMPAIGN RHETORIC

1. Presidential candidates should display a special degree of caution in the number and scope of promises they make in the foreign field.

2. To ensure that harmful statements are not made inadvertently out of a lack of information, incumbents should offer, and opposition candidates should accept, full and objective briefings during the election campaign. To the extent possible, these briefings should include information on projected actions as well as the current world situation.

3. All candidates should take special care to refrain, even at the expense of political advantage, from disparaging the career services on whom they will later need to rely for the wise conduct of the country's foreign policy.

4. Once elected, the President-elect should carefully review campaign promises in light of all the facts then available in order to make his decisions afresh away from the pressures of the campaign.

### APPOINTMENTS

5. Each candidate should begin gathering necessary information on potential appointees immediately after the candidate has been nominated. Even if the candidate assumes that his selection of Cabinet and sub-Cabinet nominees during the campaign would be unwise, and in any event politically impracticable, an early start on determining the pool from which nominees will later be drawn is a farsighted step that will pay dividends.

6. Large teams created exclusively for the purpose of analyzing departmental effectiveness during the transition should be abolished. Small task forces concerned with issues, and composed of persons experienced in foreign policy and placed as soon as possible under the direction of the incoming department or agency head, will prove more helpful.

7. Only those members of task forces who will be receiving confidential information need obtain security clearances.

8. Members of existing congressional staffs should not be members of these study groups. However, they may usefully serve as sources of information.

9. The incoming President should select his key officials having major responsibilities in areas of U.S. foreign and security relations—including secretary of state, secretary of defense, secretary of the treasury, director of the Central Intelligence Agency, director of the Office of Management and Budget, and national security assistant—within four weeks after the election. He should fill all the sub-Cabinet posts in these departments and agencies within ten weeks.

10. The incoming President and his department and agency heads should agree at the outset on procedures for appointing sub-Cabinet officers. Under one successful precedent, the President and secretary agree that there should be mutual concurrence on all appointments.

11. Greater consideration should be given to appointing to high-level posts career officials and those who have served in previous administrations.

12. Nominees should be given better preparation for their confirmation proceedings than has often been the case in the past.

13. All aspects of the appointment process—White House decision making, FBI investigation, and congressional review—should be examined afresh for ways of responsibly expediting appointments. Representatives of the White House, the FBI, and Congress should share responsibility for drawing up new guidelines to speed the process.

## ADVICE AND INFORMATION

14. All documents necessary to the implementation of ongoing policy or required as background for future decisions should be reproduced before their transfer to the National Archives and a copy retained at the White House for the information of the succeeding President and his team. In selecting documents, copies of which should be retained in the White House, a distinction is made between those reflecting intimate, personal and political advice to the President and those that record decisions and actions or the reasoning leading to such choices. Those documents which fall in the latter category should be retained in the White House. Although the final decision on the disposition of files must remain with the outgoing President, the initial selection should be in the hands of a person or persons implicitly trusted by both administrations, perhaps a career officer.

15. OMB should be restored as the institutional memory of the Executive Office by depoliticizing it. This would be facilitated by substantially reducing the number of non-career political appointees at the top of OMB from the present fifteen.

16. The institutional memory of the White House proper should be strengthened by retaining some persons on the NSC staff from one administration to the next, at least temporarily.

17. To encourage a new administration to ask an official of the preceding administration to stay on temporarily as counselor, special funds should be made available for this purpose.

18. For those appointees who lack prior experience in political life, efforts to strengthen their preparation should be increased. Seminars for officials-designate, such as those provided by several of the leading schools and centers of public affairs and at times the White House itself, have proved their worth and should be expanded. The State Department's orientation sessions for non-career appointees to ambassadorships are an encouraging effort; they should be strengthened and extended to appointments in Washington as well.

19. Outgoing officials should be expected to pass along to their successors in informal discussion their evaluations of the abilities of

career personnel in their agencies. More formally, they should leave behind job descriptions for the important posts under their jurisdiction and their ideas on the qualities required for holding those posts.

20. The President-elect should give serious early consideration to the different ways in which the national security adviser and NSC staff may be used, and to their authority relative to that of the State Department and the Defense Department.

21. Each new President, together with his principal advisers, either before or shortly after the inauguration, should receive a thorough briefing or participate in an abbreviated exercise to equip himself and key members of his new team to meet their responsibilities in the event of a nuclear crisis. He should also begin to gain familiarity, in concrete and specific terms, with his options in a nonnuclear crisis, in meetings with the Joint Chiefs of Staff and other relevant security advisers.

22. Transition planning by the candidate's staff should begin during the campaign, but not under a separately funded formal organization.

23. Public funding of post-election transition activities should continue.

### THE BUDGET

24. In years in which a regular transition occurs, the outgoing President should submit a budget of "current services," that is, an estimate of spending for programs and activities already mandated by law and adjusted for predicted changes in economic conditions (such as inflation, economic growth, and unemployment) and the number of recipients of government programs (such as welfare).

25. The outgoing President should open the files of OMB to his successor immediately after the election. Although the Congressional Budget Office and various nongovernmental budget studies are valuable sources of budgetary data, OMB remains the central repository of such information; that information should be used to educate Presidents-elect and their staffs as early as possible.

26. The new President should submit his revisions to this budget only after taking the time to think them through. The deadline for

his submission should be extended from the present April 10 to the end of May. We believe that this schedule will still give Congress ample time to consider the budget in a deliberate way.

27. The outgoing President will continue to produce a lame-duck economic report. We urge that he not fill this document with unrealistic assumptions designed to embarrass his successor. If he wishes to make a political statement or to leave behind his views on budgetary policy, let him do so in his final State of the Union message or a Farewell Address.

### INTERREGNUM DIVISION OF AUTHORITY

28. The incoming administration should refrain from publicly or privately urging unrequested advice on the incumbents and the outgoing administration should be wary of needlessly tying the hands of its successor. On the other hand, we urge informal consultation between the incoming and outgoing secretaries of state to consider whether certain sensitive issues can and should be dealt with by the outgoing administration in its last days in office.

29. Pre-inaugural meetings between representatives of the incoming administration and foreign diplomats or leaders should be sharply limited. They should be confined to a few persons clearly authorized by letter to speak for the incoming administration by the President-elect or the secretary of state–designate. These discussions may be for the educational purpose of allowing new officials to inform themselves about the problems they will face, or they may be substantive talks that will allow the new administration to act immediately upon taking office. In either case, the incumbent administration should be kept informed to the extent possible. Nothing should give the impression that the President-elect has any authority to act before the inauguration or interfere with ongoing actions by the incumbent administration.

# SELECTED BIBLIOGRAPHY

## BOOKS

Acheson, Dean. *Present at the Creation: My Years in the State Department.* New York, 1969.

Adams, Bruce, and Kathryn Kavanaugh-Baran. *Promise and Performance: Carter Builds a New Administration.* Toronto, 1979.

Barrett, Russell H. *Promise and Performance in Australian Politics.* New York, 1959.

Beyle, Thad, ed. *Gubernatorial Transitions.* Durham, N.C., 1985.

Blanke, W. Wendell. *The Foreign Service of the United States.* New York, 1969.

Borklund, O. W. *The Department of Defense.* New York, 1968.

Brauer, Carl M. *Presidential Transitions: Eisenhower Through Reagan.* New York, 1986.

Brown, Peter G., and Douglas Maclean, eds. *Human Rights and U.S. Foreign Policy: Principles and Applications.* Lexington, Mass., 1979.

Brzezinski, Zbigniew. *Power and Principle: Memoirs of the National Security Adviser, 1977–1981.* New York, 1983.

Bunce, Valerie. *Do New Leaders Make a Difference? Executive Succession and Public Policy Under Capitalism and Socialism.* Princeton, 1981.

Cannon, Lou. *Reagan.* New York, 1982.

Carter, Jimmy. *Keeping Faith: Memoirs of a President.* New York, 1982.

Christian, George. *The President Steps Down: A Personal Memoir of the Transfer of Power.* New York, 1970.

Clark, Keith C., and Laurence J. Legere, eds. *The President and the Management of National Security.* New York, 1969.

David, Paul T., ed. *The Presidential Election and Transition, 1960–1961.* Washington, D.C., 1961.

David, Paul T., and David H. Everson. *The Presidential Election and Transition, 1980–1981.* Carbondale, Ill., 1983.

Destler, I. M., Leslie H. Gelb, and Anthony Lake. *Our Own Worst Enemy: The Unmaking of American Foreign Policy.* New York, 1984.

Donovan, Robert J. *Eisenhower: The Inside Story.* New York, 1956.

Eisenhower, Dwight D. *Mandate for Change, 1953–1956.* Garden City, N.Y., 1963. Vol. I of Eisenhower, *White House Years.* 2 vols.

———. *Waging Peace, 1956–1961.* Garden City, N.Y., 1965. Vol. II of Eisenhower, *White House Years.* 2 vols.

Evans, Rowland, Jr., and Robert D. Novak. *Nixon in the White House: The Frustration of Power.* New York, 1971.

Ferrell, Robert H., ed. *The Eisenhower Diaries.* New York, 1981.

———. *Off the Record: The Private Papers of Harry Truman.* New York, 1980.

Fishel, Jeff. *Presidents and Promises: From Campaign Pledge to Presidential Performance.* Washington, D.C., 1984.

Ford, Gerald. *A Time to Heal.* New York, 1979.

Gaddis, John Lewis. *Strategies of Containment: A Critical Appraisal of Postwar American National Security Policy.* New York, 1982.

Gordon, Kermit, ed. *Agenda for the Nation.* Washington, D.C., 1968.

Greenstein, Fred I. *The Hidden-Hand Presidency: Eisenhower as Leader.* New York, 1982.

———, ed. *The Reagan Presidency: An Early Assessment.* Baltimore, 1983.

Haig, Alexander M., Jr. *Caveat: Realism, Reagan, and Foreign Policy.* New York, 1984.

Heclo, Hugh, and Lester M. Salamon, eds. *The Illusion of Presidential Government.* Boulder, 1981.

Heineman, Ben W., Jr. *Memorandum to the President: Managing the Domestic Agenda in the 1980s.* New York, 1981.

Heller, Francis H., ed. *The Truman White House: The Administration of the Presidency, 1945–1953.* Lawrence, Kan., 1980.

Henderson, John W. *The United States Information Agency.* New York, 1969.

Henry, Laurin L. *Presidential Transitions.* Washington, D.C., 1960.

Hersh, Seymour M. *The Price of Power: Kissinger in the Nixon White House*. New York, 1983.

Hilsman, Roger. *To Move a Nation: The Politics of Foreign Policy in the Administration of John F. Kennedy*. Garden City, N.Y., 1967.

Holsti, Ole R., and James N. Rosenau. *American Leadership in World Affairs: Vietnam and the Breakdown of Consensus*. Boston, 1984.

Hoxie, R. Gordon, ed., *The Presidency and National Security Policy*. New York, 1984.

*Jimmy Carter on the Presidency*. Washington, D.C., 1984.

Johnson, Lyndon B. *The Vantage Point: Perspectives of the Presidency, 1963–1969*. New York, 1971.

Kissinger, Henry. *White House Years*. Boston, 1979.

Lodge, Henry Cabot. *As It Was: An Inside View of Politics and Power in the '50s and '60s*. New York, 1976.

McCauley, Martin, and Stephen Carter, eds. *Leadership and Succession in the Soviet Union, Eastern Europe, and China*. Armonk, N.Y., 1985.

Macy, John W., Bruce Adams, and J. Jackson Walter. *America's Unelected Government: Appointing the President's Team*. Cambridge, Mass., 1983.

Melanson, Richard A., and Kenneth W. Thompson, eds. *Foreign Policy and Domestic Consensus*. Lanham, Md., 1985.

Miller Center of Public Affairs. *Transferring Responsibility: The Dangers of Transition*. Lanham, Md., 1987.

Mosher, Frederick C., ed. *Political Transitions and Foreign Affairs in Britain and France: Their Relevance for the United States*. Lanham, Md., 1985.

National Academy of Public Administration. *Leadership in Jeopardy: The Fraying of the Presidential Appointment System*. Washington, D.C., 1985.

———. *Occasional Papers on the Presidential Appointment Process*. Washington, D.C., 1983.

———. *The Presidential Appointee's Handbook*. Washington, D.C., n.d.

Neustadt, Richard E. *Presidential Power: The Politics of Leadership from FDR to Carter*. New York, 1980.

Newhouse, John. *Cold Dawn: The Story of SALT*. New York, 1973.

Nixon, Richard M. *RN: The Memoirs of Richard Nixon*. New York, 1978.

———. *Six Crises*. Garden City, N.Y., 1962.

Ramazani, Rouhallah K. *Iran's Foreign Policy, 1941–1973*. Charlottesville, 1975.

———. *The United States and Iran: The Patterns of Influence*. New York, 1982.

Roosevelt, Kermit. *Countercoup: The Struggle for the Control of Iran*. New York, 1979.

Schlesinger, Arthur M., Jr. *The Crisis of the Old Order, 1919–1933*. Boston, 1957.

———. *A Thousand Days: John F. Kennedy in the White House*. Boston, 1965.

Schlesinger, Arthur M., Jr., and Fred L. Israel, eds. *History of American Presidential Elections, 1789–1968*. 4 vols. New York, 1971.

Schott, Richard L., and Dagmar S. Hamilton. *People, Positions, and Power: The Political Appointments of Lyndon Johnson*. Chicago, 1983.

Schnapper, M. B., ed. *New Frontiers of the Kennedy Administration: The Texts of the Task Force Reports Prepared for the President*. Washington, D.C., 1961.

Shogan, Robert. *Promises to Keep: Carter's First Hundred Days*. New York, 1977.

Silva, Ruth C. *Presidential Succession*. Ann Arbor, Mich., 1951.

Smith, Gerard. *Doubletalk: The Story of the First Strategic Arms Limitation Talks*. Garden City, N.Y., 1980.

Stanley, David T. *Changing Administrations: The 1961 and 1964 Transitions in Six Departments*. Washington, D.C., 1965.

Talbott, Strobe. *Endgame: The Inside Story of SALT II*. New York, 1979.

Thompson, Kenneth W., ed. *Problems and Prospects*. Lanham, Md., 1986.

Tompkins, Dorothy Louise (Campbell) Culver. *Presidential Succession: A Bibliography*. Berkeley, 1964.

Truman, Harry S. *Years of Trial and Hope*. New York, 1956. Vol. II of Truman, *Memoirs*. 2 vols.

Vance, Cyrus. *Hard Choices: Critical Years in America's Foreign Policy.* New York, 1983.

Vatcher, William H., Jr. *Panmunjom: The Story of the Korean Military Armistice Negotiations.* New York, 1958.

ARTICLES

Benedict, Stephen G. "Changing the Watch in Washington." *Virginia Quarterly Review,* XXXVIII (Winter, 1961), 15–33.

Bloomfield, Lincoln P. "What's Wrong with Transitions." *Foreign Policy,* LV (Summer, 1984), 23–39.

Brody, Richard A. "Public Evaluations and Expectations and the Future of the Presidency." *Problems and Prospects of Presidential Leadership in the Nineteen-Eighties,* edited by James Sterling Young. Vol. I of 3 vols. Washington, D.C., 1982.

Carnegie Corporation. "Transferring the Presidency." *Carnegie Corporation of New York Quarterly* (October, 1960), 1–2.

Drew, Elizabeth. "A Reporter at Large: Human Rights." *New Yorker,* July 18, 1977, pp. 36–62.

Feinrider, Martin. "America's Oil Pledges to Israel: Illegal but Binding Executive Agreements." *New York Journal of International Law and Politics,* XIII (Winter, 1981), 525–68.

Glazer, Nathan. "On Task Forcing." *Public Interest,* XV (Spring, 1969), 40–45.

Goodwin, Richard. "The Art of Assuming Power." *New York Times Magazine,* December 26, 1976, pp. 7–33.

Graebner, Norman A. "From Carter to Reagan: An Uneasy Transition." *Australian Journal of Politics and History,* XXVII (1981), 304–29.

Graff, Henry F. "Transition at the White House." *New Leader,* LI (December 30, 1968), 3–7.

Haider, Donald H. "Presidential Transitions: Critical, if not Decisive." *Public Administration Review,* XLI (March–April, 1981), 207–11.

Henry, Laurin L. "Presidential Transitions: The 1968–69 Experience in Perspective." *Public Administration Review,* XXIX (September–October, 1969), 471–82.

————. "Transferring the Presidency: Variations, Trends and Patterns." *Public Administration Review,* XXII (Fall, 1960), 187–95.

Johnson, Robert H. "The National Security Council: The Relevance of Its Past to Its Future." *Orbis,* XIII (Fall, 1969), 709–35.

Lincoln, Franklin B., Jr. "Presidential Transition 1968–1969." *American Bar Association Journal,* V (June, 1969), 529–33.

Lissitzyn, O. J. "Duration of Executive Agreements." *American Journal of International Law,* LIV (October, 1960), 869–73.

Mathias, Charles McC., Jr. "Politics or Merit." *Foreign Service Journal,* LIX (April, 1982), 28–32, 36.

Mosher, Frederick C. "Presidential Transitions and Foreign Policy: The American Experience." *Public Administration Review,* XLV (July–August, 1985), 468–74.

Mussman, Michael Angelo. "Changing the Date for Congressional Sessions and Inauguration Day." *American Political Science Review,* XVIII (February, 1924), 108–18.

Neustadt, Richard E. "Staffing the Presidency: Premature Notes on the New Administration." *Political Science Quarterly,* XCIII (Winter, 1978), 1–9.

Pfiffner, James P. "The Carter-Reagan Transition: Hitting the Ground Running." *Presidential Studies Quarterly,* XIII (Fall, 1983), 623–45.

Polsby, Nelson W. "Presidential Cabinet Making: Lessons for the Political System." *Political Science Quarterly,* XCIII (Spring, 1978), 15–26.

Roeder, Philip G. "Do New Soviet Leaders Really Make a Difference? Rethinking the 'Succession Connection.'" *American Political Science Review,* LXXIX (December, 1985), 958–76.

Sherrill, Robert. "The Strange Case of Transitional Washington: Johnsonville Becomes Nixonville." *New York Times Magazine,* December 15, 1968, pp. 25–27, 118–22.

Silberman, Laurence H. "Toward Presidential Control of the State Department." *Foreign Affairs,* LVII (Spring, 1979), 872–93.

Somers, Herman Miles. "The Federal Bureaucracy and the Change of Administrations." *American Political Science Review,* XLVIII (March, 1954), 131–51.

Stevenson, James. "A Reporter at Large: Moving Out, Moving In." *New Yorker,* December 27, 1976, pp. 31–51.

Stoll, Richard J. "Presidential Reelections and the Use of Force." *Journal of Conflict Resolution,* XXVIII (June, 1984), 231–46.

Strauss, Robert S. "What's Right with U.S. Campaigns." *Foreign Policy,* V (Summer, 1984), 3–22.

Wellford, Harrison, "Staffing the Presidency: An Insider's Comments." *Political Science Quarterly,* XLIII (Winter, 1978), 10–12.

Wise, David. "The Twilight of a President." *New York Times Magazine,* November 3, 1968, pp. 27–29, 122, 124, 126, 128–31.

Zentner, Joseph L. "Presidential Transitions and the Perpetuation of Programs: The Johnson-Nixon Experience." *Western Political Quarterly,* XXV (March, 1972), 5–15.

GOVERNMENT DOCUMENTS

*Public Papers of the Presidents of the United States: Dwight D. Eisenhower, 1953; 1960–61.*

——. *Gerald Ford, 1976–77.*

——. *Harry S. Truman, 1952–53.*

——. *Jimmy Carter, 1977; 1980–81.*

——. *John F. Kennedy, 1961.*

——. *Lyndon B. Johnson, 1968–69.*

——. *Richard Nixon, 1969.*

——. *Ronald Reagan, 1981.*

Smith, Stephanie. *Presidential Transitions and the Presidential Transition Act of 1963.* Washington, D.C., 1980.

U.S. Congress. Senate. *Human Rights and U.S. Foreign Assistance: Experiences and Issues in Policy Implementation (1977–78): A Report Prepared for the Senate Committee on Foreign Relations by the Foreign Affairs and National Defense Division, Congressional Research Service, Library of Congress.* 96th Cong., 1st Sess.

——. Senate. *Meeting with President-Elect Carter, Briefing Before the Committee on Foreign Relations, United States Senate, on President-Elect Jimmy Carter's Views Concerning Foreign Policy.* 94th Cong., Transition Period, 1976.

——. Senate. Committee on Government Operations. *Organizational History of the NSC.* 86th Cong., 2nd Sess.

——. Senate. Committee on the Judiciary. *Commencement of*

*Terms of Office of the President and Members of Congress: Hearing Before the Subcommittee on the Constitution of the Committee on the Judiciary, United States Senate, 98th Cong., 2nd Sess.*

U.S. Department of State. *Foreign Relations of the United States, 1952–1954.* Washington, D.C., 1983. Vol. I, Part I; Vol. XV, Part I.

U.S. General Accounting Office. *Audit of Ford-Carter Presidential Transition Expenditures. Report to the House Committee on Government Operations by the Comptroller General of the United States.* December 23, 1977.

## UNPUBLISHED WORKS

Breslauer, George W. "Soviet Politics and the U.S. Presidential Cycle." Paper Delivered at the Annual Meeting of the American Association for the Advancement of Slavic Studies, Washington, D.C., 1982.

Brookings Institution. "Memorandum No. 6: Transition in the Conduct of Foreign Affairs." In "Study of the 1960–61 Presidential Transition." Washington, D.C., 1960.

Figliola, Carl L. "Considerations of National Security in the Transfer of Presidential Power: An Analysis of Decision-Making, 1960–1968." Ph.D. dissertation, New York University, 1971.

Fisher, Joel M. "The Presidential Transition of 1968: Decision-Making in the Interregnum." Paper delivered at the Annual Meeting of the American Political Science Association, Los Angeles, 1970.

Franklin, Daniel. "Departure or Debacle: Congressional Resurgence in the Aftermath of Watergate and Vietnam." Ph.D. dissertation, University of Texas, 1984.

Grossman, Michael B., Martha Joynt Kumar, and Francis E. Rourke. "The Ageing of Administrations: The Waning of Power and the Opportunity for Rejuvenation During Second Terms." Paper Delivered at the Annual Meeting of the American Political Science Association, New Orleans, 1985.

MacKenzie, G. Calvin. "Cabinet and Subcabinet Personnel Selection in Reagan's First Year: New Variations on Some Not-so-Old Themes." Paper Delivered at the Annual Meeting of the American Political Science Association, New York, 1981.

Tucker, William, and Harrison Wellford, "Transition of the President and President-elect." 1981. Manuscript in Miller Center Transition Files, University of Virginia, Charlottesville.

Wyszomirski, Margaret Jane. "In the Service of the President: The Reagan Executive Office Takes Shape." Paper Delivered at the Annual Meeting of the American Political Science Association, Presidency Research Group, New York, 1981.

# INDEX